汉语作为外语教学丛书

Teaching Chinese as a Second Language: Vocabulary Acquisition and Instruction

汉语字词教学

Helen H. Shen   沈禾玲

Chen-hui Tsai   蔡真慧   Lisha Xu   徐丽莎   著
Shu Zhu   朱殊

图书在版编目(CIP)数据

汉语字词教学 / 沈禾玲,蔡真慧,徐丽莎,朱殊著. — 北京:北京大学出版社,2011.7
(汉语作为外语教学丛书)
ISBN 978-7-301-18940-5

Ⅰ.汉… Ⅱ.①沈… ②蔡… ③徐… ④朱… Ⅲ.汉语－词汇－对外汉语教学－教学研究 Ⅳ.H195.3

中国版本图书馆 CIP 数据核字(2011)第 099830 号

书　　　　名:	汉语字词教学
著作责任者:	沈禾玲　蔡真慧　徐丽莎　朱殊　著
责 任 编 辑:	沈岚
标 准 书 号:	ISBN 978-7-301-18940-5/H·2840
出 版 发 行:	北京大学出版社
地　　　　址:	北京市海淀区成府路205号　100871
网　　　　址:	http://www.pup.cn
电　　　　话:	邮购部 62752015　发行部 62750672　编辑部 62767349　出版部 62754962
电 子 邮 箱:	zpup@pup.pku.edu.cn
印　　　　刷 者:	河北滦县鑫华书刊印刷厂
经　　　　销 者:	新华书店
	787毫米×1092毫米　16开本　16.25印张　285千字
	2011年7月第1版　2011年7月第1次印刷
定　　　　价:	40.00元(含1张DVD)

未经许可,不得以任何方式复制或抄袭本书之部分或全部内容。
版权所有,侵权必究　举报电话:010-62752024
电子邮箱:fd@pup.pku.edu.cn

Acknowledgement

As the first author of this book, I am grateful to the University of Iowa for awarding me a Career Development Award at a very difficult financial period, which allowed me to take a one-semester leave and dedicate the time to write this book. I also would like to express my gratitude to the Center for Asian and Pacific Studies at the University of Iowa for awarding me a Faculty Research Award that allowed me to hire a research assistant to assist me in collecting reference materials needed for my writing. I wish to extend my appreciation to my students who participated in the demonstration classes for the DVD shooting, and to the ProVideo Company for undertaking the DVD shooting project. In addition, I wish to thank three instructors: Katherine Fillebrown from the Bergen County Technical Schools at Paramus, New Jersey, Xiaoyuan Zhao from the University of Iowa, and Fengping Yu, from the University of Iowa, for their generously contribution of the relevant teaching examples for this book. Fengping Yu also participated in the Chinese translation for the teaching examples. All of this support has made this book and DVDs available to our readers.

Helen H. Shen
Department of Asian Languages and literature
The University of Iowa
U.S.A.
May 2011

致 谢

  作为本书的第一作者,我非常感谢美国爱荷华大学能在财政困难时期仍批准我一个学期的学术休假来撰写此书;感谢美国爱荷华大学亚洲太平洋研究中心为我提供了研究基金,使我能聘用研究助教帮助收集有关的研究材料。我更要感谢美国爱荷华大学中文部学生参与了与本书配套的字词教学示范课教学录像的拍摄和美国 Cedar Rapids 的 ProVideo 公司承担教学录像的拍录与剪辑工作。另外,我还要感谢费凯云老师(Bergen County Technical Schools at Paramus, New Jersey)、赵晓媛老师(The University of Iowa)、余丰萍老师(The University of Iowa)为本书有关章节提供了相关的教学示例。余丰萍老师还参与了部分教学示例的中文翻译。由于以上这些单位及人员的大力支持,才使得本书及与其配套的教学录像与我们读者见面。

沈禾玲
美国爱荷华大学亚洲语言文学系
2011 年 5 月

Preface

In the past two decades, scholars in the area of second language acquisition have paid increased attention to research on vocabulary instruction. The reason is simple, studies have shown that vocabulary knowledge is not only a strong predictor for reading comprehension but also an indicator of the learner's ability in other academic skills (Henriksen, Albrechtsen, & Haastrup 2004; Laufer 1997). These observation hold true in the area of learning Chinese as a second language. A study on the relationship between word knowledge and reading comprehension showed that an increase of one percent of new words in a reading material decreases reading comprehension in a fixed reading time by 2%-4% (Shen 2005). Without a doubt, vocabulary acquisition plays a key role in successful reading comprehension. Within this context, for CFL (Chinese as a foreign language) learners written vocabulary acquisition is a slow developmental process. One study indicated that American students with 26 credits in Chinese language, acquired only about 2,229 words on average from the 8,500 high-frequency-word listed in the Modern Chinese Word Frequency Dictionary 现代汉语频率词典 (Beijing Language and Culture University Press, 1986). The acquisition of active vocabulary was only about 59% of the 2,229 words (Shen 2009).

What is learning Chinese characters so difficult to western learners? One major difficulty can be attributed to the fundamental differences in orthography, phonology, and morphology between Chinese and the students' native languages. Phonologically, Chinese is a tonal language with four lexical tones. Chinese characters do not have a sound-to-script correspondence which creates difficulty in memorizing the sound of characters. Although there are phonetic radicals that cue the sound of compound characters, the accuracy rate of phonetic radicals cuing the pronunciation of compound characters is only about 26% without considering the tonal difference (Fan, Gao, & Ao 1984). We all know that almost all the phonetic radicals are independent characters. According to statistics, about 1,348 phonetic radicals are used for 6,542 commonly used compound characters(周有光 1978). This means that students first need to learn the pronunciation of the 1,348 characters before they can use them effectively as phonetic radicals for learning compound characters. Orthographically, characters are composed of strokes and there is no fixed rule regarding the number of strokes

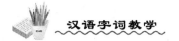

and composition of individual characters, which is drastically different from the roman letters in students' first languages. Morphologically, Chinese words have no inflections and there are no visible space boundaries between words. Characters serve as orthographic units rather than words. All of these differences require a cognitive restructuring for students who have acquired a western language as their native language in order to learn this unique language. Western learners encounter at least two major cognitive difficulties in learning the Chinese language. The first difficult is to establish a new cognitive structure that is suitable for leaning a logographic language; the other difficulty is to overcome the interference from the existing cognitive structure used to process their first language. Due to these difficulties, western learners need to spend about three-fold more time to learn Chinese in order to reach an equivalent proficiency in learning a western language (Everson & Xiao 2009).

Without a doubt, these cognitive difficulties have brought challenges to vocabulary instruction in Chinese. Understanding learners' cognitive processes in character learning and exploring effective vocabulary instruction approaches have been a strategic effort among educators. The purpose of this book is to focus our viewpoints on Chinese vocabulary acquisition and instruction with the hope of promoting more discussion and research on this topic in the field.

This book consists of nine chapters. The first six chapters written by the first author Helen H. Shen, deal with theoretical and pedagogical issues on vocabulary acquisition and instruction. Chapter 1 defines important terms used in this book to allow the readers to share a common understanding of these terms with the author while reading this book. Chapter 2 addresses studies on students' orthographic knowledge acquisition and how instruction can facilitate this acquisition. Chapter 3 presents unique psycholinguistic and cognitive models for Chinese vocabulary acquisition to help readers understand the general process of vocabulary learning and how instruction should keep in line with the learner's learning process. Chapter 4 addresses five cognitive theories from an information process perspective and their application in vocabulary instruction to maximize learning effects. Chapter 5 discusses the identification of good character learning strategies and how to train students to use effective learning strategies during learning. Grounded on the discussion in these five chapters, Chapter 6 proposes a CFL vocabulary instruction framework that consists of three dimensions: meaningful learning; skill integration, and a three-tiered instructional approach.

Chapters 7-9 present sample teaching methods for teaching vocabulary at three different instructional levels predicated on the instructional framework proposed by the first author of this book. These three chapters are written by three former graduate students at the

University of Iowa. Chapter 7, written by Lisha Xu, presents 10 vocabulary teaching methods for beginning level students; Chapter 8, written by Chen-hui Tsai, introduces 10 vocabulary teaching methods for intermediate students; and Chapter 9, written by Shu Zhu, to presents 10 vocabulary teaching methods for advanced students. These 30 methods are accompanied by real-life demonstrations recorded as three accompanying DVDs. In order to give an authentic feeling to the instruction, the teaching-demonstrations in the DVDs are recorded from authentic classroom teaching sessions and include some minor oral slips of instructors during their teaching. We appreciate your understanding. A sample DVD is accompanied by this book, the set of 3 DVDs is for sale as well.

The intended readers for this book are CFL educators (including high school teachers), graduate students who are seeking careers in teaching CFL, and researchers in CFL acquisition and instruction, particularly in vocabulary instruction.

前　言

　　近二十年来,国际二语教学中,专家学者们已经对词汇教学的研究引起了高度的重视,理由很简单,众多的研究证明,词汇知识不仅仅是阅读理解的强有力的预测者,它还是学习者能否成功掌握其他专业知识的标志 (Henriksen, Albrechtsen, & Haastrup 2004; Laufer 1997)。这些发现也在汉语作为二语学习领域中得到了证实。(Shen 2009)的关于字词知识与阅读理解关系的研究表明,阅读材料中每增加百分之一的生字就会导致阅读理解率下降2%～4% (Shen 2005)。毫无疑问,词汇的书面习得对能否成功地阅读是至关重要的。但是从另一方面来说,汉语字词的书面习得十分缓慢。研究表明,以美国学生为例,以北京语言学院出版社1986年出版的《现代汉语频率词典》列出的8500常用词为参照,修了二十六个中文学分的学生,他们平均掌握的消极词汇是2229,积极词汇只占其中的59%。

　　为什么掌握汉语字词这么难？原因不难追溯。因为汉字作为一种表意文字与印欧语言的由罗马字母组成的表音文字在语音、正字法、构词法方面有着很大的差异。从语音方面来说,汉字没有直接的音形之间的联系,掌握汉字的字音,十分困难。汉字合体字虽然有声旁,但是声旁表音的准确率只有约26% (Fan, Gao, & Ao 1984),而且绝大部分声旁都是独立的汉字。据统计,现代汉语常用的6542合成字中大约有1348个声旁,这意味着学生先要学会这些汉字才能很好地利用它们(周有光 1978)。而表音文字却有很强的音形之间的联系,看到形就可以知其音,与汉语相比,掌握表音文字的音的困难度很小。汉字有四声,四声的错读会引起对音节所代表的语义的误解,表音文字不存在这个问题。从正字方面来看,汉字是由笔画组成,这与学生第一语言的表音文字有很大不同。而每个汉字的笔画数与它字形的关系是没有规律可循的。从构词方面来说,汉语的词没有由语法规则带来的词形的变化,而且书面形式上没有标出词与词的界限。汉语中,汉字,而不是词,是最小的有意义的语言单位。由于这些差别,对已习惯于表音文字的西方学习者来说,学习中文,需要在他们的大脑中进行认知结构重组。他们在学习汉字中会面临双重认知困难。第一重困难是他们必须改变大脑在学习表音文字过程中建立起来的已经习以为常的认知系统和风格,而建立一种适合于认知汉字的新的认知系统;第二重困难是,在学习过程中,他们不仅仅需要发展一种新的认知系统,而且必须在发展新系统过程中,有意识地抑制来自于感知拼音文字认知系统的干扰。由于这些困难,学生必须花比学习一种新的印欧语言的三到四倍的时间来学习汉语(Everson & Xiao 2009),才能达到同等流利水平。

　　毋庸置疑,上面提到的汉语二语字词学习上的困难也给汉语字词教学带来了极大的挑战。对于从事汉语教学的教师来说,了解汉字习得的认知规律,探索行之有效的字词教学途径,是当前并在今后相当长一段时间内的具有战略意义的举措。本书旨在就字词习得和教学方面提出我们的一己之见,以促进这一方面更多的讨论和研究。

　　本书共有九章。第一到六章由本书的第一作者撰写。主要阐述汉语字词习得与教学方面的理论和实践问题。第一章,先对本书涉及的几个重要的概念加以界定,使读者对这些概念的理解上能与作者保持一致;第二章阐述学习者正字知识的习得过程,以及教学如何能促进其习得;第三章描述字词习得的独特的心理语言学模式和认知模式,使读者了解字词学习的心理过程以及教学如何顺应学生的字词学习认知过程;第四章从认知心理信息加工的角度讨论了五种认知理论及在字词教学上的应用;第五章阐述如何帮助学生找出良好的学习策略,并如何进行学习策略的训练。基于上述五章的讨论,在第六章中,作者提出了一个综合性的汉语二语字词教学模式。这一模式包含三个维度。第一维度是有意义学习;第二维度是听说读写技能综合;第三维度是三层次的渐进式教学途径。第七到九章,根据第六章提出的汉语作为第二语言字词教学模式为读者展示具体的教学方法。这三章分别由爱荷华大学汉语二语习得专业的三位研究生撰写。徐丽莎老师在第七章中列举十种大学(也适合高中)初级汉语字词教学方法,蔡真慧老师在第八章中列举了十种大学中级字词教学方法;朱殊老师在第九章中列举了十种大学高级汉语字词教学的方法。这三十种教学方法配有录像演示。为了给读者一个真实的教学情景的感受,这些录像都是课堂实况记录,所以录像中教师的教学语言可能有些口误,请读者谅解。本书所附DVD为演示版,配套的完整录像将专门另售。

　　本书的阅读对象是汉语二语教育者(包括中学汉语教师),在校的汉语二语专业的研究生以及汉语二语习得的研究者,尤其是对汉语字词习得和教学感兴趣的学者。

References 参考文献

周有光 (1978) 现代汉字中声旁的表音问题,《中国语文》,第3期,173-177。

Everson, M.E., & Xiao, Y. (Eds.) (2009) *Teaching Chinese as a foreign language.* Boston: Cheng & Tsui Company.

Fan, K.Y., Gao, J. L., & Ao, X. P. (1984) Pronunciation principles of Chinese characters and alphabetic script. *Chinese Character Reform*, 3, 23-27.

Henriksen, B. Alberechtsen, D., & Haastrup, K. (2004) The relationship between vocabulary size and reading comprehension in the L2. *Angles on the English– Speaking World*, 4, 129-140.

Laufer, B. (1997) *The lexical plight in second language reading*, in Coady, J. and T.

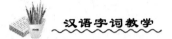

Huckin(eds.) (1997) *Second language vocabulary acquisition*, 20-34, Cambridge University Press: Cambridge.

Shen, H. H. (2005) Linguistic complexity and beginning-level L2 Chinese Reading. *Journal of Chinese Language Teachers Association*, 40, 1-28.

Shen, H. H. (2009) Size and Strength: Written vocabulary acquisition among advanced learners. *Chinese Teaching in the World*, 23, (1), 74-85.

Contents
目　　录

Chapter 1 Characters, radicals, words, and vocabulary knowledge
第一章　关于汉字、部首、词、词汇知识的概念 ··· 1
  1.1 What are characters? 什么是汉字？ ··· 1
  1.2 What are radicals? 什么是部首？ ·· 4
  1.3 What are words? 什么是词？ ·· 7
  1.4 What is the scope of word knowledge? 怎么界定词汇知识？ ················ 7

Chapter 2 Orthographic knowledge acquisition and instruction
第二章　正字知识的习得与教学 ·· 12
  2.1 Phonological awareness in character recognition and Pinyin learning
      语音意识在汉字认读中的作用以及拼音学习 ·································· 12
  2.2 Orthographic awareness and character learning
      正字意识和汉字学习 ·· 24
  2.3 The role of the first language in Chinese word acquisition
      第一语言在汉语字词习得中的角色 ··· 38

Chapter 3 Cognitive and psycholinguistic models for Chinese vocabulary acquisition
第三章　汉语字词习得的心理语言模式和认知模式 ······································· 46
  3.1 Cognitive processing models for word acquisition
      字词习得的认知模式 ·· 46
  3.2 Psycholinguistic models on lexical access
      词义提取的心理语言模式 ··· 54

Chapter 4 Cognitive theories and vocabulary learning
第四章　认知理论与字词学习 ··· 67
4.1 Dual coding theory
　　双编码理论 ··· 67
4.2 Cognitive load theory
　　认知负荷理论 ·· 72
4.3 Level-of-processing theory
　　认知加工深度理论 ·· 79
4.4 Multisystem account
　　多种通道理论 ·· 88
4.5 Competition theory
　　竞争理论 ··· 92

Chapter 5 Character learning strategies and training
第五章　汉语二语字词学习策略及训练 ······································· 102
5.1 Vocabulary learning strategies: concept and scope
　　汉语字词学习策略：定义和内涵 ··· 102
5.2 Studies on Chinese vocabulary learning strategies
　　汉语二语字词学习策略的研究 ·· 105
5.3 Identifying and training on vocabulary learning strategies
　　识别和训练字词学习策略 ··· 112

Chapter 6 A framework for CFL vocabulary instruction
第六章　汉语二语字词教学模式 ··· 126
6.1 Fostering meaningful word learning
　　培植有意义的字词学习 ·· 127
6.2 Promoting skill automatization
　　促进技能自动化 ·· 138
6.3 Adopting a three-tiered instructional approach
　　采用三层次教学途径 ··· 141

Chapter 7 Vocabulary instruction methods demonstration: Beginning level
第七章　汉语字词教学方法举例：初级 …………………………………… 179

Chapter 8 Vocabulary instruction methods demonstration: Intermediate level
第八章　汉语字词教学方法举例：中级 …………………………………… 190

Chapter 9 Vocabulary instruction methods demonstration: Advanced level
第九章　汉语字词教学方法举例：高级 …………………………………… 213

Appendixes　附录
　　Appendix A　附录 A ……………………………………………………… 240
　　Appendix B　附录 B ……………………………………………………… 241
　　Appendix C　附录 C ……………………………………………………… 242
　　Appendix D　附录 D ……………………………………………………… 243

Chapter 1 第一章

Characters, radicals, words, and vocabulary knowledge
关于汉字、部首、词、词汇知识的概念

1.1 What are characters? 什么是汉字？

A character is an individual written unit separated by a space boundary, with each character corresponding to one oral syllable. From a western scholar's view point, characters are monosyllabic morphemes and represent the smallest meaningful units in a word (Ramsey 1987). Unlike the case in English where most morphemes are bound morphemes in words, most of Chinese characters are free morphemes. They can stand alone to be a word. Only a very few characters lacking independent meanings are required to combine with other characters to form two-syllabic morphemes such as 蟋蟀 (xīshuài) *cricket*. Characters are constructed by individual strokes. In general, according to 张静贤 there are seven basic strokes. The different combinations of the seven basic strokes yield another 24 types of strokes (张静贤 1992: 31-32). Please refer to Appendix A for the strokes. These 31 types of strokes are used to create about 50,000 Chinese characters, of which only 5,000-8,000 are in common use. Of these, 3,000 - 4,000 are commonly used in daily communication.

汉字是书写单位，每个汉字对应于一个音节。从西方的学者的角度来看，汉字是单音节词素，是词的最小单位(Ramsey 1987)。在英文中，大部分词素是黏着词素，而汉语中，大部分词素是自由词素，它们可以独立成词，只有极少数汉字没有独立的意义需要跟其他汉字一起组成双音节词，比如"蟋蟀"(xīshuài)。汉字由笔画组成。笔画可以分成两类：基本笔画和派生笔画。基本笔画7种，由这7种笔画的不同组合，派生出24种笔画(张静贤 1992：31-32)。具体请见附录A。这31种笔画的不同组合形成了约5,0000汉字，这些汉字中只有其中5000到8000是常用的。在常用汉字中，3000到4000是日常生活中最常用的。

Characters can be classified into two categories in terms of their physical structure: simple characters and compound characters. A simple character such as 日 (rì) *sun* or 月 (yuè) *moon* is composed of a number of strokes and it cannot be decomposed into meaningful orthographic units. A compound character consists of two or more orthographic units such as 明 (míng) *bright* which contains 日 and 月. How are these two categories of Chinese characters formed? In the study of the composition of Chinese characters, a traditional theory known as 六书 (liùshū) *six writings*, explains that six types of characters are developed based on the characteristics of their formation. The six types of characters are termed pictographic, indicatives, ideographs, phonetic-semantic compounds, mutual explanatory, and phonetic loans (谢光辉、项昌贵、谢爱华 1997). Precisely speaking, the last two are not methods of creating new characters, because the **mutual explanatory** is a way of explaining the meaning of a character through comparison with another existing character with similar meaning. The **phonetic loans** are ways of borrowing existing characters to represent new ideas. That is, to give an existing character a new meaning. Neglecting these two types for the moment, let us take a close look at the other four methods of character creation.

　　根据汉字的结构,我们可以把它分成两类:独体字和合体字。独体字由笔画组成,不能拆分成有意义的缀字部件,例如"日"(rì)、"月"(yuè)。而合体字是由两个或两个以上的缀字部件组成,比如,"明"(míng)是由"日"、"月"组成。汉字是怎么形成的呢? 传统的六书理论介绍了汉字造字的六种方法。它们是象形、指事、会意、形声、转注、假借(谢光辉、项昌贵、谢爱华 1997)。确切地说,最后两种不属于造新字方法,因为转注是借用已有的汉字来注释另一已有的汉字的义。假借是借用一个已有的汉字来表示与其音相同或相近的另一个不同意思的口头字,所以是赋予已有汉字一个新的意义。除去这两种后,我们来仔细考察一下剩下的四种造字方法。

The first type is the **pictograph** in which each graph depicts an object. For example, 日 (rì) and 月 (yuè) are originated from pictographs of ☉ and ☽. Pictographs are based on the external form of objects, so it is difficult to express abstract ideas. This probably is the reason why the use of pictographs is very limited. Approximately, 1,700 pictographs are identified from the oracle bone inscriptions (韩鉴堂 2005:20). Nonetheless, pictographs showed us that the origin of Chinese characters is rich in meaning-shape connection.

　　第一种是象形,也就是一个汉字表示它所代表的物的形状。比如现代汉字的"日"和"月"的象形字是 ☉ 和 ☽。因为象形字只描绘出事物的形状,一些抽象概念就很难用象形字来代表,所以象形字的数量很有限。目前,我们已从甲骨文中考证了大概1700象形字(韩鉴堂 2005：20)。尽管数量少,象形字揭示了汉字的起源,告诉我们最早的汉字有着意形之间的紧密联系。

The second type is the **Indicative** which refers to the way of forming abstract characters using indicative symbols. There are two subtypes of indicatives: one is created by adding an indicative marker to a pictograph. For example, 刀 (刃 rèn; *blade*) is composed by adding a dot to a knife to indicate that part of knife is the knife-edge. The character 本 (本 běn; *root*) is constructed by adding a horizontal stroke to the pictograph 木 (木 mù; *tree*). The other type of indicatives is created by using symbolic signs to represent abstract ideas (e.g. 上 shàng; *above*) indicates an object is above the cursive line; (下 xià; *underneath*) indicates that an object is underneath the cursive line. Due to the simplification and standardization of characters over history, pictographs in modern script have been obscured because the cursive strokes are all straightened.

第二种是指事,即用一种指示符号来创造抽象字。具体地说,有两种造字方式。第一种是在原有的象形文字上加上指示符号。例如,刀 (刃 rèn; *blade*) 是在刀子上加一点表示刀锋。本 (本 běn; *root*) 是在 木 (木 mù; *tree*) 字下边加一笔表示树的根。另一种是用一种形象符号来表示抽象概念。例如, (上 shàng; *above*)表示一个物体在中线的上面, (下 xià; *underneath*)表示一个物体在中线的下面。由于历史上汉字不断简化和标准化,汉字的笔画已从曲线形发展到直线形,所以现代汉字中,象形字的痕迹已经不明显了。

The third type, the **ideograph**, is composed of two or more existing pictographs. For example, a single pictograph 木 (木 mù) means *tree*. By adding another 木 to it, the character becomes 林 *woods*. By putting three 木 pictographs together which is 森, gives the meaning *forest*.

第三种是会意字,一般由两个或两个以上的象形字组成。例如,一个象形字 木 (木 mù) 表示 树木,再加上一个木,两个木在一起就是林 (树林),三个木就是森 (森林)。

The fourth type is the **phonetic–semantic compound** which refers to characters consisting of a semantic and a phonetic component within. The semantic component of the compound character indicates the meaning category of the character while the phonetic radical signifies its pronunciation. To cite two examples 根 gēn(*root*) and 花 huā (*flower*). For the character 根 , the left component 木 is a semantic component indicating this character has a meaning related to a tree. The right component 艮 gěn cues the sound of the character without considering the tonal difference. For the compound character 花 huā, the top component ⺾ signifying the meaning category "plant" and the bottom component 化 huà cuing the sound of the character although the tone of 化 is different from 花. Here, we would need to point out that the semantic component in a compound character shows only the meaning category of the character, but not its specific meaning. For a phonetic component, due to the phonological changes in the history, only about 26% of phonetic components in the phonetic-semantic compounds can reliably indicate the sound of the characters even ignoring tonal differences (Fan, Gao, & Ao 1984).

第四种是形声字。形声字都是合体字。该类字每个字包含至少一个表音(称为音旁)和一个表义(称为形旁)部件。形旁标明着该字的意义类属,声旁则标出该字的读音。比如,根 gēn(*root*)和 花 huā (*flower*) 这两个字都是形声字。根的左边"木"是形旁,代表这个字与树木有关;右边艮 gěn 是声旁,虽然声调不一致,但它标示着"根"字的读音 gēn。"花"huā 的上部"⺾"代表着该字的意思是跟植物有关;下部"化 huà"标明"花"字的读音,虽然调不同。我们必须记住的是,形旁只代表该字的意义类属,但不能给出确切的字义。声旁虽然标音,但是由于历史上汉语语音的演化,现代汉语中,即使不考虑声调的差异,它的标音的可靠性大概也只有26%(Fan, Gao, & Ao 1984)。

From the above description, we can understand that pictograph and indicatives are simple characters. Ideographs and phonetic-semantic compounds are compound characters. According to 《汉字信息字典》(1988) (the *Dictionary of Chinese Character Information*) about 7462 of the commonly used 7,785 characters belong to compound characters. Among these compound characters, the phonetic-semantic compounds are the predominant compounds.

从上述描述中,我们可以推知,象形字和指示字基本上是独体字。会意和形声字为合体字。根据《汉字信息字典》(1988),7785个常用汉字中,其中7462是合体字,而绝大部分的合体字是形声字。

1.2 What are radicals? 什么是部首?

In the previous section, we have mentioned that pictographs and indicatives are simple characters, and majority compound characters are phonetic-semantic compounds. Each consists of semantic and phonetic components within. Traditionally, we refer to semantic components as radicals. What does "radical" mean and who invented the term? In the Eastern Han dynasty, a scholar named Xu Shen 许慎 (30-124) classified 9,353 compound characters into 540 categories based on the common simple characters they contained. He used their common simple character as their heading and referred to this common simple character as a "radical." The radicals that Xu Shen identified are semantic radicals. Each radical signifies the meaning of the compound character containing the radical. For example, characters 松、柳、杨 all share the same semantic radical 木 (*tree*), we can guess that the meaning of these characters are all related to tree. This groundbreaking method--classifying characters based on their shared radicals, allowed Xu to compile the first Chinese dictionary 《说文解字》*Character and Word Annotations* (Shen, Wang, & Tsai, 2009) to index characters based on their common components—radicals. Later scholars further analyzed the characters and reduced the number of semantic radicals. In the *Modern Chinese Word Dictionaries*《现代汉语词典》(2005) published in mainland China, we usually find 201 semantic radicals in the radical index section. For pedagogical convenience, in the CFL character instruction, we expand the definition of radical. In this book, we define a "radical" as the smallest meaningful orthographic unit. For the purpose of convenience, the term "radicals" include three types of character components: semantic radicals, phonetic radicals, and perceptional radicals (Shen & Ke 2007).

前面我们提到象形和指事字基本上是独体字,而绝大部分的形声字是合体字,每个形声字各含有表声和表义部件。传统上,我们称表义的部件为部首。部首是什么意思,谁发明了这个词？在东汉年间,一个叫许慎(30—124)的学者,对9353个字进行了分析,归纳出了540个部件。这些部件是某些汉字共有的。他把所有的9353按照它们共有的部件进行归类,归成540个部,把每类汉字中共有的部件拿出来作为该类的标识称为部首。例如,"松、柳、杨"字的部首就是"木"。我们可以从其部首推断,这一类的汉字的意思都跟木有关。许慎根据这一具有历史意义的汉字分类方法,编纂了第一本汉字字典《说文解字》(Shen, Wang, & Tsai 2009),即用部首作为索引来检索汉字。后来的学者在许慎的研究上继续减少部首的数量。在《现代汉语词典》(2005)上我们通常看到201部首。为海外教学上的方便,我们对原来的部首的定义进行了扩大。在本书中,我们把部首定义为:最小的有意义的缀字单位。部首包括汉字中三类部件:形旁、声旁和知觉部件。

As we mentioned above, a semantic radical indicates the meaning category of a compound character and a phonetic radicals signifies the pronunciation of the compound character. In addition to the semantic and phonetic radicals, we refer to character components that provide neither semantic nor phonetic cues to the compound character as perceptual radicals. A perceptual radical in a compound character plays a perceptual role. Visually it is an integral unit and is separated by a visible diminutive space from other components. To illustrate, the compound character 瞥, piē (*to glance at*), 敝 as the upper part of the character 瞥 is a stand-alone character that serves as the phonetic radical in 瞥. The bottom part 目 is the semantic radical. Perceptually, 瞥 consists of three components 尚, 攵, and 目 which we refer to as perceptual radicals. This means that the phonetic radical 敝 in this character consists of two perceptual radicals 尚 and 攵. Although 攵 itself is a semantic radical and has its own pronunciation (pū), it has lost its semantic and phonetic functions in the compound 瞥. Although the perceptual radicals do not cue either meaning or sound of the compound character, they are important cognitive units. Cognitively, if students can perceive a compound character as a combination of radicals rather than a pile of strokes, this will greatly reduce their memory load. Therefore, learning the perceptual radical is part of character learning content. Scholars have different opinions on the definition and categorization of perceptual radical. One study defines it as "it is larger or equal to a stroke and smaller or equal to a character." (费锦昌 1996: 20). This study analyzed 3,500 commonly used characters and identified 384 perceptual radicals. The 384 radicals were further classified into two categories: basic radicals 290 and commonly used compound radical 94. For the basic radicals, they were further divided into two groups: single stroke radicals (a total of 8) and multi-stroke radicals (a total of 282). This classification method is new to the field but we will be open-minded if the classification criterion will help reduce the complication in linguistic study, computer information processing, and classroom instruction. We hope that scholars can reach consensus in perceptual radical categorization in the near future which will bring greater convenience to language instruction.

我们在前面提到,形旁和声旁分别标示合体字的义和音。除此之外,我们称那些既不表音,也不表义的部件为知觉部首,因为在合体字中它们有知觉上的意义。从视觉的角度上说,知觉部首是一个知觉单位,部首之间有细小的空间隔开。比如,合体字"瞥",(piē, *to glance at*),上面的"敝"是一个独立的汉字,但是在这里是声旁。下面是"目"也是一个独立的汉字,在这里是义旁。从视觉上来看,"瞥"由三个部件构成,"尚"、"攵"、"目",声旁"敝"是由两个知觉部首组成:"尚"和"攵"。虽然"攵"本身是一个义旁读成pū,但是在"瞥"这个合体字中,它失去了作为义部的音和义。虽然知觉部首对合体字的音和义没有标示作用,但是,它是重要的认知单位。从认知心理的角度看,如果学生能把一个合体字从知觉上分解为部首而不是一堆笔画,那么记忆的负荷就会大量地减少,因此学习知觉部首是汉字学习的有机组成部分。学者们对知觉部首的界定和分类有不同的见解。在费锦昌(1996)的研究中,它被定义为:大于或等于笔画,小于或等于汉字。那项研究分析了3500常用字,从中界定了384个知觉部首。这384个知觉部首进一步被划分为两大类:基本部首290和常用复合部首94个。在基本部首中又分出8个一笔部首和282个多笔部首。这种分类方式很新异,但是如果分类的方法有利于减少语言学、计算机信息加工及课堂教学方面的复杂性,我们应该虚怀若谷。我们希望学者们不久将来能在知觉部首的分类上达成一致的看法,这会对汉语作为第二语言教学带来诸多方便。

1.3 What are words? 什么是词?

We mentioned earlier that most of characters are free-morphemes and that they can serve as words. However, most individual characters have multiple meanings and they can combine with other characters to form a new word. Therefore, a character can serve as a word when it is stand-alone; it can also serve as a component of words when combined with other characters to express meaning. According to the *Modern Chinese Frequency Dictionary*《现代汉语频率词典》(1986) single character words comprise about 27% percent of the daily use corpus, while two-character words account for 65%. Therefore, two-character words are predominant in the Chinese vocabulary corpus.

前面我们提到绝大部分汉字是自由词素,它们能单独成词。但是大部分单音节词有多重意思,它们都可以跟其他汉字组合成双音节或多音节词。因此,汉字可以单独成词,但当它们与其他汉字合成词时则成为词中的一个词素。根据《现代汉语频率词典》(1986),日常生活中的词汇,单字词大概占27%。双字词占65%左右。所以双字词在汉语词汇中占了绝大部分比例。

1.4 What is the scope of word knowledge? 怎么界定词汇知识?

In the classroom, what do we expect students to learn about words? That is, to what extent do we consider that a student has learned a particular word? In vocabulary acquisition, we use the term "breadth" and "depth" to measure a person's vocabulary knowledge. Breadth refers to how many words a person can recognize. However, recognition of a particular word does not mean that a learner has a full knowledge of the word. Thus we need the term "depth" to determine how much a learner knows about a particular word.

在课堂教学中,我们希望学生掌握什么词汇知识?在何种程度上我们可以说学生已经掌握了某个词?在词汇习得方面,我们使用"广度"和"深度"这两个概念来界定个体的词汇知识。广度是指个体能认读多少词。能认读词并不意味着个体对某个词有了全面的掌握。因此我们还用深度这个概念来界定个体对某一词掌握的程度。

Reed (2004) proposed a construct for defining the depth of vocabulary knowledge for alphabetic language. The construct consists of three components: precision of meaning, comprehensive word knowledge, and network knowledge. This construct cannot be directly applied to the Chinese language as it is designed for an alphabetic language. Based on this knowledge, we propose a construct defining the depth of Chinese word knowledge consisting of four components: definitional knowledge, syntactical knowledge, pragmatic knowledge, and networking knowledge.

Reed (2004) 提出了一个英文词汇掌握深度的测定标准。这个标准包含三个成分:对意义的准确掌握,词汇知识的丰富性,以及词汇网络知识。这一标准不能直接在汉语教学中应用,因为它只适应于西方语言。根据这一标准的精神和汉语词汇的特点,我们提出测定汉语词汇知识深度的标准,应该包含四个因素:定义知识,句法知识,语用知识和网络知识。

The term **definitional knowledge** refers to the knowledge of word as an isolated item; that is, the sound, shape, and meaning of the word. The learner knows the pronunciation of a particular word which includes its tonal variation (such as 任 can be read as rèn and rén); different readings (such as 解 can be read as jiě and xiè); and multiple meanings as defined in the dictionary. The term **syntactical knowledge** involves knowledge of grammar, collocation, and constraints for using the word. Grammar knowledge includes part of speech (how many part of speeches a particular word can serve in a syntax (e.g.工作 is a noun in the sentence 我有一个很好的工作 but it also can be a verb in another sentence such as 我每天都工作); the knowledge of sentence components for a particular word and its position in a sentence (e.g. 解放 can serve as predicate in the sentence 北京解放了, but it also serves as an attribute in another sentence such as 解放战争是1945年开始的). The collocation knowledge refers to how a particular word can be regularly used together with another word in a sentence (e.g. in the sentence 他的声音里含着脉脉深情, the word 声音 cannot be used together with 脉脉深情; as 脉脉 is used to convey a feeling with the eyes but not to convey a voice (see 李芳杰 1993:212). The constraints of using words refers to customized use of words (e.g. we say 两个人 but not 二个人; we say 二人转 but not 两人转). The term **pragmatic knowledge** refer to word usage in oral and written communication that fits into a social setting or environment, such as using 年纪 to ask an elder person's age but 几岁 for a younger person. The term **network knowledge** refers to knowledge of possible relationships between words, such as knowledge of synonyms, antonyms, coordinate and subordinate relationships.

字词定义知识指的是对单个字词的音、形、义的了解,包括知道某个字词的读音其中一字多调(比如,"任"可以读成 rèn 或 rén);一字多音(比如"解"可以读成 jiě 或 xiè)。以及一字多义如字典中所界定的。词汇的句法知识包括语法、词语搭配、词语使用范围的知识。词汇的语法知识包括词性(例如"工作"在"我有一个很好的工作"中是名词,但是在"我每天都工作"中是动词),句子成分(例如"解放"在"北京解放了"中是谓语,但是在"解放战争是1945年开始的"中是定语)。词语搭配知识是指懂得一个词通常与哪些词搭配以及它的固定搭配(例如,"他的声音里含着脉脉深情"中的"声音"不能跟"脉脉深情"搭配,因为"脉脉"是指用眼神传达的情感而不是由声音传达(李芳杰 1993:212)。固定搭配是指传统上词的固定用法(例如,我们说"两个人"不说"二个人";我们说"二人转"但不说,"两人转"。)词汇语用知识是指在进行口头和书面交流时词语使用得体,适合交流的场合或环境。比如,用"年纪"问年长者的年龄,而用"几岁"问年少者的年龄。词汇网络知识是指一个词与其他字词的各种关系,例如同义(近义)词,反义词,字词之间的联合关系或隶属关系。

In this chapter we first briefly discussed the linguistic features of Chinese characters and words. By doing so, we wish to highlight that Chinese is a logographic writing system which is drastically different from European languages in terms of its orthography. Therefore, learning Chinese characters requires unique cognitive process which we will address in detail in the subsequent chapters. Next, we discussed that the scope of word knowledge consists of four aspects. It should be pointed out that the accumulation of the four aspect of the word knowledge is not hierarchical and linear; rather, it is interrelated and spiral. A learner who has not acquired all necessary definitional knowledge of the target word may possess certain pragmatic knowledge. The development of these four aspects of knowledge is also not synchronous. One aspect of knowledge may increase faster than others, which is determined by learners' factors, curriculum factors, instructional factors, and environmental factors. We also need to bear in mind that the development of the four aspects of word knowledge takes time, but our appropriate instruction can facilitate the developmental process to a great extent. We need to keep in mind that word knowledge accumulation is incremental; it may take life-long accumulation. Therefore, trying to explain a certain word exhaustively in a single teaching session is not a wise strategy. Students may not process the knowledge that exceeds their comprehensible span. We will discuss effective vocabulary instruction in detail in the subsequent chapters.

　　这一章,我们先简要讨论了汉字和词的语言学上的特征。我们这样做的目的是为了强调汉语有着与西方语言完全不一样的正字法。因此汉字学习具有独特的认知加工过程,我们在后面的章节中会详细论述这一问题。接下来,我们讨论了字词知识界定的四个层面。需要指出的是,这四个层面知识的积累不是等级递增型的或线性的,而是交互型的或螺旋型的。个体对某个词的定义知识还没完全掌握时,有可能已经具备了某些语用知识。这四个层面知识的发展也不是共时的,某一层面的知识的掌握的递增可能会快于另一层面的知识。这种发展,受制于个体的认知因素、课程因素、教学因素及环境因素等等。我们必须切记,这四个层面字词知识的发展需要时间,虽然,教学在很大程度上能促进这种发展。我们必须尊重这一事实,也就是,字词知识的积累是渐进的,它也许需要一生的积累。因此,教师想在一节课上把某个词的知识进行全面详尽的讲解并不是一个明智的教学策略,因为当知识的量超过认知负荷时,个体无法进行加工。我们在以后章节中将对有效的字词知识教学方法进行深入的探讨。

In this chapter, we discussed the definition of characters and words. We recognize the overlap and the difference between characters and words. Since individual characters can serve as single-character words, for convenience, in the English sections of the following chapters, the term "word" also includes "character" unless it is specified.

　　这一章,我们对字和词的概念进行了界定,字和词的概念范围有不同面,但也有重合面和交叉面,因为单字可以成词,词由字组成。为了方便起见,在此后的章节中,除非特别指明,在英文部分,通常我们提到的"word"也包括字。

References 参考文献

北京语言学院语言教学研究所编(1986)《现代汉语频率词典》,北京:北京语言学院出版社。
费锦昌(1996)汉字部件探究,《语言文字应用》第二期,20-26。
韩鉴堂(2005)《汉字文化图说》,北京:北京语言大学出版社。
《汉字信息字典》(1988)上海:上海科学出版社。
李芳杰(1993)《汉语语法和规范问题研究》,武汉大学出版社。
谢光辉、项昌贵、谢爱华(1997)《常用汉字图解》,北京:北京大学出版社。
张静贤(1992)《现代汉字教程》,北京:现代出版社。

中国社会科学院语言研究所词典编辑室（2005）《现代汉语词典》（第五版），北京：商务印书馆。

Fan, K.Y., Gao, J. L., & Ao, X. P. (1984) Pronunciation principles of Chinese characters and alphabetic script [in Chinese]. *Chinese Character Reform,* 3, 23-27.

Ramsey, Robert S. (1987) *The language of* China. Princeton, New Jersey: Princeton University Press.

Reed, J. (2004) Plumbing the depths: How should the construct of vocabulary knowledge be defined? In P. Bogaards & B. Laufer (Eds.), *Vocabulary in a Second Language,* pp. 209-227. Amsterdam: John Benjamins Publishing Company.

Shen, H. H. & Ke, C. (2007) An investigation of radical awareness and word acquisition among non-native learners of Chinese, *The Modern Language Journal,* 91, 97-111.

Shen, H. H., Wang, P., & Tsai, C-H. (2009) Learning *100 Chinese radicals.* Beijing, China: Reking University Press.

Chapter 2   第二章
Orthographic knowledge acquisition and instruction

正字知识的习得与教学

2.1 Phonological awareness in character recognition and Pinyin learning
语音意识在汉字认读中的作用以及拼音学习

Chinese characters have no sound to spelling correspondence. Can readers recognize the meaning of characters without knowing their pronunciation? During reading, when a leaned character visually presented, how do CFL readers recognize the meaning of the character? Do they need to recall the sound of the character in order to recall the meaning of the character or the reverse?

汉字没有直接的音形联系,那么读者能否不知音而知其义？在阅读中,当一个熟悉的汉字出现时,学习者是怎么提取字义的？他们是否先要提取字音然后再提取字义或是相反？

The dual-route theory initially proposed by Baron and Strawson (1976) and then further developed by Coltheart, Curtis, Atkins, and Haller (1993) addresses the activation of phonological knowledge in word recognition in English. This theory assumes that a reader can employ two routes to recognize a word. One is the direct route in which the reader could sound out the word by using sound-to-spelling correspondence knowledge, thereby, activating the meaning of the word. The other is the indirect route, where the reader looks at the whole word and retrieve the sound of word previously stored in the memory which in turn help to access to the meaning of the word. No matter which route is used, in general, scholars accept that phonological knowledge plays an important role in recognizing word meaning in English.

双通道理论,最初由 Baron & Strawson (1976)提出，Coltheart, Curtis, Atkins, Haller (1993) 为其进一步发展做了努力。该理论阐述了英文认读过程中语音知识激活的几种假设。这一理论假设个体对词的认读经由两个通道。其一是直接通道,个体可以运用音形对应知识见词后直接读出词的音,由此而激活词义。其二是非直接通道,个体见词形后从大脑中提取先前存储的关于该词的发音,在这过程中同时激活词义。不管采用哪种通道,学者们一般都认可语音知识在词义提取中起了重要作用。

In Chinese writing, there is no sound-to-spelling correspondence. What then is the role of phonological knowledge in character recognition? Bulk of studies has been conducted on this topic. Some studies have showed that the time course of character recognition is from orthography to sound to meaning (Perfetti & Zhang 1991; Perfetti & Li 1998). Other studies have reported that both orthographic and phonological information function interactively to activate the meaning of a character (Zhou & Marslen-Wilson 1999, 2000). Although scholars hold different views with regard to the time course of activation of the phonological information in character recognition, they have reached a consensus that phonological information plays a role in character recognition for native Chinese speakers (Feng, Miller, Shu, & Zhang 2001; Myers, Taft, & Chou 2007; Chan & Siegel 2001).

 汉语没有直接的音形联系。那么语音知识在汉字的认读中起什么样的作用?这方面已有大量的研究。有些研究认为,汉字认读的过程是从字形到字音再到字义提取(Perfetti & Zhang 1991; Perfetti & Li 1998)。另一些研究认为,字形和字音知识交互影响达到对字义的提取(Zhou & Marslen-Wilson 1999 2000)。虽然学者之间就汉字认读过程中字音激活的时间问题存在不同看法,但是他们都认为对汉语母语者来说,语音知识在汉字认读中起了重要作用。

What does research say about the role of phonological information in character recognition among CFL learners? So far, no study has yet revealed the exact time course of phonological activation in character recognition. A number of studies from classroom learning perspective, however, have shown the connections between phonological information and character recognition.

 那么在这一问题上,汉语二语的研究告诉了我们什么?迄今为止,还没有研究明确说明在汉字认读中,语音知识究竟是在哪一个环节上激活的。尽管如此,一些关于课堂教学方面的研究表明语音知识与汉字认读存在相关性。

One study (Everson 1998) on word recognition among English-speaking college students who were beginning CFL learners was conducted in the United States. In that study, students were asked to write out *pinyin* for the sound and character meaning in English for 46 disyllabic words. A strong correlation was noted between being able to correctly pronounce the

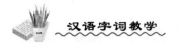

character and being able to correctly recall the meaning of the character (r = .96; p< .001). This result was confirmed by a later study conducted in Beijing (赵果 2003). In that study, the participants were all beginning level students at the Beijing language and Culture Universities and all participants' first language were European languages. Participants were first asked to write out Pinyin for 102 characters, then they were asked to use the target characters to form a new word or sentence to show whether they understood the meaning of the target characters. A strong correlation was found between knowing the sound and knowing the meaning (r = 0.91; p = .000). Another interesting study was conducted by 江新 (2003) with college CFL learners in Beijing who had different linguistic back ground. A strong correlation was again found between knowing the sound and knowing the meaning of a character (r = .97, p < .01) for students who's English as their first language. A moderate correlation was detected for students with Hindi as their first language (r = .50, p < .01).

 Everson（1998）进行了一项关于美国大学初级汉语二语学习者的汉字认读的研究。在该研究中,参与者被要求为46个双音节词写出拼音和英文意思。结果表明正确写出拼音与正确写出词义存在高相关(r = .96; p< .001)。这个结论在赵果(2003)的研究中进一步得到了证实(2003)。在那个研究中,参与者是北京语言大学初级汉语学生,他们的母语都是西欧语言。参与者被要求给102单字词写出拼音,然后给每一个单字词组成多音节词或用它造句。用此方法测试学生是否懂得这些单字词的意思。结果表明,正确写出字音与正确写出词义之间存在高相关(r = 0.91; p = .000)。另一个很有意思的相关研究是江新(2003)在北京做的。参与者来自不同语言背景。研究结果也表明,对于母语为英文的学习者来说,知音与知义之间存在高相关((r = .97, p < .01);对于母语为印度语的学生来说,知音与知义之间存在中度相关(r = .50, p < .01)。

In summary, albeit lacking sound-to-spelling correspondence in Chinese writing, to CFL learners, the availability of phonological information is crucial for CFL learners for character recognition. Therefore, phonological awareness, or the awareness of the sound structure of a language is important for character recognition. In an alphabetic writing system, phonological awareness refers to the ability to conceive of spoken words as sequences of smaller units of sound segments such as syllables, onsets, rimes, or phonemes (Siok & Fletcher 2001). In modern Chinese, we adopt *pinyin*, phonetic alphabet system, to help pronounce characters. Therefore, phonological awareness in Chinese can be defined as the ability to perceive syllables, to detect initial and final sounds of a syllable, and to differentiate tones.

综上所述,虽然汉语缺乏音形之间的直接联系,相关的语音知识对汉字认读至关重要。因此,对于汉语二语学习者来说,是否具备语音意识对汉字认读是十分必要的。语音意识指的是对语言的发音结构的意识。对拼音文字的语言体系来说,语音意识是指对听到的词的音节及其组成成分的认识,例如,音节的区分,识别音节中音节头、音节尾、音素等(Siok & Fletcher 2001)。现代汉语中,我们用拼音(语音字母系统)来帮助发音,因此,对汉语来说,语音意识可以定义为区别音节,识别音节中的韵头、韵尾及区分不同的声调的能力。下面我们来讨论教学中如何增强学生的语音意识。

Pedagogical suggestion for developing students' phonological awareness
关于发展学生语音意识的教学建议

- Introducing Pinyin prior to formal character learning
  拼音教学先于正式汉字教学

Most of institutes in western countries adopt Hanyu Pinyin as a Mandarin phonetic alphabet. In general, two practices are used for introducing *pinyin*. The first introduces Pinyin prior to learning characters and the second incorporates Pinyin into regular lesson learning and therefore introduces only a few Pinyin sounds in each lesson. Either way will eventually lead students to mastery of Pinyin. However, for adult CFL learners who are non-Asian language speakers, we strongly favor having a good knowledge of Pinyin prior to formal character learning. Thus, an intensive Pinyin learning period should be scheduled in our curriculum prior to formal character learning. However, our emphasis on learning Pinyin prior to character learning does not mean that characters should not been introduced during Pinyin learning, it only means that the focus of learning is on Pinyin rather than on characters. We may introduce characters in order to learn Pinyin in a meaningful way but students are not quizzed on character recognition or production during the period of Pinyin learning. The linguistic and cognitive arguments for doing so are presented below.

　　在西方国家,大部分学校采用汉语拼音作为汉语的语音字母系统。一般来说,汉语拼音教学以两种方式展开。一种是拼音教学在先,汉字学习在后。另一种是拼音教学与汉字学习同步进行。用后一种方法教学拼音,一般是在每课上只学习与本课汉字学习有关的几个拼音。无论用哪种方法,最后都能达到学会拼音的目的。但是,对于大学成人汉语二语教学,我们主张学生在正式汉字学习之前应该先有一个良好的拼音基础。这里,我们强调拼音教学在先并不是说在教拼音时不能出现汉字,而是强调教学的重点放在拼音上而不是汉字上。为了让拼音学习有意义,我们可以在介绍拼音的同时伴随介绍

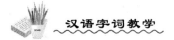

汉字,但是在拼音学习阶段并不要求学生进行汉字的认读和听写测验。下面我们讨论这样做的语言学和认知心理学的依据。

First, students from non-Asian language backgrounds have been introduced to the Roman alphabet, which is the alphabet we used for the Pinyin system. The merit for this is that students do not need to learn a new set of written symbols in order to learn *pinyin*. The cognitive difficulty is that students need to try hard to resist the negative transfer or interference from the pronunciation of the alphabetic language that they have been very familiar with when learning the new Pinyin sounds. Introducing characters would demand extra cognitive resources from the working memory, which may cause cognitive overload to students, hence, it would take longer time for them to master Pinyin. Second, Introducing Pinyin prior to character learning allows students to master Pinyin in a short time and to use it as an aid for pronouncing unknown characters. Therefore, they will be able to learn new characters that they may encounter after the class even at the very beginning stage of learning. Third, at the initial stage of learning, if Pinyin is not fully introduced, then students can use only the very limited characters introduced in their spoken and written communication. This may dampen students' learning enthusiasm if they feel that they cannot communicate effectively with others. With Pinyin assistance, students can communicate with Pinyin to get message crossed even though they have not fully mastered the corresponding characters. Lastly, it is common practice for students to use Pinyin input methods for typing in Chinese. Without a solid Pinyin knowledge, a substantial difficulty will be created for students in the efficient use of word processors. In sum, early exposure of students to Pinyin allows for a better mastery of the phonological knowledge that aids character learning.

首先,母语为非亚洲的语言学习者在学汉语前已经学了罗马字母,它跟我们用的拼音字母的书写形式一样。拼音采用罗马字母的优点是学生不必再去学一套新的字母书写系统。但是认知上的困难是学生必须在学拼音过程中很努力地去排除他们十分熟悉的罗马字母发音造成的负迁移。在这个时候同时要求学生记忆汉字,这必定要求工作记忆给予额外的认知资源,由此而造成工作记忆超负荷工作,使拼音学习不那么有效,因此,学生得花更长的时间来学拼音。第二,如果先介绍拼音,学生会在较短时间中掌握拼音从而用之帮助学习新字的音。这样,在学习的初级阶段,他们就可以在课外借助拼音去学那些课堂上没见过的生词。第三,在学习的初级阶段,如果不把全部的拼音介绍给学生,那么学生在他们的口头和书面交流中只能用非常有限的汉字进行交流,如果交流很费劲或常常受阻,就会很容易伤害他们的学习积极性。如果允许学生用拼音交流,那么他们如果一时想不起汉字就能借助与之对应的拼音进行交流,使交流畅通。最后,一般学生都用拼音输入法打汉字,没有一个坚实的拼音基础,会对学生有效运用汉字软件带来很大影响。简而言之,学生越早学会拼音,他们就能越早利用语音知识来学习汉字。

- Topic-based Pinyin instruction
  以话题为依托的拼音教学

We encourage the introduction of Pinyin prior to introducing characters but we discourage teaching Pinyin without context as it makes learning monotonous and inefficient. We propose topic-based Pinyin instruction, an approach to learning Pinyin that is based on language content. By adopting this approach, Pinyin is introduced together with words and sentences, and is practiced in a meaningful language situation. practicing Pinyin in a meaningful language situation not only increases efficiency of memory but it also helps student to accumulate spoken words and sentences during Pinyin learning, which in turn helps them to learn characters. Please see Teaching Example 1 for details of the topic-based Pinyin instruction.

我们鼓励拼音学习先于汉字,但是反对孤立的拼音教学使学习变得单调而低效。我们建议拼音教学以语言内容为依托,也就是拼音学习是在语境中进行。采用这种方法教学,使拼音学习与学习字词、句子相结合,让练习在有意义的交际过程中进行。这种教学方法不仅增强记忆的效率而且帮助学生积累口头词汇和句子从而帮助汉字学习。具体的教法,请参看教学示例1。

Teaching example 1. Topic-based *pinyin* instruction:Thanksgiving Holiday
教学示例1 话题型拼音教学:感恩节

Content教学内容:《汉语拼音入门》第八课Lesson 8: 前鼻韵母 an en in ün ian uan üan uen(un)

(from *Introduction to Standard Chinese Pinyin System* by Helen H. Shen, Chen-hui Tsai, Yunong Zhou, Beijing Language and Culture University Press, 2006)

Targeted learners教学对象:Beginners汉语初学者
Teaching objectives教学目标:

  Learn the eight front nasal simple and compound sounds
  学习并掌握八个前鼻韵母的发音。
  Review previous learned vowels and consonants
  综合练习已学过的声韵母的发音。

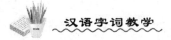

Teaching approach 教学方法: Learn *pinyin* sounds in vocabulary and sentence patterns around the topic "Thanksgiving Holiday" 拼音学习和操练围绕与"感恩节"话题相关的词汇及句型

Teaching Steps 教学步骤:

Step 1. Introduce the theme and learn pronunciations of eight *pinyin* sounds 学习八个韵母的发音。

1) 学习an, en, ün

① Introduce Chinese pronunciation of "Thanksgiving" and drill an, en, ün by using pictures.
导入主题"感恩节"(gǎn'ēnjié)讲解三个前鼻韵母an, en, ün的读音,结合图片操练。

② Ask the question "Whom do you give thanks to?" and practice relevant vocabulary by answering this question 利用问题"感恩节,你感谢谁?"引出相关词语,操练发音。
感谢 gǎnxiè 我们 wǒmen 你们 nǐmen 他们 tāmen 爸爸 bàba 妈妈 māma 哥哥 gēge 姐姐 jiějie 弟弟 dìdi 妹妹 mèimei 爷爷 yéye 奶奶 nǎinai 老师 lǎoshī……很多 hěnduō 很多人 hěnduōrén 一群人 yīqúnrén

③ Review the three *pinyin* sounds by using the sentence pattern "Gǎnēn jié, wǒyàogǎnxièyīqúnrén/hěnduōrén, yǒu……"通过操练"感恩节,我要感谢一群人/很多人,有……"来复习发音。

2) 学习in, ian, uan

① Drill in, ian, uan by using pictures 讲解这三个前鼻韵母的读音,结合图片操练。

② Practice following words by answering the question "Why do you want to give thanks to...?"利用问题"我们为什么感谢他们?"操练发音"为什么 wèishénme 因为 yīnwèi 钱 qián 关心 guānxīn 很好 hěn hǎo."

③ Students group in pairs. They review the three *pinyin* sounds by creating dialogues and using leaned words such as "Nǐ yào gǎnxiè shéi, wèishénme? Wǒ yào gǎnxiè…… Yīnwèi……"
学生两人一组,复习发音,互相问答"你要感谢谁,为什么? 我要感谢……。因为……"

3) 学习üan, uen(un),然后在句子中复习八个前鼻韵母。

① Drill the pronunciations of üan, uen(un) by using pictures 讲解前鼻韵母 üan, uen(un)的读音,结合图片操练。

② Showing a photo to students and ask students to answer the questions based on the photo. Questions include "Where is it? Who are they? What are they doing? What do you think of the family?" students answer the questions by using the following words 出示一张家庭图片,利用问题"这是哪儿？他们是谁？他们在做什么？这是一个什么样的家？"引出相关词语,操练下列字词的发音。

"家 jiā 爸爸妈妈 bàba māma 爷爷奶奶 yéye nǎinai 和 hé 孙子 sūnzi 孙女 sūnnü 吃饭 chīfàn 温暖 wēnnuǎn 团圆 tuányuán

③ Review the eight Pinyin sounds by saying the following sentences and practicing them in a relay game：Jīntiān shì gǎn'ēnjié. Wǒmen yīqúnrén chī tuányuánfàn. Wǒ shì sūnzi/sūnnü. 复习八个拼音,学生接龙操练"今天是感恩节。我们一群人吃团圆饭。我是孙子/孙女"。

Step 2. Comprehensive review Activities 综合复习活动
Activity 1: Thanksgiving Dinner 活动一：感恩节晚餐

Question：What did you have for the Thanksgiving dinner?
问题：感恩节你吃什么？Gǎn'ēn jié nǐ chī shénme?

Numerous food pictures are presented to students via PPT（see vocabulary list below）; each student has one of the pictures in hand to indicate this is the food he/she had for the Thanksgiving dinner. One student comes to the front of the class without showing his/her photo to the class. Other students in the class take turn to guess this student's picture. After a correct guess is made, the student in the front needs to say whether he/she likes the food or not.
教师用PPT呈现食物的图片(见参考词汇)。学生每人也有一张图片,代表他/她感恩节所吃的食物。一个学生上前不让其他人看他/她的图片,其他人一个接一个猜测他手中的图片。如猜中了,拿图片的学生要说明自己是否喜欢这种食物。

Vocabularies to be used in the activity 参考词汇
晚餐 wǎncān 蛋糕 dàngāo 玉米面包 yùmǐ miànbāo 汉堡包 hàn bǎobāo 米饭 mǐfàn 干果 gānguǒ 火鸡 huǒjī
南瓜派 nánguāpài 点心 diǎnxin 意大利面 yìdàlì miàn

Sentence patterns to be used in the activity 参考句型：
感恩节你吃的是……吗？Gǎn'ēnjié nǐ chī de shì……ma?

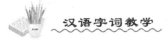

不是,感恩节我吃的不是…… Bú shì, Gǎn'ēnjié wǒ chī de bú shì……
是的,感恩节我吃的是…… Shì de, Gǎn'ēnjié wǒ chī de shì……
你喜欢不喜欢吃…… Nǐ xǐhuan bu xǐhuan chī……?
我很喜欢/不喜欢吃…… Wǒ hěn xǐhuan/bu xǐ huan chī……

Activity 2: Thanks giving Travel Plan 活动二:感恩节旅游计划

Each student receives a task sheet indicating an identity as a family member, supposed arriving time and destination of the trip during Thanksgiving break. Students need to ask each other to find whether they belong to a "family" (those members who are planning a trip to arrive in the same destination on the same day). The "family" team reuniting in the shortest time wins.

学生先每人拿到一张任务单,写有家庭成员身份(爸爸/妈妈/……),旅游时间(……月……号)和旅游地点(美国城市名)然后学生互相询问来找到和自己同一天去同一个地方的"一家人"。最短时间内完成家庭"团圆"的组获胜。

Sentence patterns to be used in the activity 参考句型:

你好,我是……(爸爸/妈妈/爷爷/奶奶/……)
Nǐ hǎo, wǒ shì……(a family member)
你打算什么时候去旅游?
Nǐ dǎsuan shénme shíhou qù lǚyóu?
你打算去哪儿旅游? Nǐ dǎsuan qù nǎr lǚyóu?
我打算……月……号(感恩节假期内的一天)去旅游。
Wǒ dǎsuan……yuè……hào qù lǚyóu.
我打算去……(美国城市名)旅游。
Wǒ dǎsuan qù……(a city name in the U.S.) lǚyóu……
我们是一家人,打算……月……号去……旅游。
Wǒmen shì yī jiā rén, dǎsuan……yuè……hào qù……lǚyóu

Step 3. Assessment 评估

Students are required to take a quiz involving reading and writing the words and sentences by using the eight newly or previous learned *pinyin* based on the pictures presented to them.

要求学生用学到的拼音根据提供的图片说和写前面学过的8个拼音,对学生进行测试。

(Teaching example 1 is contributed by Fengping Yu, teaching assistant, the University of Iowa, U.S.A)

- Use of Pinyin and phonetic radical as memory pegs for character learning
  用拼音和声旁作为汉字记忆的支点

An excellent way to increase student phonological awareness during character learning is to use the Pinyin of the character and the phonetic radicals of the character as memory hooks. We discourage the use of phonetic radical to guess the sounds of new characters because this is a random guessing game. One reason as we mentioned earlier is that phonetic radicals have only 26% percent reliability in cuing the sound of compound characters and there are no regularities or patterns in terms of phonetic radicals cuing the sounds of the compound characters. The other reason is that a phonetic radical itself does not carry lexical tone. Even though students can guess the sound correctly based on phonetic radicals, they still cannot figure out the tone. However, Phonetic radicals are very useful in aiding character memorization if we use them as memory pegs. When a new character is introduced, students should be encouraged to recall the previously learned sound same characters to build a phonetic connection between the new character and the old character. Once this type of connection is established, the sound for the new character is no longer new to students. If the new character is a compound character, encourage students to find out its phonetic radical and its relationship to the pronunciation of the compound character. If the phonetic radical can be used to cue the sound of the new compound, then the leaner can effortlessly memorize the sound of the compound character as the phonetic radical will serve as a memory peg for the new compound.

利用声旁作为汉字记忆的支点是增强学生语音意识的一个很好的方法。我们不鼓励在遇到生字时盲目地运用声旁猜测字音。原因之一是我们前面提到,声旁的表音准确率只有大概26%且声旁表音没有规则可循。原因之二是声旁并不标示声调。即使学生猜对了读音,他们也不知道准确的声调,所以盲目猜测近乎于一种瞎猜。虽然如此,我们可以利用声旁作为记忆支点来记忆汉字。当我们把一个新字词介绍给学生时,我们要鼓励学生回想以前学过的同音字,把新字词的发音与相关的学过的字词的发音联系起来。这种联系一旦建立,新字词的发音就不再是新的,记忆就会变得容易。如果新字词是一个形声字,让学生找出声旁,让学生讲一讲声旁与该汉字的表音关系。如果声旁有直接的表音功能,学生就可以利用声旁来记住该字词的读音。

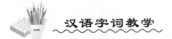

- Practicing oral reading in the classroom
在课堂上运用朗读法

Within a short period of intensive studying of the Pinyin sounds at the initial stage of learning, students can fluently read *pinyin* and syllables, but this does not mean that they can also accurately and fluently read words. It takes time to make a connection between a Pinyin sound and a particular character. After initial Pinyin instruction, instructors should adopt the oral reading method during normal classroom teaching sessions, especially in the beginning level class. Oral reading means asking students to read lessons out loud. This is a traditional teaching method rooted in its linguistic, cultural, and social grounds (Tao & Zuo 1997). Some scholars consider oral reading lead to be a form of rote memorization, but this is a misconception. Oral reading can be meaningful if used appropriately. Oral reading has two major purposes: one is to practice accurate pronunciation of each word and to establish sound to script connections; the other is to aid text comprehension. For lower level language classes, the lesson contents usually are not difficult, so oral reading mainly helps develop phonological awareness of individual words, allowing accurate and fluent pronunciation of words. As Chinese has no sound-script connections in written form, it takes much more effort for learners to establish a sound-shape connection for a character. When students sound out the word, they can actually hear the sound. This aural effect will help build connections in the learner's brain between a particular pronunciation and its corresponding character. In the classroom we may observe that western learners are not sensitive to the lexical tone that each *pinyin* word carries, because this feature is absent from their native language. Reading out loud can help the instructor detect if students have pronounced the character with accurate tone, so that their pronunciation errors can be noticed. In addition, as we mentioned earlier since phonetic radicals bear no lexical tones, the best method for reading a character with accurate tone is actually to say it out loud frequently.

在初始阶段进行拼音集中学习后,学生基本上能流利地朗读拼音或音节,但这并不意味着学生以后就能流利地读汉字,建立汉字的音和形的联系需要时间。因此,在初始的拼音教学后,尤其是在初级汉语课上,在学习汉语课文时,教师应该采用朗读法。朗读是传统的汉语教学方法,有其深厚的语言学、文化和社会根基(Tao & Zuo 1997)。有些学者认为朗读会导致机械记忆。这种看法有片面性。朗读如运用恰当可以是很有意义的。运用朗读方法的主要目的有二:其一是练习对每个字的正确的发音,并在头脑中建立音形之间的联系;其二是有助于对文本的理解。对于初级汉语课来说,文本的内容很容易,朗读主要是帮助学习者增强语音意识,能够准确和流利地读每个汉字。因为汉语没有直接的音形联系,对于非母语学习者来说,需要加倍努力才能在头脑中建立每个汉字的音形联系。当学生朗读汉字的时候,他们能听到汉字的音,这种听力效应能促进他们建立汉字的音与形的联系。在课堂上,我们可以观察到,西方学习者对汉语拼音的声调的变化不敏感,因为在他们的母语中没有这一现象。朗读能帮助教师及时发现学生是否读准某个汉字的声调,这样,学生的错误会得到及时的注意并被纠正。另外,我们提到汉字的声旁并不标示声调,如果要让学生正确地掌握每个汉字的发音,那么最好的方法是让他们经常大声地把汉字的音说出来。

Repeated oral reading could risk reducing learning interests. How can we make oral reading more meaningful? Variation in methods is important. A number of methods can be used for meaningful oral reading:

1. Individual expressive reading. Readers read with expression to convey their own or the feeling of the characters in the text.
2. Paired reading. Two students take turn to read and also ask and answer reading comprehension questions of each other.
3. Role-based reading. Students read in small groups and each student take a role in the text.
4. Question-directed reading. The teacher asks a question and the student answers the question by reading a relevant sentence or a paragraph.
5. Error detecting reading. One student reads while the other students listen to and evaluate his/her reading quality.
6. Demonstration reading. The teacher can ask students to recommend each other and have good oral readers to demonstrate oral reading in the class.

　　重复朗读课文有时会使学习变得单调乏味,使学生失去学习兴趣。怎样才能使朗读变得有意义?方法的变化是关键。我们可以采用下面一些方法使朗读变得不那么单调:

1. 个别表情朗读。轮流让每个学生进行表情朗读。在朗读中融进自己独特的感受。
2. 两个人一组对读。在读的过程中,学生互相向对方就课文提问。
3. 分小组角色朗读。每个学生担任课文中的一个角色。
4. 问题导入式朗读。教师就课文提问,学生只朗读与该问题的答案有关的句子。
5. 错误发现式朗读。两个人一组对读。一个学生朗读时,另一学生根据既定的评分标准,对该学生的朗读进行评估。
6. 示范朗读。教师让学生推荐优秀朗读者在班上进行示范性朗读。

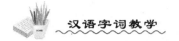

2.2 Orthographic awareness and character learning
正字意识和汉字学习

Orthographic awareness refers to the awareness of the graphic construction of the language. For English, this is about the awareness of how the word is constructed and spelled. For Chinese, it is the awareness of how a character is constructed which includes two aspects: one is the awareness of the physical structure of a character such as how a simple character is constructed by strokes and how a compound character is constructed by radicals, and the patterns of the physical structure of these radicals such as left-right, top-down, half-enclosure, and enclosure structures. The other is the awareness of the function of radicals in a compound character such as how they signify the sound and meaning of the compound character. We will discuss these two aspects separately below.

  正字意识是指对语言的书写形式的意识。就英文来说,是对于一个词的构成和拼法的认识。就中文来说,是对于一个汉字的构成和书写形式的认识。具体包括两个方面:一方面是对汉字结构的认识,包括一个独体字是由哪些笔画组成的;一个合体字又由哪些部首组成的;合体字组成的结构规则,譬如左右结构:上下结构、半包围结构以及全包围结构等。另一方面是对部首在合体字中的作用的认识包括声旁、形旁的作用。下面,我们分别对这两个方面进行详细的讨论。

2.2.1 CFL students' awareness of physical structure of Chinese characters
汉语二语学习者的字形结构意识

When do CFL learners start to develop their awareness of the physical structure of compound characters? Studies on CFL students' awareness of perceptual radicals within a compound character (Wang, Perfetti, & Liu 2003; Wang, Lu, & Perfetti 2004) showed that adult English-speaking beginning Chinese learners showed strong evidence of quickly acquiring the orthographic structure of Chinese compound characters. Students could master the internal structural complexity and compositional relationship of the radicals within a compound character even with very little knowledge of Chinese radicals, very limited character knowledge, and no explicit instruction on the orthographic structure of characters. This observation is firmly supported by a later study (Shen & Ke 2007) in which the authors reported that English-speaking CFL learners could decompose unknown compound characters into radical units and reproduce the compound characters by radical units. This capacity emerged at the very beginning stage of learning—after only a few weeks of exposure to characters. The authors attributed this to the two factors: one is learners' cognitive maturity in perceptual organization which allows them to detect the diminutive space boundaries between radicals within a compound character. The other important factor is the students' experience with the graphic structure of Chinese, although very brief. As Chinese compound are comprised of radicals, when new characters are introduced, instructors generally demonstrate to students how the character is constructed from radicals and then write out the characters by radical units following a particular order. Those studies hinted that adult beginning CFL students are cognitively ready for the perceiving the internal structure of compound characters. Instruction and practice play a key role in facilitating awareness of physical structure of Chinese characters.

　　汉语二语学习者什么时候开始逐渐形成字形结构意识？有关研究表明,汉语二语大学初级学习者在汉语学习起始阶段就能很快地掌握汉字的字形结构形式(Wang, Perfetti, & Liu 2003; Wang, Liu, & Perfetti 2004)。即使在他们的声旁和形旁知识,汉字知识十分有限,又没有接受过正规的正字知识方面学习的情况下,学生也能很快地掌握合体字中知觉部件的复杂性和部首之间的空间关系。这一现象在另一个稍后的研究中进一步得到了证实(Shen & Ke 2007)。该研究调查了英语母语的汉语学习者在学习的初始阶段——只有几个星期的汉字学习就能够把不认识的合体字分解为知觉部首,并能按部首抄写汉字。该文作者认为这是由两方面的因素决定的。一个因素是学习者对符号感知的认知成熟度,他们能够从合体字中觉察到部首之间的细小的空间。这种空间意识使他们能够把构成合体字的部首分辨出来。另一重要因素是学生学习汉字的经历,即使这种经历非常的短暂。因为合体字是由部首组成的,教学中教师一般都会向学生示范如何写汉字,在示范过程中,学生可以了解到合体字是怎样组成的,写的时候又是怎样按部首为单位书写的。这些研究的结果告诉我们,在学习起始阶段,成人汉语二语学习者在认知上已具备了认知合体字中的部首,但教学和练习在促进汉字结构意识建立中起了关键的作用。

A number of studies have also reported students' error pattern when they reproduce characters. One study (杜同惠 1993) reported seven types of errors: 1. miswriting character component such as writing 刀 as 九; 2. switching character position within a character; e.g. writing 和 as 口禾 ; 3. Missing character component such as writing 些 as 此 4. adding or missing strokes; 5. changing the shape of strokes such as writing 见 as 贝 6. changing the structure of characters such as changing the top-down structure to left-right 宿 as 偖 ; and 7. homophone substitution such as using 坐 for 座. Another study (范可育 1993) identified eight types of errors which were largely similar to the patterns reported by 杜同惠 . It should be pointed out that the character writing error-patterns 1-6 reported by 范可育 belongs to structural errors which relate to how students perceive the graphic structure of the characters. The error pattern 7, a substitution error such as homophonic character substitution or substituting a target character with another irrelevant character in students' discourse writing (composition) do not result from students' inaccurate recall of the physical structure of characters rather they are errors caused by inaccurate perception of the meaning of the character (if they are not a result of carelessness). Therefore, substitution errors (别字) are related to students' knowledge of vocabulary especially the strength and depth of vocabulary knowledge. Another study (江新、柳燕梅 2004) showed that students with the more character knowledge made fewer character structural errors.

一些研究报告了学生在汉字书写时出现的一些错误。杜同惠(1993)总结了学生汉字书写中的七种类型的错误:(1) 部首错写,比如将"刀"写成"九";(2) 部首换位,比如将"和"写成"口禾";(3) 少了部件,比如将"些"写成"此";(4) 增减笔画;(5) 改变部首的笔画,比如将"见"写成"贝";(6) 改变汉字的间架结构,比如把上下结构"宿"写成左右结构;(7) 同音字替代,比如用"坐"来替代"座"。另一相似的研究 (范可育 1993) 报告了学生错字的八种类型,大部分类型与杜同惠报告的是一致的。值得注意的是范可育报告的1—6类错误是属于书写结构的错误,这些错误与学生对汉字书面形式的感知有关。但是第7类错误,学生在写作中用同音字替代目的字,这类错误不是因为学生对汉字结构的知觉不正确,而是由于对汉字字义的错误理解而造成的。所以替代错误(写别字)是跟学生的字词知识的广度和深度有关。另一研究 (江新、柳燕梅 2004) 表明,学生掌握的字词知识越多,他们的汉字书写结构上的错误越少。

In summary, the structural errors in writing characters can be divided into two types: One type is miswriting stroke or radicals within a character; the other type of is configuration error — the radicals within a character are incorrectly positioned.

综上所述,学生的汉字书写错误可以分成两大类,一类是笔画错误,另一类是间架结构错误。

This raises a pedagogical question that the instructor may want to ask: Should students follow the fixed standard order of strokes in practicing handwriting of the characters? With the increased popularity of computer technology, increasingly more students are interested in using Chinese word processors for character writing instead of handwriting. CFL educators now are debating the amount of time and efforts that students should devote to handwriting characters. Due to the fact that *pinyin* input methods are used for typing characters, students do not need to have a knowledge of stroke order to type in Chinese characters. Consequently, some instructors and students consider the knowledge of stroke order no longer to be crucial and that practicing handwriting of characters is not very necessary. At this point, we have no intention of arguing how much time and effort students should devote to writing characters, but we consider that practicing handwriting of characters is indispensible in learning Chinese language at the beginning stage even though the computer may replace most handwriting tasks in CFL learning. We support the notion that students should be taught about the order of strokes for writing each individual character. The reason behind this is that study showed the order of stroke writing can serve as a cue for retrieval of characters during character recognition; namely, the order of stroke writing is an important feature of the orthographic and lexical representation of characters in memory. The learners store the information about the order of writing the strokes of a character especially the beginning strokes of a character as motor schema that are and internalized as a code in memory. When the character is recalled, the sequence of stroke order is likely to be activated as a useful retrieval cue for the memory representation of that character (Flores d'Arcais 1994). Another study (Ke 1996) on Chinese character recognition and production among English-speaking beginning CFL learners showed a moderate correlation between character recognition and production (r = .68, p = .05). Although this study did not investigate the role of stroke orders in the character memorization the result of correlation analysis indicated that the stroke writing order may also served as a retrieval cue for character recognition.

　　上述讨论引出一个教学法上的问题,那就是学生在练习写汉字时是否必须严格地按照规范的笔顺进行？由于电脑技术的普及,越来越多的学生用电脑打字来代替手写。由此引发了学者们对学生应该花多少时间来练习手写汉字的讨论。基于电脑打字用拼音输入法这一事实,学生不需要有笔顺知识就能打字,所以有些教师和学生觉得笔顺知识对汉字学习不是那么重要,用大量的时间来练习手写汉字也没有那么必要。在这里,我们无意争论学生究竟要花多少时间来学习手写汉字的问题,但是我们认为在初级学习阶段让学生练习手写汉字是不可或缺的。我们支持这样的观点:学生应该学习每个汉字书写的正确的笔顺。这样做的理由是因为有研究证实汉字的书写笔顺可以成为汉字认读时的提醒线索。也就是说,汉字的书写笔顺可以成为大脑对该汉字的记忆表征。学习者在练习汉字书写时,自动地把笔顺的先后作为一种运动码存储在大脑中,尤其是起始笔画顺序。当汉字认读时,笔画顺序就会成为提醒线索之一被激活从而导致对汉字的正确认读(Flores d'Arcais 1994)。另一关于英文为母语汉语学习者的汉字认读与书写关系的调查表明(Ke 1996),汉字认读与书写存在中度相关(r = .68, p = .05)。虽然这一调查没有特别调查汉字笔顺记忆,但是认读与书写的中度相关性不排除汉字笔顺记忆是这种相关的其中一个因素。

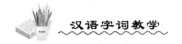

Pedagogical suggestions for reducing errors in Character writing
关于减少汉字书写错误的教学建议

- Accurate perception of strokes and accurate execution of stroke order
  准确感知汉字笔画和正确书写笔顺

Character writing practice should follow the sequence of strokes → radicals → characters. Before practicing radicals, students' skill on stroke execution should reach automaticity. Thus, when they are working on radicals and characters, they can pay full attention to the physical configuration of the character rather than to the individual strokes. In general, students should follow the conventional rules of executing strokes in character writing. 张静贤 (1992) summarized this into six basic rules and eight supplemental rules (Please refer to Appendix B for details). During character writing practice, individual students may deviate slightly from the standard stroke order in executing strokes. The instructor should make efforts to reduce this kind of deviation by using a character copying book in which each stroke for a character is clearly illustrated, or by using software programmed with animated stroke orders for characters.

汉字书写练习应按照笔画→部首→合体字的顺序进行。在学习写部首之前,学生对基本笔画的书写应该达到自动化。这样,在他们写部首和汉字时,他们的注意力可以集中在汉字的间架结构上,而不是每个笔画怎么写。一般来说,学生应该按照标准的汉字书写笔顺规则来练习书写。张静贤(1992)总结了六条基本笔顺规则和八条补充规则(请参看附录B)。在初始的练习中,个别学生可能没有完全按照规则书写而出现偏误,教师应该设法减少这种偏误。比如,汉字练习本上明确标示汉字的书写笔顺,也可以利用动画的汉字书写电脑软件,让学生在电脑上练习。

- Knowledge of radicals and character configurations
  汉字部首及间架结构知识

As we mentioned earlier that compound characters are composed of three types of radicals: perceptual radicals, semantic, and phonetic radicals. For the beginning learner, studies have indicated the pedagogical feasibility of introducing them high frequency semantic, phonetic, and perceptual radicals. A study (张旺熹 1990) analyzed 1000 high frequency characters from the book of《常用字和常用词》(1985) by the Beijing Language and Culture University and classified radicals into two categories: the perceptual radicals which cannot serve as an independent character; and the radicals that can serve as independent characters. In total, the author identified 42 perceptual radicals and 76 independent characters that served as phonetic or semantic radicals. Another study (崔永华1997) analyzed 801 characters which comprised 1,033 Level 1 word (甲级词) listed in the《汉语水平词汇与汉字等级大纲》(1992) and identified 330 radicals based on the 578 radicals classified by the National Language Reform Committee 国家语言文字工作委员会（费锦昌1996）. Classroom teachers may wish to use the research results of these analyses and incorporate them into character writing instruction and introduce high frequency radicals to students.

　　我们在前面提到合体字大致由三类部首组合而成：知觉部首、表义部首、表音部首。对于初级汉语学习者来说，先介绍给学生一些高频率部首是可行的，因为有些研究已经提供了高频部首的信息。张旺熹(1990)从北京语言学院出版的《常用字和常用词》一书中分析了1000个高频率汉字，把1000个汉字中的部首分成两类。一类是不能单独成字的知觉部首，共42个；另一类是可以独立成字的表音或表义部首，共76个。另一个研究(崔永华1997)分析了《汉语水平词汇与汉字等级大纲》(1992)列出的1033甲级词中的801字，找出了330个部首，这些部首是国家语言文字工作委员会（费锦昌1996）分类的578个部首中的一部分。教师们可以利用这些研究成果在教学中向学生逐步介绍高频部首。

Although compound characters number in the thousands, in terms of physical configurations, they are formed based on certain regulations. Traditionally, we classify compound character structures into four basic categories such as left-right structures 和、河，top-down structures 男、雷，half-enclosure structures 庆、压 and full enclosure structures 国、回. Each category has a number of variations. Please refer to Appendix C for the variations in compound character structures. Students should be introduced these basic character configurations and should learn to identify the character structure for newly introduced words. This knowledge will help them in the efficient memorization of characters.

　　虽然合体字有几千个，分析它们的间架结构，传统上，根据它们的部首的组合规律，这些汉字可以大致上分成四类：左右结构（和、河）、上下结构（男、雷）、半包围结构（庆、压）、全包围结构 (国、回)。在每一类中还可以根据其变化分小类，具体请参看附录C。我们应该把这些知识介绍给学生，让学生自己分析新字词的间架结构，以帮助对汉字的识记。

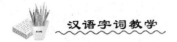

- **Amount of meaningful practice**
  有意义练习的量

Introducing knowledge of strokes, radicals, and configurations of characters are the first steps in character writing instruction. Plenty of meaningful practice should follow to enable accurate character writing by the students. Meaningful practice includes two dimensions: meaningful learning and meaningful copying. Meaningful learning can arise during character learning by informing students about how a particular character is formed so that they understand the etymology of the character. Another way is by giving students the freedom to create their own story for memorizing character structure. For example, one student commented on how to memorize the character 背, as "two persons sit back to back on the moon." This is an individualized way to remember the structure of the character.

　　介绍笔画、部首和汉字的间架结构只是汉字书写教学的第一步。大量的有意义的练习应该跟上去使学生能学会正确地书写汉字。有意义的练习包括两个方面：有意义地学汉字和有意义地抄写汉字。有意义地学汉字的方法之一是让学生学习汉字的字源知识。另一种方法是让学生自己动脑筋说说如何识记某个字词。例如，有个学生介绍他用"两个人背靠背坐在月亮上"这一形象的方法记住"背"。这是一种体化的汉字记忆的方法。

For meaningful copying, we encourage using methods such as asking students to recall the image of character right before writing it (柳燕梅、江新 2003), or asking students to report strokes, radicals, and configurations of a particular character before copying it. These activities require students to devote more cognitive effort in memorizing characters rather than just simply mechanically copying them.

　　至于有意义地抄写，我们鼓励比如让学生在抄写前不看汉字，先回忆一下汉字的形状(柳燕梅、江新 2003)，或者让学生在写某个汉字之前对自己报告一下该字的笔画、部首和间架结构，因为这些活动需要学生运用更多的认知资源去记忆汉字而不只是机械地抄写它们。

We understand that students' character writing speed and accuracy is also directly influenced by the way of character learning and teaching. We will address character instruction in detail in later chapters.

　　学生汉字书写的速度和准确度跟教学有直接的关系，在后面的章节中我们将会详细讨论字词教学的问题。

2.2. 2 CFL students' awareness of radicals in recognizing compound characters
汉语二语学生汉字认读中的部首意识

Radical awareness is defined as "functional understanding of the role of radicals in forming Chinese characters and the ability to consciously use this knowledge in character learning. To be specific, this radical awareness relates to knowing and using Chinese orthographic knowledge at three levels: 1) understanding that Chinese compounds are formed out of radicals rather than clusters of arbitrary strokes and be able to visually decompose unfamiliar compounds into radical units and to reproduce unfamiliar compounds in terms of radical units; 2) possessing a good knowledge of semantic radicals--knowing the sound, shape, and meaning of semantic radicals; and 3) understanding the orthographic structure of phonetic-semantic compounds, namely the role of semantic and phonetic radicals in a compound character, and being able to use this knowledge in learning new compound characters" (Shen & Ke 2007: 100).

部首意识是指"功能性地理解部首在合体字中的作用以及有意识地运用这一知识学习汉字的能力。具体地说,部首意识是关于了解和运用正字法知识,它包括三个层面:1)理解合体字是由部首组成,而不是笔画的随机堆砌;能在视觉上把不熟悉的合体字分解成部首,并能按部首抄写合体字。2)对表义部首有很好的了解,知道常用表义部首的音、形、义。3)了解形声字的构成,能运用有关的声旁和义旁知识来学习新的形声字"(Shen & Ke 2007:100)。

A number of studies have explored the phonetic radical awareness among adult CFL learners. For example, beginning learners were found to be well aware of using phonetic radicals to pronounce compound characters. Their performance on using phonetic radicals for accurate pronunciation of compound characters was affected by word frequency and the regularity of phonetic radical cuing of the sound of compound characters. They performed better on high frequency words, and made fewer mistakes for phonetically transparent words (陈慧 2001;陈慧、王魁京 2001). Another study on CFL students' awareness of phonological cues in phonetic-semantic compound characters reported that intermediate and advanced western CFL learners performed significantly better on the sound of characters that contained reliable phonetic radicals, which indicated that students were using phonological cues to pronounce compound characters. As grade level increased, students' awareness of the limitations of phonetic radical cuing the compound words also increased (江新 2001).

对成人汉语二语学习者的部首意识的调查发现,初级学习者已经意识到可以利用声

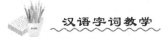

旁来发合体字的音,但是这种利用声旁学习合体字的发音是受制于汉字的频率和形声字表音的透明度。对高频率和高透明度的合体字,学生发音的准确度也高(陈慧2001;陈慧、王魁京2001)。另一关于汉语二语学生声旁意识的研究发现母语为西语的中级和高级汉语学习者对声旁表音透明度高的合体字发音的掌握显著要比透明度低的合体字好,这说明,学生是运用了声旁知识来学习合体字的发音。随着年级水平的提高,学生对声旁表音的有限性的意识也逐渐增强(江新2001)。

Some other studies focused on students' semantic radical knowledge and character learning. A study on semantic radical and character learning among English-speaking adult CFL learners showed that beginning students could apply semantic radical knowledge in learning new semantic transparent characters. Students with good semantic radical knowledge performed significantly better on the recognition and production of these characters (Shen 2000). Another study (Shen & Ke 2007) investigated semantic radical awareness and character learning among English-speaking adult CFL learners who had completed first and second year Chinese courses and showed a moderate correlation between semantic radical awareness and character learning (r.46. p = .000).

有几个研究是调查表义部首知识与汉字学习的关系的。Shen (2000) 探讨关于成人英语母语的汉语学习者的表义部首知识和汉字学习的关系。结果表明,初级汉语学习者能利用部首知识来猜测透明度高的合体字的字义。表义部首知识掌握得好的学生对合体字的认读和听写成绩显著地高于差的学生。另一研究调查初级和中级母语为英语的汉语学习者的部首意识和他们汉字学习的情况,发现学生的表义部首知识与他们汉字学习呈中级相关(r.46. p = .000) (Shen & ke 2007)。

During character recognition, do learners recognize the character as a whole or do they identify radicals and strokes prior to character recognition? Studies on processing units in character recognition (张武田、冯玲 1992; 彭聃龄、王春茂 1997) among native Chinese speakers reported that readers use both strokes and radicals as visual processing units. As readers get more familiar with radicals, they will tend to use radicals as processing units, as reported in a study on character recognition among skilled native Chinese speakers (Chen, Allport, & Marshalls 1996). Radicals were found to be the functional units in character recognition and readers identified the radicals within the compound characters, which then led to recognition of characters. Similar evidence was also observed among beginning CFL college-level learners, whose awareness of orthographic structure demonstrated implicit knowledge of the semantic radicals in recognizing compound characters. After receiving explicit instruction, the students' performance on using semantic radicals in learning compound characters significantly improved (Wang, Liu, & Perfetti 2004). A recent study on radical knowledge development among beginning English-speaking CFL learners reported that an overwhelming majority of the beginning learners (93%) considered semantic radical knowledge to be a help in learning characters. Students reported that this knowledge helped them learn the meanings, sounds (when a semantic radical served as a phonetic radical), and the graphic structure of characters (Shen 2010).Cognitively, if students are able to perceive radicals in the compound character and use radicals as memory chips instead of strokes, it will save memory space and increase recall speed and efficiency.

在汉字认读时,学生是整体识别汉字,还是先辨认出部首或笔画再达到对汉字的整体认读? 在这个问题上,我们先看看汉语为母语的读者对汉字的认知加工情况。一些研究表明读者同时用笔画和部首来作为汉字视觉加工的单位(张武田、冯玲1992;彭聃龄、王春茂1997),但是,随着部首知识的增长,读者倾向于使用部首为加工单位(Chen, Allport, & Marshalls 1996)。部首是功能性的加工单位,在对合体字的加工时,读者先辨认出合体字中的部首,由此导入认读合体字。同样的情况也在大学初级汉语二语学习者中观察到。研究表明,学生的隐性的表义部首知识促进了对合体字的认读。当学生受到显性的表义部首知识的训练后,他们用表义部首来学习合体字的能力显著提高(Wang, Liu, & Perfetti 2004)。最近的一个关于英语母语的大学初级汉语学习者的部首发展情况的研究显示,绝大部分的初级学习者(93%)认为表义部首对汉字学习有帮助。学生报告了表义部首知识帮助他们学习汉字的义和音(当表义部首在有些汉字中成为表音部首时)以及识别汉字的间架结构(Shen 2010)。从认知的角度来说,如果学生能辨认合体字中的部首并用部首作为记忆组块而不是笔画,这会节省记忆空间,增进汉字提取的速度和效度。

Pedagogical suggestions for increasing radical awareness
关于增加部首意识的教学建议

- Practicing decomposition of compound characters into perceptual radicals
  练习把合体字分解成知觉部首

We understand that a character can be decomposed into radicals and that a radical can be further decomposed into strokes. After learning certain types of radicals, exercises that require students to identify radicals from the compound characters or decompose the characters into radicals should be incorporated into radical learning, because this type of exercise will help students to reach automaticity in radical recognition, and hence, facilitate character recognition. Below are two examples of exercises: (cited from the workbook of *Learning 100 Chinese Radicals, Lesson 11 by Shen, Wang, Tsai, Beijing University Press, 2009*)

我们知道,合体字是由部首组成,而部首是由笔画组成。当学生学了一定数量的部首以后,在生词学习中我们应该结合一些把合体字分解成部首的练习,这种练习有助于达到对部首认知的自动化,由此促进汉字认读。下面是这一类练习的两个例子:

1. Please identify the radicals you have been introduced to, and copy the components into the brackets on the right 请找出你学过的部首并把它们抄在右边的空格中:

   谢 [　] [　] [　]　　　　新 [　] [　] [　]
   砸 [　] [　] [　]

2. Please find component shared by the three characters in the list below and copy the radical into the bracket 请找出三个字中的共同部首并把它抄在左边的空格中:

   [　] 巨 医 区　　　　[　] 时 封 导
   [　] 嘴 武 些

- **Systematically introduce high frequency semantic radicals**
  系统介绍高频率表义部首

High frequency semantic radicals are the radicals that have higher combinability with other radicals to form compound characters. We mentioned earlier that modern Chinese dictionaries published by mainland China usually list 201 semantic radicals. By analyzing 9999 characters from the《现代汉语词典》(商务印书馆 2005), we identified 100 high frequency radicals (please see Appendix D for details) and used these 100 high frequency radicals to write a radical textbook (Shen, Wang, & Tsai 2009). Instructors may wish to use this type of radical textbook for systematic introduction of radical knowledge to students.

高频率表义部首是指那些组字能力极强的部首,我们前面提到通用的现代汉语字典,列出201部首。通过对《现代汉语词典》(商务印书馆2005)的9999汉字的分析并结合教学上的实践经验,我们整理出了100个高频率部首(请参看附录D)。我们用这一百个部首编了一本部首教材《汉字部首教程》(沈禾玲、王平、蔡真慧2009)。教师们可以使用这一类课本向学生系统地介绍高频部首。

We strongly favor the systematic introduction of students to semantic radicals at the initial stages of character learning, for three reasons: First, almost all semantic radicals originated from pictographs that are root characters. Introducing these semantic radicals with connecting pictograph origins will help students in effectively memorizing the radicals (characters). A study (Chan, C.C. H. Leung, A. W.S, Luo, Y-J, Lee, T. M.C. 2007) reported that native Chinese students recognized characters having directly meaning connections with pictographs (such as 马) faster and also more accurately than the characters with no direct meaning connection with their pictographs (such as 南). From a cultural learning perspective, learning the high frequency radicals will expose students to the rich culture behind the characters, which will increase their learning interest. Second, since high frequency radicals will appear more frequently in the commonly used compound characters, it will alleviate the difficulty level of learning compound characters. Third, quite a number of semantic radicals also serve as phonetic radicals, such as the radical 土 in character 吐。Therefore, mastery of these high frequency radicals helps students to process not only the meaning of compound characters, but also their sounds.

　　我们主张在初级学习阶段系统地向学生介绍表义部首的原因有三。其一是几乎所有的表义部首起源于象形字,除了极个别失去了独立性之外,它们都是基本字。学习这些部首时与相应的象形字结合起来能帮助学生有效地记忆这些部首或基本字。研究表明汉语作为母语的学生认读那些直接起源于象形字的汉字(例如"马")比那些不是直接起源于象形字的汉字(例如"南")要快和准确(Chan, C.C.H. Leung, A.W.S, Luo, Y-J, Lee, T.M.C. 2007)。从文化学习的角度来看,学习这些高频率表义部首可以让学生了解文字后面的深厚的中华文化,这能增强学生的学习兴趣。其二是因为高频表义部首经常出现在高频字中,学了高频部首就能促进学习高频字,减轻记忆负担。其三是有相当一部分高频表义部首同时也在合体字中充当表音部首,譬如部首"土"在"吐"中起表音作用,所以掌握这些高频表义部首不仅是帮助学习合体字的义,也帮助记住音。

How should radicals be introduced? Should we introduce radicals as radical lessons, separate from regular lessons, or should we introduce radicals based on their appearance in the new characters of a regular lesson? We consider that both strategies have their advantages and disadvantages. Introducing semantic radicals prior to compound character learning allows students to direct all of their attention to radical learning, as semantic radicals can serve as independent characters; therefore, students are also learning simple characters. Proceeding from simple character learning to compound character learning converges to learners' cognitive processing. Furthermore, this focused learning can help students quickly and effectively learning radicals, which provides a strong foundation for compound character learning. The disadvantage, however, lies in the subsequent lesson learning; it is not possible to have a character containing all previously learned radicals, especially if the lessons are theme-based rather than orthographic-based. Consequently, students may forget the previously learned radicals if they do not appear sufficiently often in the subsequent lessons. Introducing semantic radicals as they appear in the lesson will help to build strong connections between a particular radical and a compound character containing the radical. This will produce an immediate effect on facilitating the character memorization. Especially during introduction of a new character, radical learning was followed by learning the compound character of the radical within (Taft & Chung 1999). However, introducing radicals based on appearance of radicals in the lesson may take a much longer time to learn high frequency radicals as the lesson organization is not radical-based; consequently, each lesson may contain very few new radicals or even no new radicals. Instructors will have to decide which method is better based on learning reality.

在课堂上我们应该如何向学生介绍部首？我们应该单独开部首课先教部首，还是在部首随课文出现时教？我们认为两种方法各自有它的优缺点。如果部首教学先于汉字教学，这能让学生把全部的注意力集中到部首学习上，而且表义部首本身就是独体字也是基本字。从学独体字过渡到学合体字符合由简单到复杂的认知规律。另外，这种有重点的强化学习能帮助学生在短时间内快速有效地学习部首，从而为合体字学习打下一个坚实的基础。它的缺点是：如果教材采取以话题为纲的，而不是正字知识为纲的课文编排方式，那么学过的部首很可能不再在后续课文中出现，这会导致学生忘记先前学到的部首，因此教师必须组织有计划地复习才能减少遗忘。如果部首介绍随课文的生字出现，它的优点是容易建立特定的部首与包含该部首的合体字的联系。尤其是当介绍新字时，立即介绍组成该字的部首会对汉字的学习产生即时效应，使学生有效地记住所学的合体字(Taft & Chung 1999)。这种教学方法的缺点是：需要比较长的一段时间学生才能学完高频部首，因为课文的组织不是以部首为纲，所以每课中可能包含很少新部首，甚至没有新部首。鉴于上述情况，教师要根据教学实际采用合适的部首教学方法。

- Emphasizing radical knowledge application
  强调部首知识应用

A study among beginning to advanced English-speaking CFL learners (Shen & Ke 2007) revealed that students' ability to apply semantic knowledge in learning compound characters was not synchronous with the development of radical knowledge. Radical knowledge increased steadily from year 1 of study to year 3 of study, but the ability for accurate application of the semantic radical knowledge in learning characters did not show a significant increase until the end of the second year of study. Thus, a gap exists between knowledge gained and accurate knowledge application. We understand that, cognitively, it takes time to transfer knowledge into skills. Nonetheless, this gap could be shortened if our instruction paid attention to radical knowledge application after the radicals are introduced. Exercises such as requiring students to guess the meaning of a new compound character based on its known semantic radical or to choose an appropriate radical for an uncompleted character based on its meaning or sound given are all helpful in facilitating radical knowledge allocation. Below are a few examples of this type of exercise: (cited from the workbook of *Learning 100 Chinese Radicals, Lesson 11 by Shen, Wang,Tsai, Beijing University Press, 2009)*

　　Shen & ke (2007) 的关于英语为母语的大学汉语学习者的部首意识的研究表明学生部首知识的应用能力的发展不与部首知识的习得同步。学生从一到三年级学习期间，部首知识每年都稳定增长，但是有效地运用部首知识学习汉字的应用能力则到第二年学习结束后才有明显的增强。因此，我们应该理解，从认知的角度上来说，把知识转化为技能技巧是需要时间的。虽然如此，如果教师能在教学中重视部首知识的应用练习，那么，部首知识习得与部首知识应用之间的时差是可以缩小的。应用练习可以包括让学生根据已知的表义部首来推知新字的义，或让学生给一个缺少部首的汉字根据字义或字音填上合适的部首。下面列举几种这类的练习：

1. Based on your understanding of each radical's meaning, please choose the appropriate meaning from the list and fill in the bracket on the left:
   根据部首的意思为汉字选适当的义，填入左边空格：
   [　] 甜　a. sad　　b. sweet　　c. broken
   [　] 房　a. room　b. waist　　c. ring

2. Based on the sound of each radical you have learned, please choose the correct *pinyin* for the characters from the list to fill in the bracket on the left:
   根据声旁的读音为汉字选适当的读音，填入左边空格：
   [　] 沪　a. hù　　　b. luàn　　c. xiàng
   [　] 址　a. chōng　b. zhǐ　　 c. láo

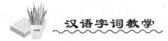

3. Based on the sounds and meanings of radicals that you have learned, please match the characters on the left to their sounds and meanings on the right with a line:
根据部首的音和义为汉字找到相应的音和义，用线连接：

    a. 趾   · gōng   bow
    b. 护   · cūn   village
    c. 躬   · zhǐ   toe
    d. 村   · gōng   achievement
    e. 功   · hù   protect

In addition to providing meaningful exercises, when introducing new characters, students should be asked to analyze the characters and identify the relationship between the radical and character. These are all excellent ways to encourage students to apply learned radical knowledge in learning new characters.

除了提供有意义的练习以外，教师在教生字时，要请学生自己来分析汉字，找出部首与有关汉字之间的联系。这是鼓励学生应用部首知识学汉字的一种很好的方法。

2.3 The role of the first language in Chinese word acquisition
第一语言在汉语字词习得中的角色

For adult CFL learners, prior to learning Chinese, they already have acquired their mother language. Therefore, learning a second language inevitably will be influenced by their first language. Studies in L2 word acquisition have confirmed the hypothesis of the existence of cross-linguistic variations in word recognition processes and that reading a particular orthography entails processing mechanisms unique to its system (Koda 1996).

A study on first language influences on second language word reading reported that speakers of different native languages may bring processing strategies specific to their L1s' to their learning of L2 words (Wade-Woolley 1999). Another study that investigated orthographic effects on CFL word recognition concluded that students with prior knowledge of the Chinese writing system performed better in both word naming and word meaning identification (Yang 2000). We will discuss what we have observed about the influence of students' first language, English, on acquisition of phonology, orthography, and semantics of Chinese words.

对于成人汉语二语学习者来说，在学汉语之前，他们已经掌握了自己的母语。因此，第二语言的学习势必要受到母语的影响。第二语言词汇习得的研究已经证实了在词的认知过程中存在着跨语言变异,由于缀词(正字)法的不同带来不同语言字词认知加工的独特性(Koda 1996)。另外,不同母语的学生在学习第二语言词汇时,他们各自的学习策略会受到加工母语词汇的策略的影响(Wade-Woolley 1999)。另一关于(正字)知识的效应的研究证实汉语二语学习者过去接受过汉语学习的,在字词认读时他们的成绩优于没有接受过汉语学习的学生(Yang 2000)。接下去我们将讨论我们所观察到的学生的第一语言——英语对汉语字词的语音、正字、语义方面习得的影响。

Phonology 语音

In terms of phonological knowledge acquisition, students often use English pronunciation to pronounce Chinese sounds. Table 1 presents a few samples.

从语音知识习得方面来说,学生经常借用英文的发音来发汉字的音,见表一列出的几个例子:

Table 1　表 1

Pinyin 拼音	English 英文	Difference 不同点
chi	chili	The tongue position is higher in pinyin 拼音的舌位稍高
zhi	college	Zhi is unvoiced but college is voiced 拼音 zhi 是清音但 college 是浊音
ji	jeep	Ji is unvoiced but *jee*p is voiced 拼音 ji 是清音但 *jee*p 是浊音
s	plea*se*	S is unvoiced but plea*se* is voiced 拼音 s 是清音但 plea*se* 是浊音

From Table 1, we can appreciate the similarities of English sounds and Chinese Pinyin, but we also notice the differences between. Some students often ignore these differences and use English pronunciation to produce Chinese Pinyin sounds, which will cause their Chinese pronunciation to sound like Eng-Chinese not Chinese *pinyin*.

从表 1 中,我们看到拼音与英文在某些音上有相同方面,但是也有不同方面,可是我们的学生经常记住相同点却忽视不同点,他们习惯于用英文发音来发拼音,结果他们的发音成为英中音,而不是纯粹的汉语拼音。

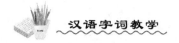

Orthography 正字

English writing is very different from Chinese. English uses 26 roman letters. Each letter has only a few strokes, varying from 1-3 strokes. Most letters use only one or two strokes and many strokes in the letters are cursive strokes. Students who have developed English writing habits, when writing Chinese characters, demonstrate problems in stroke writing and radical writing within a character. With regard to stroke writing, students are insensitive to adding or dropping strokes in a character. They do not consider that adding or dropping a stroke is a serious problem in Chinese, because they think that, on the whole, adding or dropping a stroke will not change too much about the character. In a study (范可育 1993), the author pointed out an interesting phenomenon that western students often write straight or angular strokes as cursive ones. The author considered that this type of error may have resulted from their writing habits in the first language, as English letters often have cursive strokes. With respect to radical writing, students shift the position of radicals or change the structure of the character such as by changing left-right structures into top-bottom ones by shifting the radicals within the compound characters, as we discussed in an earlier section. These kinds of errors are commonly made by western learners. Cognitively, students have not become accustomed to figure-like orthography. It takes time for them to develop sensitivity in perceiving Chinese characters.

英文的拼音文字系统与汉语表意文字完全不同。英文用26个罗马字母,每个字母只有1到3个笔画。而大部分字母只有1到2笔,笔画是曲线形的。学生因为已经习惯了这种写法,在写汉字的笔画和部首中就出现了问题。在写笔画方面,他们对汉字多一笔或少一笔不敏感,他们不认为多一笔少一笔是很大的错误,因为他们认为一个笔画并不影响汉字的整体视觉效应,看上去还是差不多。范可育(1993)在他的一项汉字书写方面的研究报告中,作者指出了一个有趣的现象,这就是,学生经常把直线或有角度的笔画写成曲线的形。范认为这是受到英文的影响,因为英文字母是以曲线为主。在写部首时,就像我们前面提到的,学生会改变汉字的间架结构,把左右结构写成上下结构,他们随意移动一个合体字中部首的位置。这类错误在西方的学习者中很常见,因为从认知方面来说,他们还不习惯图形式的汉字构字形式,他们需要时间来逐渐增强对汉字字形的敏感度。

◆ *Semantics* 语义

In learning word meaning, adult L2 learners often rely on their pre-existing semantic system. Jiang (2004) proposed the occurrence of a two-stage semantic transfer and development in adult L2 vocabulary acquisition. The first stage is comprehension. In this stage, when a new word is introduced, the learner will search for a pre-existing English translation of this word to establish an L2-L1 link. Based on this link, the learner is able to comprehend the meaning of the new L2 word. For example, if the Chinese word 滥用 is introduced, the learner will find an English equivalent "abuse" for 滥用 from their existing L1 mental lexicon. However, since they have not realized that translation equivalents from two different languages may not always share identical semantic properties and boundaries, they may produce an inaccurate sentence like 美国的法律不允许滥用小孩. The second stage is a developmental stage where the learners gradually realize that the L2 word meaning and the equivalent L1 word meaning do not perfectly overlap. The learners begin to be aware of the differences in the corresponding L2 and L1 words, which results in restructuring the semantic content originally transferred from L1. For example, they realize that 滥用 not only has the meaning of "abuse" but also has meanings of misuse (错用), inappropriate use (乱用), and indiscriminate use (妄用). While the English word "abuse" not only has the meaning of 错用、乱用、妄用, it also has the meaning of 虐待, which is not included in the Chinese word 滥用. Therefore, they gradually understand that 滥用药物，滥用权力 are correct, but 滥用犯人 (abuse prisoner) is incorrect in Chinese.

在学习字词的义的方面，成人汉语二语学习者在很长一段时间内依赖已经存在的语义系统。Jiang (2004) 提出了一个两阶段成人二语词汇的语义转换和发展模式。第一阶段是理解阶段。在这一阶段，当新词出现时，学习者就会在头脑中寻找已有的对应的英文翻译，建立二语与一语词之间对应联系。基于这种联系，学习者才能理解新介绍的二语词。例如，如果"滥用"这一词介绍给学生，学生就会在他的心理词库中找到相应的英文翻译—abuse。但是，由于学生没有意识到汉语词跟英文翻译不是百分之百在语义和使用范围上对应，他们很可能会用目的词造一些不正确的句子，比如，"美国的法律不允许滥用小孩"。第二阶段是语义发展阶段。在这个阶段，学习者逐渐地认识到了二语的词与母语的词不是完全的对应关系，他们开始注意到这种不对应性，这样，原来的简单翻译的二语语义结构开始重组。譬如，他们意识到"滥用"不仅有 abuse 的意思，但是还有 misuse（错用），inappropriate use（乱用），indiscriminate use（妄用）等意思。而英文的 abuse 还有"虐待"的意思，但是中文中的"滥用"没有"虐待"这个意思。因而，他们逐渐明白，"滥用药物"、"滥用权力"是正确的，但是"滥用犯人"在汉语中是不正确的。

Some instructors underestimate the importance of the role that L1 plays in L2 word learning (Jiang 2004). They hold the idea that students are learning Chinese, so the teacher just needs to have knowledge of Chinese. Mentioning anything about the learners' L1 in a Chinese class is viewed as a waste of time. This is a misconception. To classroom teachers, understanding the role of the first language in Chinese vocabulary acquisition is important because appropriate instructional intervention will greatly facilitate Chinese word acquisition. Excellent Chinese teachers should have a substantial knowledge of the students' first language and culture, which allows them to point out the similarities between the two languages so that students can use the first language as memory hook to accelerate their memorization of the sound, shape, and meaning of Chinese characters. Teachers should also pinpoint how learning problems are caused by over-generalization of the similarity between L1 and L2, while neglecting the differences, when applying pre-existing L1 word knowledge to L2 word learning. Directing students to compare the similarities and differences between L1 and L2 words in the aspects of phonology, orthography, morphology, and semantics are useful in facilitating L2 Chinese word acquisition.

有些教师在教学中低估了第一语言对第二语言词汇学习的影响(Jiang 2004)。他们认为,学生是在学中文,所以教师只要有中文知识就可以了。如果在汉语课堂上提及学生的第一语言——英文,那是浪费时间。必须指出,这是一个错误的观点。对于教师来说,懂得第一语言在第二语言词汇习得中起的作用是十分重要的,因为相应的教学干预可以在很大程度上促进二语词汇学习。一个优秀的教师应该对学生的第一语言和文化有充分的了解,这能使教师及时地指出母语词与目的词之间的相同点,学生可以利用母语词作为记忆支点,记住目的词的音形义。教师更应该诊断学生的哪些问题是由于第一语言词汇知识的过度推广而造成的。引导学生比较母语词与目的词之间在语音、正字、构词及语义上的不同,才能更好地促进学生的二语词汇习得。

References 参考文献

陈慧(2001)外国学生识别形声字错误类型小析,《语言教学与研究》第2期,16-20。

陈慧、王魁京(2001)外国学生识别形声字的实验研究,《世界汉语教学》第2期,75-80。

崔永华(1997)汉字部件和对外汉字教学,《语言文字应用》第3期,49-54,62页。

杜同惠(1993)留学生汉字书写差错规律试析,《世界汉语教学》第1期,69-72。

范可育(1993)从外国学生书写汉字的错误看汉字字形特点和汉字教学,《语文建设》第4期,28-31。

费锦昌（1996）汉字部件探究，《语言文字应用》第2期，20-26。

国家对外汉语教学领导小组办公室、汉语水平考试部（1992）《汉语水平词汇与汉字考试等级大纲》，北京：北京语言学院出版社。

《汉字信息字典》(1988) 上海：上海科学出版社。

江新 (2001) 外国学生形声字表音线索意识的实验研究，《世界汉语教学》第2期，68-74。

江新（2003）不同母语背景的外国学生汉字知音和知义之间的关系的研究，《语言教学与研究》第6期，51-57。

江新、柳燕梅（2004）拼音文字背景的外国学生汉字书写错误研究，《世界汉语教学》第1期，60-70。

柳燕梅、江新（2003）欧美学生汉字学习方法的实验研究——回忆默写法与重复抄写法的比较，《世界汉语教学》第1期，1-9。

彭聃龄、王春茂（1997）汉字加工的基本单元：来自笔画数效应和部件数效应的证据，《心理学报》第1期，8-16。

《现代汉语词典》(第五版) (2005) 北京：商务印书馆。

《现代汉语频率词典》(1986) 北京：北京语言学院出版社。

谢光辉、项昌贵、谢爱华（1997）《常用汉字图解》，北京：北京大学出版社。

赵果（2003）初级阶段欧美学生识字量与字的构词数，《语言文字应用》第3期，106–112。

张静贤（1992）《现代汉字教程》，北京：现代出版社。

张旺熹（1990）从汉字部件到汉字结构——谈对外汉字教学，《世界汉语教学》第2期，112-120。

张武田、冯玲（1992）关于汉字识别加工单位的研究，《心理学报》第4期，379-385。

Baron, J., & Strawson, C. (1976) Use of orthographic and word-specific knowledge in reading word aloud. *Journal of Experimental Psychology: Human Perception and Performance,* 2, 386-393.

Chan, C.C. H. Leung, A. W.S, Luo, Y-J, Lee, T. M.C. (2007) How do figure-like orthographs modulate visual processing of Chinese words? *Cognitive Neuroscience and Neuropsychology,* 18, 8, 754-761.

Chen, Y-P., Allport, D. A., & Marshalls, J.C. (1996) What are the functional orthographic units in Chinese word recognition: The stroke or the stroke pattern? *The quarterly Journal of Experimental Psychology,* 49A, 1024-1043.

Coltheart, M., Curtis, B., Atkins, P., & Haller, M. (1993) Models of reading aloud: Dual-route and parallel-distributed-processing approaches. *Psychological Review,* 100, 589-608.

Chan, C. K. K., & Siegel, L. S. (2001) Phonological processing in reading Chinese among normally achieving and poor readers. *Journal of Experimental Psychology,* 80, 23-43.

Everson, E. M. (1998) Word recognition among learners of Chinese as a foreign language: Investigating the relationship between naming and knowing. *Modern Language Journal,* 98, 194-204.

Fan, K.Y., Gao, J. L., & Ao, X. P. (1984) Pronunciation principles of Chinese characters and alphabetic script [in Chinese]. *Chinese Character Reform,* 3, 23-27.

Feng, G.; Miller, K., Shu, H., & Zhang, H. (2001) Rowed to Recovery: The use of phonological and orthographic information in reading Chinese and English. *Journal of Experimental Psychology: Learning, Memory, and Cognition,* 27, 4, 1079-1100.

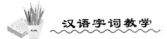

Flores d'Arcais, G. B. (1994) Order of strokes writing as a cue for retrieval in reading Chinese characters. *European Journal of Cognitive Psychology,* 6, (4), 337-355.

Ho, C.S. H.,& Bryant, P. (1997) Phonological skills are important in learning to read Chinese. *Developmental Psychology,* 33, 946-951.

Jiang, N. (2004) Semantic transfer and development in adult L2 vocabulary acquisition. In P. Bogaards and B. Laufer (Eds.), *Vocabulary in a Second Language,* pp. 101-126.

Ke, C. (1996) An empirical study on the relationship between Chinese character recognition and production. *The Modern Language Journal,* 80, 340-350.

Koda, K. (1996) L2 word recognition research: A critical review. *The Modern Language Journal,* 80 (4), 450-460.

Myers, J., Taft, M., & Chou, P. (2007) Character recognition without sound or meaning. *Journal of Chinese Linguistics,* 35, 1-57.

Perfetti, C. A. & Li, H-T. (1998) The time course of graphic, phonological, and semantic activation in Chinese character identification. *Journal of Experimental Psychology: Learning, Memory, and Cognition,* 24, 101-118.

Perfetti, C. A. & Zhang, S. (1991) Phonological processes in reading Chinese characters. *Journal of Experimental Psychology: Learning, Memory, and Cognition,* 17, 633-643.

Ramsey, Robert S. (1987) *The language of China.* Princeton, New Jersey: Princeton University Press.

Reed, J. (2004) Plumbing the depths: How should the construct of vocabulary knowledge be defined? In P. Bogaards & B. Laufer (Eds.), *Vocabulary in a Second Language,* pp. 209-227. Amsterdam: John Benjamins Publishing Company.

Shen, H. H. (2000) Radical knowledge and character learning among learners of Chinese as a foreign language, *Linguistic Studies,* June, 85-93.

Shen, H. H. (2010) Analysis of radical knowledge development among beginning CFL learners. In M.E. Everson & H.H. Shen (Eds.), Research among learners of Chinese as a foreign language (*Chinese Language Teachers Association Monograph Series,* Vol. 4), pp. 45-65. Honolulu: University of Hawaii, National Foreign Language Resource Center.

Shen, H. H. & Ke, C. (2007) An investigation of radical awareness and word acquisition among non-native learners of Chinese, *The Modern Language Journal,* 91,97-111.

Shen, H. H., Wang, P., & Tsai, C-H. (2009) *Learning 100 Chinese Radicals.* Beijing, China: Beijing University Press.

Siok, W-T., & Fletcher, P. (2001) The role of phonological awareness and visual- orthographic skill in Chinese reading acquisition. *Developmental Psychology,* 37, 6, 886-899.

Tao, L. & Zuo, L. (1997) Oral reading practice in China's elementary schools: A brief discussion of its unique roots in language, culture, and society. *The Reading Teacher,* 50, (8), 654-665.

Taft, M. & Chung, K. (1999) Using radicals in teaching Chinese characters to second language learners. *Psychologia,* 42, 243-251.

Wade-Woolley, L. (1999) First language influences on second language word reading: all roads lead to Rome. *Language Learning,* 49, 3, 447-471.

Wang, M., Perfetti, C., & Liu, Y. (2003) Alphabetic readers quickly acquire orthographic structure in learning to read Chinese. *Scientific Studies of Reading,* 7, 183-208.

Wang, M., Liu, Ying, & Perfetti, C. A. (2004) The implicit and explicit learning of orthographic structure and function of a new writing system. *Scientific Studies of Reading,* 8, (4), 357-379.

Yang, J. (2000) Orthographic effect on word recognition by learners of Chinese as a foreign language. *Journal of the Chinese Language Teachers Association,* 35, 1-18.

Zhou, X., & Marslen-Wilson, W. (1999) Phonology, orthography, and semantic activation in reading Chinese. *Journal of Memory and Language,* 41, 579-606.

Zhou, X., & Marslen-Wilson, W. (2000) The relative time course of semantic and phonological activation in reading Chinese. *Journal of Experimental Psychology: Learning, Memory, and Cognition,* 26, 1245-1265.

Chapter 3　第三章
Cognitive and psycholinguistic models for Chinese vocabulary acquisition
汉语字词习得的心理语言模式和认知模式

How do students actually learn words? What are the processes that students go through from initial perception of words to the final mastery of words? How can instruction facilitate a learner's vocabulary acquisition process? These questions are important for us to know in order to understand the nature of vocabulary learning and instruction. This chapter will provide answers to these questions by presenting a number of cognitive and psycholinguistic models on Chinese vocabulary acquisition and the corresponding pedagogical measures.

学生是如何学习字词的？他们从最初的字词感知到最终的字词掌握经历了哪些认知过程？教学怎样才能推进学生的字词习得过程？为了了解字词习得与教学的真谛，我们必须知道这些重要问题的答案。这一章中我们将探讨汉语字词习得的认知和心理语言模式以及相应的教学措施。

3.1 Cognitive processing models for word acquisition
字词习得的认知模式

We first discuss two cognitive models. One is the five-stage word acquisition model and the other is the multilevel interactive-activation word identification model. The former provide a general outline of the cognitive stages of vocabulary acquisition; the latter specifically describes individual word identification during reading.

我们先介绍两个认知模式。第一个模式从总体上勾勒出字词习得认知的五个阶段；第二个模式则阐述具体的阅读中读者如何从书面材料中识别字词。

3.1.1 Cognitive model of five-stage word acquisition
五阶段字词习得认知模式

From a cognitive processing perspective, in the classroom environment, what stages do learners go through in acquiring words and where should the focus of instruction be placed to accelerate vocabulary learning at each developmental stage? Based on the characteristics of cognitive processing of Chinese words, we propose a cognitive model that involves five stages of word acquisition: perception, association, comprehension, memorization, and generation. We discuss this five-stage model in detail below.

从认知加工的角度来看,在课堂教学环境中,学生字词习得经过哪些阶段,在每个发展阶段上为了加速学生的字词习得,教学的重点是什么?基于汉字加工的认知特点,我们提出五阶段字词习得认知模式。这五个阶段分别是:感知阶段、联结阶段、理解阶段、记忆阶段和生成阶段。下面我们详细探讨这一模式并结合讨论每一认知阶段的教学重点。

Stage 1. Perception. When a new word is presented to learners, they perceive the sound, shape, and meaning of the word. At this stage, the learners will register the information of word in their minds as a mental photo. Therefore, attracting the students' attention to the target words and leaving them with a deep impression of the feature of the target words are the key points to ensure that information will be successfully retained in the learners' brains. Instructional effort should focus on how to present the new word to catch the learners' attention and arouse their intellectual curiosity in order to make a vivid initial impression of the new word in learners' minds. When introducing new words, we usually present the written form of the new word, the Pinyin for the word, and its L1 translation. How should this information be presented, and in which order, for the best retention? A study (Chung 2002) compared four types of presentation conditions for beginning English-speaking CFL learners. Condition 1 was a simultaneous presentation of character – Pinyin – English (translation), after which learners were asked to look at the character and read the Pinyin. Condition 2 was a simultaneous Pinyin—English – character condition, in which students were asked to say the sound of the character. Condition 3 was spacing character, Pinyin – English condition, in which students were asked to look at the character first as soon as it was presented, then 5 seconds later the Pinyin and English translation were also presented. The teacher then asked the students to say the sound of the word. Condition 4 was Spacing Pinyin – English, and character condition, in which the Pinyin and English translations were presented first. 5 seconds later, the character was presented. The teacher then asked the students to say the sound of the characters. At the end of the experiment, a character recognition test was administered. Of the two simultaneous conditions, the character - Pinyin - English condition resulted in better character recognition. Of the two spacing conditions, the spacing character-Pinyin - English condition had significantly better results than the spacing-Pinyin - English character condition. Comparing the four conditions, condition 3, the spacing character-Pinyin - English condition had the best results for character recognition. The reason was thought to be that presenting the character first without Pinyin and English helps learners to direct their attention solely to the characters. It also prompts their curiosity about the sound and the meaning of the character, which in turn helps them to pay attention to the Pinyin and English presented 5 seconds later. If we present three items at the same time, students have to pay attention to all three items and their attention to each item is divided and diffused, which leads to poor perception.

第一阶段：感知阶段。当一个新词呈现在学生面前时，学生感知词的音、形、义。在这一阶段学生把新词登记在大脑中，在大脑中留下了新词的视觉图。因此，如何吸引学生的注意使他们对目的词的特征有一个深刻的印象是使信息能成功地保持在他们的大脑中的关键所在。教学的要点是如何呈现目的词才能使学生对之注意，才能唤起学生求知欲，在他们头脑中留下一个鲜活的印象。在生词教学中，我们通常向学生呈现目的词的书面形式、拼音以及英文翻译。这些信息如何呈现才能有利于学生对信息的保持？(Chung 2002)比较了这些信息呈现的四种顺序。实验对象是英语为母语的初级汉语学习者。第一种情况是不间断地分别依次呈现汉字→拼音→英文翻译，之后，要求学生看汉字读拼音。第二种是不间断地分别依次呈现拼音→英文翻译→汉字，之后，要求学生读汉字的音。第三种是先出现汉字，让学生看汉字，五秒钟后，再呈现拼音和英文翻译，教师随即让学生读汉字的音。第四种是先呈现拼音和英文翻译，五秒钟后再呈现汉字，教师让学生读汉字的音。实验之后，进行了汉字认读测验。结果显示，比较第一和第二种呈现方法，第一种汉字→拼音→英文翻译顺序呈现的效果优于第一种。比较后两种五秒钟间隔方法，第三种方法优于第四种。比较四种所有的呈现方法，第三种先呈现汉字，五分钟后呈现拼音和英文翻译的方法对汉字保持最有效。原因是汉字先呈现后，因为没有拼音和英文，学习者的全部注意力都集中在汉字上，看到汉字后，即引发学生的好奇心，想知道该汉字的音和义，这种好奇心驱使他们能对五秒钟以后出现的拼音和英文翻译引起更多的注意。如果我们在同一时间中把音形义都呈现给学生，那么，他们必定要在同一时间内把注意力分配到三个信息源上，由于注意力的分散使感知效果减低。

Stage 2: Association. Once the information of the sound, shape, and meaning of the word is available, the working memory will start to process the word, which includes establishing the association between the sound, shape, and meaning within the word and the association of this word with previously learned related words. At this stage, instruction should direct students to pay attention to the internal relationship of the word, such as asking students to analyze radicals within the character to find out connections between the character and the radicals within. Instruction should also help students to find connections of the new words with previously learned relevant words. This step is important as this will help learners to integrate the new word into existing cognitive schema in their brains.

第二阶段：联结阶段。当大脑得到了目的词的音、形、义信息后，信息被立刻传递到工作记忆（短时记忆）进行进一步加工。加工过程包括建立每个字词内部的音、形、义的联结以及这些字词与先前学过的字词的联结。这一阶段教学的重点是引导学生对每个汉字或词内部之间的关系进行分析。譬如，让学生分析汉字中的部首，找出部首与该汉字的联系。教学还应该注意帮助学生建立新词与相应的旧词之间在音形义上的联系。这一教学步骤很重要，因为它能帮助学生把新词结合到他们已有的认知结构中去。

Stage 3: Comprehension. A learner may put the word 同学 into a category with other words such as 学生 or 教师，as this learner might consider that these are people we meet in an educational institute. Another sign of comprehension is that learners can understand the word when it appears in different sentences. That is, learners understand that the word may have multiple meanings in different contexts. Instruction should provide various activities to facilitate the development of skills on classification and on understanding how the word is used in different contexts.

第三阶段：理解阶段。在这一阶段，学生表现出他们对新字词的定义的理解，能根据新字词与其他字词之间的某些特征理解字词之间的关系。学习者能用自己的语言解释新字词（譬如：同学是在教室里跟你一起学习的人），他们能为新词找出同义词或反义词，能对新字词根据某种相似特征进行分类。学生可能会把同学与学生、教师等词放在一类，因为他们认为这些人都是在学校里能够遇见的。理解的另一个标志是当新词出现在不同句子中，学生能根据句子确定该字词的义。在这一阶段，教学应该侧重提供那些能帮助学生提高字词分类能力和辨析新词是如何在不同语境中使用的等活动。

Stage 4: Memorization. In this stage, the instructor should design classroom exercises that allow students to process the word in a meaningful or cognitively deeper level. Meaningful processing means that learning is not forced or a mechanical memorization. Rather, learners are fully engaged in learning activities closely related to their daily lives and their interests. They enjoy the activities to a great extent even though the activities sometimes may require considerable mental effort. Instruction should design and present comprehensive activities which varies in format such communicative based, task-based, problem-solving based, and contextual based learning activities and demands for mental efforts such as using analysis, comparison, differentiation, and evaluation mental activities. to help internalization.

第四阶段：内化阶段。当字词被理解了以后，就要把它们转到长时记忆中存储起来，成为心理词典的一部分，需要的时候可以随时提取，这个过程称之为内化。内化程度取决于对字词的记忆程度。在这个阶段，练习是帮助内化的关键。练习活动的质量会极大地影响记忆的效度。课堂练习应该让学生对字词进行有意义和有深度的加工。有意义加工是指对字词的记忆不是机械地或由外力促使，而是学生自觉地全身心地投入在与他们生活紧密联系的能引起他们兴趣的学习活动中。学生在活动中表现出极大的兴趣，尽管有些活动会需要他们相当的脑力劳动。教学的重点是设计和呈现包括交际型的、任务型的、问题解决型的、语境型的等的多种形式的综合练习活动。在活动中需要运用分析、比较、对比、评估等思维过程来帮助内化。

Stage 5. Generation. With the intensive and extensive practicing of word recognition and application in the previous stages, learners finally reach the stage of using the target words, either orally or written in a creative way. That is, they can use the word in their own language and with linguistic ease. At this stage, learners may still not have fully mastered all syntactic and semantic aspects of a particular word, but they can use the word with confidence and accuracy in most linguistic situations. At this stage, in order to help students gain abilities in using the target word, instruction should provide opportunities in which students can use the word frequently at a discourse level.

第五阶段：生成阶段。经过之前的深入和广泛的字词认读和应用练习，学习者达到了能创造性地在口头和书面上运用字词的阶段。也就是说，新字词成为他们自己语言的一部分，能得心应手地使用它们。在这一阶段，学习者可能还没有掌握某一词的全面的句法和语义知识，但是在大多数语境中，他们能自信地正确地使用该词。在这一阶段，教学的要点是提供机会，让学生能经常在相关的语境中在语段水平上使用字词。

The key features of the cognitive model of five-stage word acquisition are summarized in Figure 1. The model provides us with an outline of the psychological process that is undergone when learning new words. Instruction, in general, should observe this process and teaching activities should be designed accordingly for beginning level learners. Otherwise, learning could be time consuming and inefficient. For example, if comprehension is not achieved, internalization will be quite labored. In teaching reality, this cognitive processing order may not proceed precisely in a linear fashion. Each stage may interact with other stages. For example, at the perception stage, establishing a clear and vivid mental image of the word may directly relate to internalization of the word. If a word is not well internalized due to interference from a previously learned sound, shape, or meaning of a similar word, then we should provide another chance for learners to perceive the target word and make sure that the students have a clear perception of the difference in sound, shape, or meaning of this word from a similar word. Therefore, instruction may not be limited to a linear progression from stage 1 to 5; rather, we should allow for regression between the stages.

　　图1总结了上述的五阶段字词习得认知模式。这个模式勾画出了字词习得的一般心理过程。在初级字词课上，教学应该遵循这一心理过程设计相应教法，如果违反这一过程，教学就事倍功半。假如学生还没有达到理解阶段，就让学生对字词进行内化就会十分费劲。教学现实中，五阶段的认知过程可能不是直线式的推进，每一阶段与其他阶段是相互联系的。例如，在感知阶段，清晰、生动的词的心理图像的建立直接影响对字词的内化。如果一个词没有很好的内化是由于受到先前已经学过的音、形或义相似词的干扰，那么教学就要再一次提供机会让学生感知该词，直到学生对该词的音形义有了清晰的感知。因此，课堂上教学步骤的安排不能只限于直线式的从第一阶段到第五阶段推进，而应该允许各阶段之间的交叉。

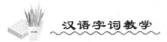

Figure 1 Cognitive model of five-stage word acquisition
图1 五阶段字词习得认知模式

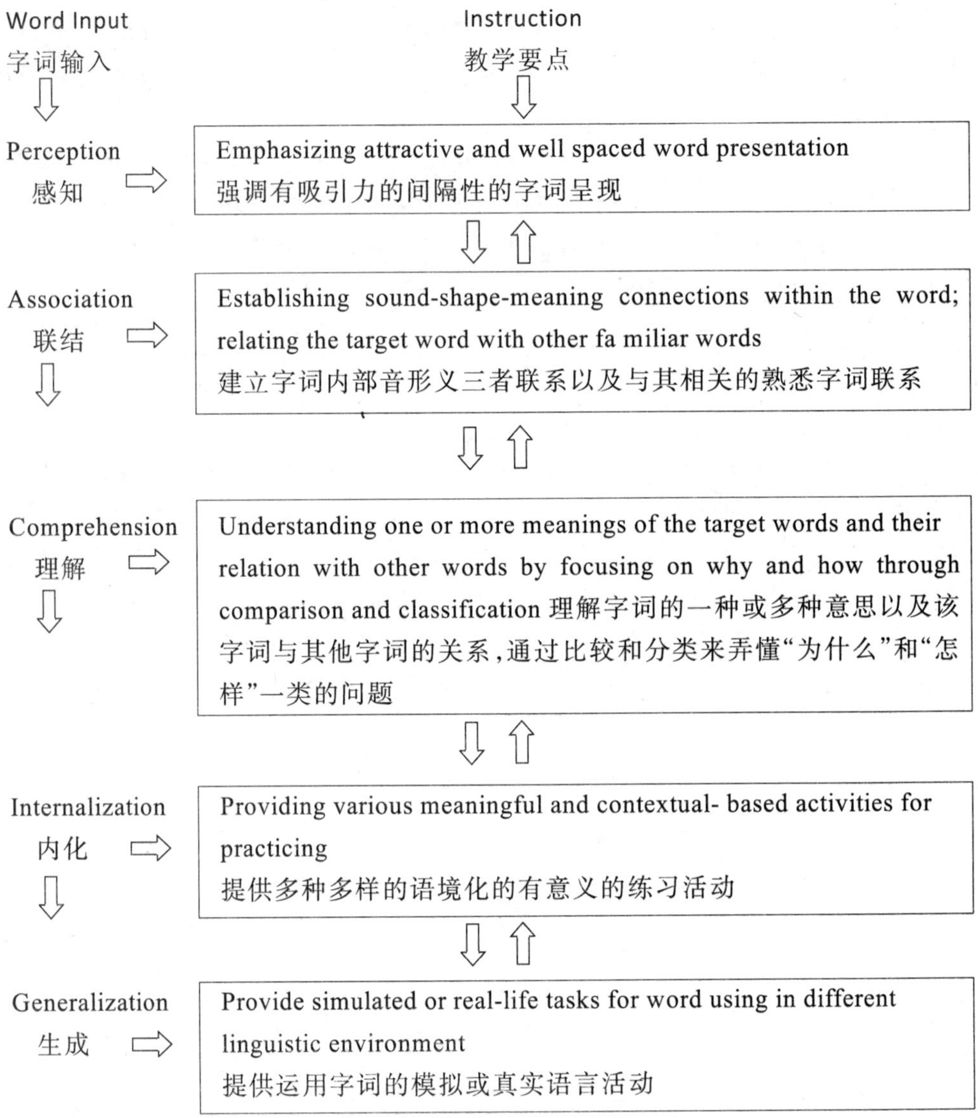

Word Input 字词输入	Instruction 教学要点
Perception 感知	Emphasizing attractive and well spaced word presentation 强调有吸引力的间隔性的字词呈现
Association 联结	Establishing sound-shape-meaning connections within the word; relating the target word with other familiar words 建立字词内部音形义三者联系以及与其相关的熟悉字词联系
Comprehension 理解	Understanding one or more meanings of the target words and their relation with other words by focusing on why and how through comparison and classification 理解字词的一种或多种意思以及该字词与其他字词的关系，通过比较和分类来弄懂"为什么"和"怎样"一类的问题
Internalization 内化	Providing various meaningful and contextual-based activities for practicing 提供多种多样的语境化的有意义的练习活动
Generalization 生成	Provide simulated or real-life tasks for word using in different linguistic environment 提供运用字词的模拟或真实语言活动

3.1.2 Multilevel Interactive-activation word identification model
多层次交互激活字词认读模式

One of the ultimate goals of vocabulary instruction is for learners to be able to recognize words automatically while reading. Naturally, we would like to know, after words are learned and stored in learners' long-term memories, how do learners identify the words when they encounter them in a reading text? Taft & Zhu (1997) proposed an interactive-activation model for word identification. This model holds that that word recognition can happen at three different levels: the word level, the character level, and the radical level. Take, for example, the word 睡觉, when it appears in 我昨天晚上很晚才睡觉因为我要做作业. If the word 睡觉 is ready to be retrieved in a reader's mental lexicon, the whole word 睡觉 will be identified as the reader reads the sentence. However, if 睡觉 is temporarily not available for retrieval due to vague memory or because the reader may have confused this word with other words such as 瞌睡, 觉得, then the reader will look at individual characters 睡 and 觉. Once the two characters are identified, then the reader will try to put these together to figure out its meaning based on the meaning of the individual characters. During this process, it is possible that the individual character process may also help to activate the word 睡觉 as a whole because individual character access could serve as retrieval cue for the word 睡觉. If the reader is not able to recall the individual character 睡 or 觉, then the reader will look at the radicals within the character and try to find clues to identify this character. For example, the radicals in the character 目 and 垂 may help to activate the meaning and sound of 睡. As 睡 is a phonetic-semantic compound in which 目 is a semantic radical and 垂 is a phonetic radical. However, 睡 is also an ideograph in which 垂 indicates a person sitting there with eyelids drooping down.

　　字词教学的最终目标是学生能够在阅读时达到字词认读自动化。自然,我们想知道,当字词存储到人脑的长时记忆系统后,个体在阅读中是怎样认读字词的? Taft & Zhu (1997) 提出了一个多层次交互激活字词认读模式,这个模式假设字词的认读可以在三种水平上进行:词水平、字水平、部首水平。以词"睡觉"为例,当它出现在"我昨天晚上很晚才睡觉因为我要做作业"这个句子中,如果"睡觉"这一词已经存储在个体的心理词典中,那么这一词是以整词的形式在句中被激活由此而完成认读。但是,如果那个读者记忆模糊,在心理词典中一时找不到"睡觉"这一词,他可能把这个词与"瞌睡"或"觉得"混在一起,那么,他就会分别辨认"睡"和"觉"。当这两个字都被辨认出来,读者会把两个字放在一起根据每个字的意思猜测"睡觉"的意思。在这一过程中,很可能对单个字的辨认会帮助读者想起"睡觉"这个词,因为,"睡"和"觉"各自都可以成为"睡觉"的提醒线索。假如,那个读者没法认读"睡"和"觉",那么,他会注意每个字中的部首,试着以部首为线索来辨认字。例如,"睡"字中的部首"目"和"垂"可能帮助激活"睡"字的音和义。因为"睡"是一个形声字,"目"是形旁,"垂"是声旁。当然,"睡"也是一个会意字,"垂"表示一个人坐在那儿眼睑下垂打盹。

The existence of radical level processing in word recognition has been confirmed. A study on adult character recognition revealed that this recognition process is affected by the number of radicals in the compound character. A character with fewer radicals is recognized more quickly. The author of the study concluded that radicals are the functional orthographic units in Chinese character recognition (Chen, Allport, & Marshal 1996). This study supports the existence of the radical level process proposed by the Multilevel Interactive-activation word identification model. The significance of the multilevel Interactive-activation word identification model is that it recognizes that radical knowledge plays a role in word recognition.

上述提及的部首水平加工已从实验中得到证实。关于成人汉字认读的研究(Chen, Allport, & Marshal 1996)揭示汉字认读过程受合体字中部首数量的影响,个体对部首少的合体字的认读速度要比对部首多的合体字快。该研究的结论是,在汉字认读中,部首是功能性的加工单位。这一研究支持多层次交互激活字词认读模式中部首水平加工的存在。这一模式的意义在于它认可了部首知识在汉字认读中的作用。

3.2 Psycholinguistic models on lexical access
词义提取的心理语言模式

In this section, we will discuss psycholinguistic models on lexical access and the establishment of lexical system. We will present two models. The first model is three-level interactive lexical access model which addresses the lower level processing during reading. The second model is four-stage lexical development model which deals how CFL learners develop their lexical system.

接下去我们将从心理语言学的角度讨论阅读中词义提取和词汇系统的建立。我们将提出两个模式。第一个模式是三层次交互词义提取模式。该模式阐释阅读中低级加工过程——即对字词的加工。第二个模式是汉语二语四阶段词汇系统发展模式,这一模式描述个体如何在大脑中建立汉语二语词汇系统。

3.2.1 Three-level interactive lexical access model
三层次交互词义提取模式

Unlike alphabetic language, in Chinese, the characters represent lexical morphemes - character boundaries rather than word boundaries are indicated by spaces. Therefore, we consider that processing Chinese words in a reading context includes at least three levels: character recognition, word segmentation, and lexical access, which initially was proposed by the first author of this book in 2008 (Shen 2008).

与拼音文字语言不同的是,在汉语中,大部分汉字代表单音节词,它们又是自由元素,可以与其他汉字组成双音节或多音节词,但在书写时汉字之间用空间隔开,词与词之间没有空间隔开。因此,在阅读过程中对词的加工至少经过三个层次:汉字辨认、断词、词义提取(Shen 2008)。

Character recognition is the activation of sound, shape, and meaning of individual characters in reading. As individual characters have multiple meanings, the exact meaning of a particular character in a reading text may not be determined at the initial stage. For example, when processing a sentence 改天再去, the first character 改 has meanings of *change, switch, transform, revise, alter etc*. The reader may activate any of the multiple meanings of 改 during the character recognition process. When the second character 天 is recognized, then the reader is able to choose a meaning for 改, as 改天 means "another day or an alternative day."

汉字辨认是指阅读过程中汉字音形义的激活。如果一个汉字是多义的,这个汉字在上下文中确切的意思在汉字辨认的初始阶段可能无法确定。比如在加工"改天再去"时,第一个字"改"有几种解释:变化、变换、转化、修改、替换等。阅读者有可能在头脑中激活这些字义,只有当第二个字"天"被正确认读后,阅读者才能在可能的字义中为"改"选择确切的意思,因为"改天"意思是"另外一天或换一天"。

Word segmentation groups relevant characters into lexical units and processes them as words in ongoing reading. In the sentence 人人都说他是一个人才, deciding which is a word or not a word is not a straightforward task. We all know that 个人 (individual) is a word 人才 (talented person) is also a word, but in this particular context, if we group 个人 together , it will lead to an inaccurate lexical access which results in inaccurate comprehension of the whole sentence.

断词是指在阅读过程中把相关的字组成词。例如,在"人人都说他是一个人才"这个句子中,决定怎样组词并不是一件直截了当的事。因为"个人"是一个词,"人才"也是一个词,但是在这个特定的语境中,如果组成"个人",就会导致错误的词义提取由此引起对句子的错误理解。

Lexical access refers to the process of gaining word meaning, syntactic properties, and pronunciation that best fits the context. The key for lexical access is to choose only a contextually relevant meaning for the word, to ensure successful comprehension of the reading text. Due to the linguistic factors, Chinese words consist of either one, two or more characters and individual character has multiple meanings. Therefore, compared with English, readers in Chinese rely heavily on a more diffused, context-dependent strategy during reading for comprehension as opposed to a more focused word-dependent strategy often adopted by readers of alphabetic systems (Chen 1992, 1999).

词义提取是指在阅读过程中激活适合上下文的正确的词义，词的语法特征以及词的发音。词义提取的关键是词义是否适合上下文，这样才能保证阅读理解的成功。由于语言学上的特点，汉语的词可以由一个汉字、两个汉字或两个以上汉字组成。每个汉字含有多种意思。因此跟英文相比，读者更加需要使用上下文来确定词义的策略(Chen 1992, 1999)。

Now, let us further discuss how the three levels of character recognition, word segmentation, and lexical access interact with each other to complete lexical access during text reading. Let us first examine character recognition in a context. One study reported that character recognition was the most rapid when it was not associated with any other characters. Recognition was faster when it was part of a word, no matter whether this word fits the meaning of the sentence, such as "人人" in the sentence (人人)都说他是一个人才. Recognition was slowest, when the character was not part of a word or it was grouped with other random characters such as in "人都" or "都人他" situations. This evidence suggests that character recognition is the initial stage of lexical access, but the word context in which the character is embedded also affects character recognition. As we mentioned earlier, to the way that characters are grouped to form a word is affected by the sentential context; therefore, initial word segmentation could be wrong. Readers will have to rely on the context information to confirm or disconfirm their decisions on word segmentation as they read. For example, in reading the sentence 人人都说他是一个人才, the reader may initially consider 人 as a word, but when the second and third characters are read, the reader will determine that 人人 should be a word. Under this type of circumstance, word decision is affected by the information obtained from the context. Word decision is based on the readers' comprehension of the individual character, but also on their initial comprehension of the context, although this comprehension is ongoing and not a final one. Thus, we can say that word segmentation is part of lexical access. A study on the segmentation of Chinese words during reading (Li, Rayner, Cave 2009) proposed a model of Chinese word segmentation. This model argued that Chinese word segmentation and word recognition are interactive processes involving top-down and bottom-up factors. The author proposed multiple levels for processing of words. The first level is a visual perception level that abstracts visual features from the stimulus. The second level is character recognition, which recognizes characters using perceptual information from the first level and feedback information from the word recognition level. The third level is the word segmentation and recognition level, this level receives information from both the character recognizers and the lexicon. Based on this evidence, the interaction between the three-stages in the lexical access process is illustrated in Figure 2.

现在,让我们进一步讨论阅读中汉字辨认、断词、词义提取这三个水平如何交互作用完成词义解码的。我们先来看一下在文本中的汉字辨认。研究表明,在没有上下文的情况下汉字辨认速度最快(Li, Rayner, & Cave 2009),辨认较快的是汉字是词的一部分,不管这个词是否对上下文合适,比如"人人"在"人人都说他是一个人才"句子中。辨认最慢的是汉字不是词的一部分,或者说跟其他字随机组在一起不成词的情况下,比如,"人都"或"都人他"。这个现象表明汉字辨认是词义提取的初级阶段,包含目的词的语境也影响着汉字辨认。前面我们提到怎样断词是由上下文决定的,所以在没有理解句子情况下的初始阶段的断词可能会发生错误。读者必须依赖上下文信息来不断确认和否认自己初始阶段的断词决定。例如,在读"人人都说他是一个人才"时,读者最初也许把"人"看成是一个词,但当读了第二和第三个字时,读者便认为"人人"应该是一个词。所以,断词依赖于对上下文的理解。如何断词是基于读者对每个汉字的理解,但是也基于读者对上下文的初步理解,虽然这种理解不是最后的而是进行性的。由此,我们可以说,断词也是词义提取的一部分。Li, Rayner & Cave (2009) 认为汉语断词和词的认读是一个自下而上、自上而下的交互作用过程。他们提出了一个词加工的多级水平模式。第一级是视觉感知水平,即对刺激物的特征的提取。第二级是汉字辨认。第三级是断词和词的认读。汉字辨认依靠第一级感知水平和第三级断词和词认读的反馈信息。而第三级水平加工依赖于前两级的加工信息。根据这些研究结果以及上述的分析,我们现在把前面提出的三层次交互词义提取模式以及他们之间的关系用图2来标示。

Figure 2 The three-level interactive lexical access model
图2 三层次交互词义提取模式

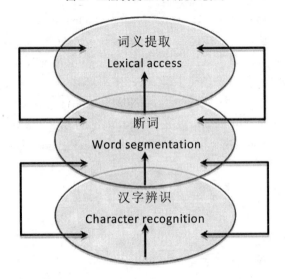

In this model, we see the overlaps between the levels of character recognition and word segmentation and between the levels of word segmentation and lexical access. The pedagogical implication of this model is that character instruction should not stop at the place where students can identify words in isolation; rather, there is a continuum from recognizing individual character to successful lexical access. Thus, context-based character instruction should be one of the important components of entire vocabulary instruction.

在图2中,我们看到第一层次与第二层次的交叉重合以及第二层次与第三层次的交叉重合。这一模式的教学法意义在于,字词教学不能满足于学生能正确地辨认汉字,而是要认识到字词教学是从汉字辨认到成功词义提取的一个动态过程。因此,语境化的字词教学应该成为整个字词教学的一个重要组成部分。

3.2.2 CFL four-stage lexical development model
汉语二语四阶段词汇发展模式

We mentioned above that lexical access is the process of gaining word meaning, syntactic property, and pronunciation that best fits the context. For English-speaking CFL learners, the development of word segmentation and lexical access skill is a slow process, especially regarding the aspect of semantic development. Shen's study (2008) revealed that English-speaking learners who completed 26 credit hours in Chinese learning gained only about 54%

accuracy in word segmentation when reading the materials at their instructional level. This slow development of lexical access prompts us to take a closer look at the lexical development process among CFL learners. Jiang (2000) pointed out the two practical constraints on lexical development in L2 vocabulary instructional settings. One is the poverty of input in terms of both quantity and quality. For learners studying in a non-target language speaking environment, when a new word is introduced, the contextualized practice available is insufficient for learners to observe the changes in word meaning in various contextual situations. The other constraint is the presence of an established conceptual/semantic system that is closely associated with the L1 lexical system. That is, L2 learners rely on their L1 lexical system in learning new words in a second language, because the meanings of L2 words can be understood through their L1 translation. However, there is no perfect match for the meaning equivalence between L1 and L2. By pointing out the two constraints in lexical development, Jiang further proposed a three-stage L2 lexical development model. The first stage is the formal stage of lexical development. At this stage, the learner's attention is focused on the formal features of the word: its spelling and pronunciation, with little semantic, syntactic, or morphological information created or established within the lexical entry in the process. At this stage, the use of L2 words involves the activation of the links between L2 words and their L1 translations. The second stage is the L1 lemma mediation stage. In this stage, the use of L2 words is mediated by the lemmas of their L1 translations. The last stage is the L2 integration stage. At this stage, a lexical entry in L2 will be very similar to a lexical entry in L1 in terms of both representation and processing. As the learners' experience in L2 increases, stronger associations are developed between L2 words and their L1 translations. The learners can simultaneously activate L2 word forms and the semantic and syntactic information of L1 equivalence. Jiang's model provided a rough framework of lexical development for L2 as an alphabetic language. Inspired by Jiang's model, and based on CFL lexical accessing characteristics, we propose a four-stage L2 Chinese lexical development model. The four-stages are the L2-L1 direct mapping stage, L1 mediated generative stage, initial formation of the L2 lexical system stage, and full development of the L2 lexical system stage, as illustrated in Figure 3 and as discussed in detail below.

  我们在前面提到,词义提取是指在阅读过程中激活适合上下文的正确的词义、词的语法特征以及词的发音。对于英语为母语的汉语学习者来说,断词和词义提取技能的发展是一个缓慢的过程,尤其是语义知识的发展。Shen(2008)的研究揭示了英语为母语的

汉语字词教学

大学汉语学习者修学完26个学分后,在阅读跟他们的年级水平相当的文章时,断词的正确率只达到54%。这一现象促使我们有必要近距离地考察汉语二语学习者的词汇系统发展过程。Jiang (2000)指出了二语学习者词汇系统发展的两个教学上的负面因素。第一个是词汇输入在量和质上的贫乏。对于在非目的语环境中学习者来说,当新词被介绍后,语境化的练习很缺乏,以致学生很少有机会观察到一个特定的词在不同语境中的语义变化。另一负面因素是已经建立的母语词汇系统的干扰。也就是说,学习者在学习二语新词时依赖于他们母语词汇的语义系统,即二语词义的获得是通过母语的翻译,但是这种翻译是不可靠的,因为母语与二语的词义并不完全对等。在指出了这两个负面因素之后,Jiang进一步提出了一个三阶段二语词汇发展模式。第一阶段是标准词汇发展阶段。在这一阶段,学习者的注意力集中在词的一些标准特征上:拼法和读音,但对某词条的词义、句法及构词法方面的知识却非常贫乏。在这一阶段,对二语目的词的应用是要通过第一语言的翻译系统。第二阶段是第一语言词目阶段(词目:词汇学中指列在西方词典中词条开头的词项)。在这一阶段,第二语言目的词的应用是通过第一语言的词目为中介。最后阶段是第二语言词汇整合阶段。在这一阶段,对第二语言词条在学习者的头脑中的表征和加工形式达到与第一语言相似程度。随着学习者二语词汇学习经验日趋丰富,第一语言词汇翻译系统与第二语言词汇系统已经建立很强的联结。学习者在看到二语词时,可以同时激活对应的第一语言的词的形式、语义和句法系统。Jiang的模式为我们提供了一个拼音文字语言作为二语的粗线条的词汇发展的轮廓。受到Jiang的模式的启发,根据汉语二语词汇发展的特征,我们在这里提出一个四阶段汉语二语词汇发展模式。这四个阶段是:二语与母语词汇直接对应阶段、母语为中介的生成阶段、汉语二语词汇系统形成初级阶段、汉语二语词汇系统完全发展阶段(请参看图3)。下面详细阐述这一模式。

Stage 1: L2-L1 direct mapping stage. At this stage, students learning Chinese target words heavily rely on L1 definitions and translations. They memorize word meanings based on English translations. Due to the very limited knowledge of the semantic aspect of target words, such as how many meanings a word may have, how and in which way a word can be connected with other words, the scope and restriction for using the word in context, etc., students hesitate to create sentences using newly learned target words and they feel more secure in memorizing the sentences from the textbook and use these whenever it is possible, both inside and outside the classroom. At this stage, we may not observe many mistakes in students' word use.

第一阶段:二语与母语词汇直接对应阶段。在这个阶段,学生学习汉语词汇十分依赖于他们的母语。他们对字词意思的理解是通过母语翻译。由于汉语语义知识匮乏,一个特定的词有多少种意思,某一词与其他词是以什么样的方式联系在一起及有多少种联系,一个词在语境中运用的范围和限制是什么等等,学生都不清楚,所以为了不犯错误,他们非常不愿意用目的词造自己的句子,而是背诵课文中的句子,在可能的时候在课堂里和课堂外运用这些背诵的句子。在这一阶段,我们可能很少发现学生的用词错误。

Stage 2: L1 mediated generation stage. As their Chinese vocabulary and syntactic knowledge increases, students gradually develop the confidence to generate L2 sentences using L2 target words. However, this generative process is still heavily mediated by L1. When they try to use the words in sentences, they will first work out a L1 sentence, then try to translate the L1 sentence into L2. Due to the drastic differences in semantics and grammar structure, this L1 mediated creative use of L2 words is often inaccurate. Due to limited communication opportunities in non-target speaking environments, L2 words are learned in the first stage mainly through association with L1 definitions or translations, rather than by extraction or learning from the authentic linguistic context by the learners themselves. Thus, we often observe various types of errors indicating that students are inappropriately applying learned orthographic, syntactic knowledge in word use. For example, a study (潘先军 2002) reported that students try to use semantic radical knowledge to understand the meaning of 切 in the word 亲切. Because 切 has a semantic radical 刀, the students guessed that the word meaning for 亲切 is 自己砍 (one himself cuts). By analyzing this error, we can tell that the student was well aware of the role of semantic radical in a compound character, but his semantic knowledge of the character 切 was still limited. A student may say that 我见面他, as result of translation from the English sentence "I see him" because the learner is not aware of the grammatical restriction of the word 见面。In producing sentences, we can observe all kinds of mistakes due to inaccurate word use. A study on the development of semantic transfer in acquisition of L2 Chinese productive vocabulary (Shen 2009b) reported that English-speaking advanced CFL learners who had completed 26 credit hours of Chinese study still heavily relied on their native language for productive vocabulary use. For example, a student would consider 这个词我学过,我 认识是什么意思 as a correct sentence because 认识 can be translated into "to know" in English. Learners will not be able to correct these types of learning errors until they encounter a communication breakdown in a situation where a native speaker or a more advanced learner points out the problem to the learner or they read correct expressions in L2 reading texts.

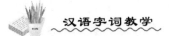

第二阶段：母语为中介的生成阶段。随着学生汉语词汇和语法知识的增加，学生开始有了用所学的词造句子的自信心。但是这个创造过程仍然十分依赖于母语中介。当他们要用汉语说一句话的时候，他们先用母语说这句话，然后把母语的句子翻译成汉语句子。但是由于母语与汉语之间在语义和语法结构上有很大差异，学生的汉语句子经常会有错误。因为在第一阶段，学生用母语翻译来理解汉语的词义，加上缺少与汉语母语者的交流机会，所以学生在第一阶段学到的汉语词汇几乎都是通过母语翻译法，而不是学生从真实的目的语语境中获得的，自然，我们会观察到学生在用词上的各种错误，包括错误地运用他们学到的关于汉语的正字知识和句法知识。例如，潘先军(2002)指出学生试图用表义部首来理解汉字"切"在"亲切"中的意思。因为"切"的表义部首是"刀"，学生就猜测"亲切"的意思是"自己砍"。通过分析这一类错误，可以得出学生对表义部首在合体字中的作用已经有很好的理解，但是对"切"的语义知识仍然很肤浅。学生可能会说"我见面他"。这一错误的原因是因为学生把英文句子"I see him"直接翻译成了中文，而没有意识到"见面"作为离合词在汉语里不带宾语。在学生汉语句子生成中，我们可以看到许多错误是由用词不当引起的。一个关于汉语二语积极词汇习得中的语义转换的研究(Shen 2009b)显示，英语母语的汉语高级学习者（已修完26个汉语课学分）在汉语词汇运用中仍十分依赖他们的母语英语。例如，一个学生会认为"这个词我学过，我<u>认识</u>是什么意思"是正确的，因为"认识"的英文意思是"to know"。在这一阶段，学生没有机会改正这一类的错误，除非他们同汉语母语者或比他们更优秀的汉语学习者交流中，对方指出了他们用词上的错误，或他们在阅读中得悉了正确的表达方式。

Stage 3: Initial formation of the L2 Chinese lexical system stage. As they continuously expand the breadth and depth of target vocabulary and increase their opportunities to use the target words in spoken and written communication, students gradually develop an L2 lexical system. During this stage, students rely less on their L1 for producing target language. They may not use L1 as mediation for those words that they feel quite confident to use them, although they may still feel restricted in word using due to deliberately avoiding making mistakes. In general, they have a good sense of the differences in orthography, semantics, and syntax between L1 and L2. They understand the limitations of L1 mediation. As a result, they produce semantically and grammatically correct sentences, but obviously, their word use is not sophisticated and lacks variation. We often observe these phenomena, where learners can present their ideas with considerable sophistication when using their native language, but when they switch to Chinese, we feel that they talk like elementary students.

第三阶段:汉语二语词汇系统形成初级阶段。随着学生不断地扩大他们的汉语词汇知识的广度和深度,以及在口头和书面形式上运用汉语词汇机会的增多,汉语二语词汇系统逐步形成。在这一阶段,学生在二语句子生成时,对母语的依赖性逐渐减少。对于他们觉得有把握的句子,他们在使用的时候,不再通过母语翻译,虽然为了避免犯错误,他们在运用时还是不那么自如。总的来说,他们对母语与汉语之间的在语义、句法等方面的不同有了更好的认识,认识到母语翻译的局限性。这一阶段,他们能生成语义和语法正确的句子。但是很明显,他们的词汇运用不那么老练,句子简单且缺少变化。我们经常注意到这种现象,学习者能用他们的母语对某种观点的表达达到一定的深度和高度,但是当他们用汉语来表达相同的观点时,我们有时会感到他们词汇和句子运用如同汉语为母语的小学生的表达水平。

Stage 4: Full development of the L2 Chinese lexical system stage. At this stage, the learners no longer look like learners they are skillful users of the target vocabulary and their language behavior is close to a Chinese native speaker. However, it is possible that most CFL learners are at the juncture of indefinitely approaching this stage, but are never quite able to reach it if they do not have an opportunity to be immersed in a target language speaking environment for a prolonged time. Due to the complex nature of semantic aspects of the Chinese lexical system, it is not surprising that we may still observe unconventional ways of word use for those CFL speakers who studied and lived in China for three or more years.

第四阶段:汉语二语词汇系统完全发展阶段。在这一阶段,他们已经能娴熟地使用词汇,他们的语言行为很接近汉语母语者。但是,大部分的汉语二语学习者如果他们没有在目的语环境中进行较长时间的沉浸式学习的话,可能处在不断接近这一阶段的途中,却不能到达这一阶段的终点。由于汉语词汇系统的复杂性,我们不难发现,一个外国学生已经在中国生活和学习了三年甚至更长的时间可能仍然会有不恰当的用词行为。

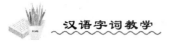

Figure 3　CFL four-stage lexical development model
图 3　汉语二语四阶段词汇系统发展模式

Stage 4: Full development of the L2 Chinese lexical system
汉语二语词汇系统完全发展阶段

Features 特征:

1. No L1 mediation is observed in word use 用词不再以第一语言为中介
2. Few error patterns are observed in word use 几乎没有规律性的用词错误
3. Chinese lexical system is well developed 汉语二语词汇系统已经完善

Stage 3: Initial formation of the L2 Chinese lexical system
汉语二语词汇系统形成初级阶段

Features 特征:

1. Fast growth of breadth and depth of vocabulary 词汇深广度知识的快速发展
2. Chinese lexicon system is formed, but lacks variation and Sophistication 汉语二语词汇系统初步形成但是比较简单缺少变化
3. Use target word with confidence and seldom requires L1 mediation 能自信地运用汉语词汇很少借助母语中介

Stage 2: L1 mediated generation 母语为中介的生成阶段

Features 特征:

1. Start generalizing own sentences by using target words, but rely on L1 translation 开始能用目的词造句但是依赖母语翻译
2. Errors observed due to 1) lack knowledge of incompatibility between L1 and L2 in syntax, semantics, and pragmatics; 2) over generalization 观察到词汇运用错误,原因有二:1)缺乏母语和二语词汇不对应的相关知识;2)过度推广
3. Start to develop L2 lexicon system 开始发展汉语二语词汇系统

Stage 1: L2-L1 direct mapping stage 汉语二语—母语词汇直接对应阶段

Features 特征:

1. Heavy reliance on L1 translation 十分依赖母语翻译
2. Rely on memorization of sentence patterns in word use 词汇使用依靠对汉语二语句子的背诵
3. No obvious errors due to little generation in word use 因为不会自造句子所以很少有词汇运用错误

L2 Chinese vocabulary input 汉语二语词汇输入

The proposed CFL four-stage lexical development model, although it still needs to be validated and refined by further empirical studies, provides a general picture of learners' lexical development in vocabulary learning. Instructors must realize that vocabulary knowledge development is restricted by the psycholinguistic reality of the learners. Students' mistakes that we observe in the lexical development should not be viewed as a result of our inappropriate instruction. Rather, they reflect the students' progress at each stage of lexical development. From this point of view, we welcome learning mistakes because, by analyzing these mistakes, we can find which developmental stage the learner is currently situated so that we can provide appropriate instructional intervention. The importance of instructional intervention is that it can shorten the developmental time between the stages. It can also arouse students' self-awareness of their problems in lexical development.

以上我们提出的汉语二语四阶段词汇系统发展模式,虽然仍需要进一步的检验和充实,这个模式无疑勾勒出了一个汉语二语词汇学习和发展的总轮廓。教师们应该意识到词汇发展受制于学习者的心理语言现实。在此发展过程中,如果我们观察到的学生词汇运用上的错误,我们不能简单地把错误归咎于教学不当。相反,这些错误反映了学生处在词汇系统发展的某个阶段。从这个角度上来看,我们欢迎学习中的错误,因为从对这些错误的分析,我们会了解到学生正处于发展的哪个阶段,教师可以制定相应的教学干预措施。教学干预的重要性在于它能加速各阶段的发展并增强学生对用词错误的自我意识。

References 参考文献

潘先军(2002)形旁表意功能在留学生汉字学习中的负迁移及对策,《汉字文化》第3期,49-52。

Chen, H-C. (1992) Reading comprehension in Chinese: Implication from character reading times. In H-C Chen and O. J. L. Tzeng (Eds.), *Language Processing in Chinese*, pp. 175-205. The Netherlands: Elsevier Science Publishers B.V.

Chen, Y-P., Allport, D.A., Marshal, J.C. (1996) What are functional orthographic units in Chinese word recognition: The stroke or the stroke pattern? *Quarterly Journal of Experimental Psychology*, 49A, (4), 1024-1043.

Chen, H-C. (1999) How do readers of Chinese process words during reading from comprehension. In J. Wang, A.W. Inhoff, & H-C. Chen (Eds.) *Reading Chinese script: A cognitive analysis*, pp. 257-287. Mahwah, NJ: Lawrence Erlbaum Associates.

Chung, K.K.H. (2002) Effective use of hanyu Pinyin and English translation as extra stimulus prompts on learning of Chinese characters. *Educational Psychology*, 22, (2), 149-164.

Jiang, N. (2000) Lexical representation and development in a second language. *Applied Linguistics*, 21, (1), 47-77.

Li, X., Rayner, K., & Cave, K. R. (2009) On the segmentation of Chinese words during reading. *Cognitive Psychology*, 58, 525-552.

Shen, H. H. (2008) An analysis of word decision strategies among learners of Chinese. *Foreign Language Annals, 41*, (3), 501-524.

Shen, H.H. (2009a) Size and strength: Written vocabulary acquisition among advanced learners. *Chinese Teaching in the World.* 23, 1, 74-85.

Shen, H. H (2009b) *The development of semantic transfer in acquisition of L2 Chinese productive vocabulary.* Paper presented at the conference on "Word Formation in Chinese", Organizer: French Association for Chinese Teaching and Research, the University Paris, Paris.

Taft, M. & Zhu, X. (1997) Submorphemic processing in reading Chinese. *Journal of Experimental Psychology: Learning, Memory, and Cognition*, 23, (3), 761-775.

Chapter 4 第四章
Cognitive theories and vocabulary learning

认知理论与字词学习

Cognitive science studies brain and brain function. From a cognitive perspective, the character learning process is the process whereby the brain processes information. How can we learn characters more efficiently and memorize characters in a better way? The answer is that we should use cognitive information processing theories to guide our vocabulary instruction. In this chapter, we will discuss five cognitive theories that deal with information encoding, processing, and their relationship to character instruction, based on the first author's previous study on this subject (Shen 2008). The five cognitive theories included in this chapter are: dual coding theory, cognitive load theory, level-of-processing theory, multi-system account theory, and competition theory.

认知心理学研究大脑和大脑的作用。从认知角度来看,汉字学习过程是大脑加工信息的过程。我们怎样才能用更有效的方法学习汉字,用更好的方法来记忆汉字?答案是我们应该用认知加工理论来指导我们的汉语二语字词教学。在这一章中,我们将在本书第一作者(沈禾玲 2008)的研究基础上进一步讨论五种关于信息编码、加工的认知理论以及它们与字词教学的关系。这五种理论分别是:双编码理论、认知负荷理论、认知加工深度理论、多种加工通道理论和竞争理论。

4.1 Dual coding theory 双编码理论

In chapter 3, we discussed the five-stage word acquisition process. The first stage for this process is perception. After a word is initially perceived by the learner and registered in the brain, the encoding process immediately follows. **Encoding** is the process by which information in one form is converted into another form, to be communicated using a set of methods or rules. For example, a written passage is coded with numbers that can be recognized by the telegraphy to be sent to another person. Therefore, a code is a method to be used to transform a message into another form. From the character-learning viewpoint, encoding is a strategy or method used to process words so that they can be easily comprehended and memorized by individuals.

在前一章,我们讨论了五阶段字词习得认知模式。这一模式的第一阶段是对字词的感知。当字词一旦被感知登记到大脑后,编码过程就立即开始了。编码是根据规定的方法把信息的一种形式转换成另一种形式。举个例子来说,一段书面话语可以用数字来编码以电报的形式传给另一个人。因此,"码"是转换信息用的方法。从汉字学习的角度来看,编码是运用一种策略或方法对字词进行加工使它们能容易地被个体理解和记忆。

Dual coding theory initially was proposed by Paivio (1969). The theory assumes that there are two cognitive subsystems in the brain, a nonverbal system specialized for dealing with nonlinguistic objects and events, and a verbal system specialized for dealing directly with language. The two systems are functionally independent, but interconnected. Cognition involves the cooperative activity of the two systems (Paivio 1986). The theory assumed three levels of meaning processing for incoming information: representational meaning, referential meaning, and associative meaning. (1) **Representational meaning** is obtained from either verbal or non-verbal representations of the information. In other words, the understanding of the new information is through verbal definition (logogen), or through imagery representation of the information (imagen). (2) **Referential meaning** is derived from the relationship between the verbal system and nonverbal system. That is, understanding of new information occurs through the connection between the verbal definition and image of the new information. (3) **Associative meaning** is gained by activation of representations within the same verbal or nonverbal system (Paivio 2007). A given task may require any or all of the three levels of processing in order to comprehend it. Here is a concrete interpretation of the three levels of meaning processing for the word 同学 classmate. If a new word 同学 is presented as new information, representational meaning of it can be gained either through presenting a definition such as 同学是跟你一起学习的人 (a verbal representation) or by a picture of a person sitting in the same classroom with you (a nonverbal representation). The referential meaning is obtained by building a connection between the verbal description of 同学 and the picture of 同学, so that we know that both the verbal and the imagery representation of 同学 are pointing to the same concept 同学. The associative meaning is accessed by understanding the connection of 同学 with other definitions or concepts within the verbal system, as well as within the nonverbal system. For example, 同学 is the person who sits in a classroom with you. It could be the person who studies with you in any time period at any learning situation. It also could be a person who is not physically present, but who is in the same group with you via a distance learning setting. Within the imagery system, images of all types of 同学 in all types of learning situations could be activated as representation of 同学 in the learner's mind. Therefore, the concept 同学 is connected with many related situations such as classroom, school, teacher, or distance education, either in verbal or nonverbal systems.

双编码理论最初由 Paivio (1969) 提出来。这一理论假设大脑中有两个认知子系统：一个是非语言系统专门于对非语言事物的加工，另一个是语言系统，专门于对语言信息的加工。认知的过程需要这两个系统的互相合作(Paivio 1986)。这一理论假设对信息的意义加工存在着三种水平：表征意义、参照意义、联想意义。(1) 表征意义是头脑中对非语言或语言信息的直接表征。换句话说，对新信息的理解是通过用语言定义（概念）或通过展示意象（具象）。(2)参照意义的获得是通过对语言系统和非语言系统之间的关系的建立。也就是说，对新信息的理解是通过把语言所传载的信息与具象所传载的信息之间形成相互的联系。(3) 联结意义的获取是通过建立语言定义系统内部和意象系统内部的表征信息之间的联系 (Paivio 2007)。对不同信息的加工可能需要其中一种或所有三种水平的意义加工参与。举个例子来说，如果"同学"是一个新词，表征意义的获得可以通过给"同学"这个词下定义："同学是在同一个学校学习的人"（概念表征），或者呈现一张跟你坐在同一个教室的人的照片（具象表征）。参照意义的获得是在头脑中让"同学"的概念表征与具象表征联系起来，因此你知道概念表征和具象表征指的是同一个信息：同学。联结表征是指对"同学"这个概念在概念表征系统内部与其他概念的关系的理解和在具象表征内部它与其他具象之间的关系的理解。比如说，在概念系统中，我们用语言来描述，"同学"可以是现在在教室里和你一起学习的任何一个人；也可以是在任何一个阶段在任何一个学习单位与你在一起学习的人；也可以是一个不与你坐在一起但与你在同一期中通过远程教育设施一起学习的人。在具象系统中，关于各种各样的"同学"的具象被激活并使具象之间产生联系。这样，"同学"这一概念在概念系统或具象系统中与许多其他的事物发生联系，如与教室、学校、老师、远程教育等概念之间的联系以及概念所代表的具象之间的联系。

Imagery code can be in different formats: visible format such as pictures and mental images, and invisible formats such as visual images, sound images, kinesthesia, tactile images, and emotional experiences. According to dual coding theory, any information can be encoded as verbal or imagery representation. If both verbal and imagery encoding methods are used, it will result in better learning and memorization than single coding (either verbal or imagery code). The reason is simple -dual codes provide dual recall cues. Thus, when newly learned information is recalled from the brain, if one code is lost, the brain still can use the other code to retrieve the information. That means that when the word 同学 is presented, a learner can recognize this word by recalling the encoding cue, the verbal description of this word. If this cue is lost (forgotten), the learner can use an imagery cue — the picture of 同学 to recognize the word.

"双码"在这里指的是用来把信息转化成个体能够理解的相应的语言码和意象码。对"同学"下定义是语言码,一张同学的照片是意象码。意象码可以有不同的形式,可以是声音觉具象、运动觉具象、触摸觉具象及情感体验。根据双编码理论,任何信息都可以用概念或意象来表征。如果语言和意象表征同时运用,那么对信息的记忆就会优于只用一种表征(只用语言码或只用意象码)。理由很简单,因为双编码提供双重提醒线索。当新近学到的信息被提取时,如果一种码被暂时遗忘,大脑可以用另一种码来提取信息。也就是说,如果"同学"这个词呈现时,个体可以通过回忆这个词的定义从而认读该词。但是如果这一定义被忘记,那么个体还可以用意象码,关于同学的具象来激活对该词的记忆达到认读这个词的目的。

Pedagogical implications
教学应用

Applying the dual coding theory to character instruction means that, when introducing new words to students, we should use dual codes (both verbal and imagery codes) to allow students to dual-encode the new words. Traditionally, scholars held the concept that adults are cognitively mature and they can accept verbal descriptions; therefore, images are not necessary in vocabulary instruction. This idea is correct from the comprehension perspective. However, we suggest that the use of dual codes not only considers comprehension, but more importantly, also promotes memorization. Dual codes not only help comprehension, but also help in information retention and retrieval.

把双编码理论应用在汉字教学中意味着在向学生介绍生词时我们应该使用双码(语言码与意象码),这样学生就能对新词加工时运用双编码。传统上,一些学者们认为成人在认知上已经成熟,他们能接受语言概念,所以呈现意象在字词教学中是不必要的。这一观念从理解的角度来看是合理的,但是我们建议运用双码不是光从理解的角度考虑,更重要的是从记忆的角度来考虑,双码不仅是有助于理解,它也有助于信息的保持和提取。

A study (Shen 2010a) compared the learning effects of two instructional encoding methods in Chinese vocabulary instruction among English-speaking beginning college CFL students. One instructional method used verbal encoding only, and the other used verbal encoding plus imagery encoding. Learning of both concrete words and abstract words was examined under these two encoding methods. When compared with the verbal encoding method, the verbal plus imagery encoding method did not show any superior effect in retention of the sound, shape, and meaning of concrete words, but a statistically significant difference was found for retention of the shape and meaning of abstract words. This confirms the effectiveness of dual encoding in Chinese vocabulary acquisition. The author explained the reason why we did not see a significant positive effect of dual encoding in learning concrete words. In teaching those concrete words, although the visual images were not presented to students in the control group, it was very possible that because of the concrete nature of these words, the students recalled mental images of these words that had previously been stored in their mental photo albums. During the instruction, when students saw these words, the relevant mental images were activated. To cite an example, when the word 起床 was introduced, an image of a person getting up from a bed could be evoked based on students' past experiences. For the abstract word, mental images were not readily retrieved from the students' mental photo album; therefore, the presence of visual images greatly facilitated encoding the words with imagery codes. The study reported that dual codes led to a better retention of the shape and meaning of the abstract words, but not the sound of the abstract words. Why? As mentioned earlier, Chinese lacks sound-to-spelling correspondence. In the study, the imagery coding method used imagery codes, but not acoustic ones; hence, retention of the sound of words was not promoted. By understanding this, in using dual codes for words instruction, and especially for abstract words, an instructor may consider three issues: One is that instruction should provide visual images such as pictures and visual actions to accompanying the word, in addition to verbal explanations. Sometimes, presenting a single concrete picture for an abstract word may not be possible; thus, it would be helpful if diagrams (including figures and charts) were presented to help students comprehend the word. The other is that in order to help students learn the sound of words, instruction must place weight on using methods that enhance acoustic encoding or evoke acoustic images, together with other encoding methods. Thus, in addition to the practice of sounding out individual words, activities such as categorizing words according to the similarities and differences in initial sounds, final sounds, or tones or searching phonetic radicals in new words should be encouraged. These types of activities help students recognize patterns of pronunciation for words and allow students to be exposed to the sound of words and to practice them in a meaningful way. Another aspect is that instruction should not focus solely on new words at the representational meaning level; rather, it should lead to the associative level. Activities that help students to establish associations between the new words and learned words and other related items in both verbal and nonverbal systems should be followed after initial presentation of the new words.

  Shen (2010a)比较了两种教学编码方法对英语母语汉语学习者字词学习的影响。一种是只用语言码教学,另一种是同时运用语言码和意象码。比较这两种方法的在学习具体字词与抽象字词的效果。在学习具体词的情况下,两种方法在对字词的音形义的保持上没有显示统计意义上的显著性不同,但是在对抽象词的形和义的保持上,双码教学明显地优于只用语言码教学。这一结果证实双编码教学在汉语字词教学中的有效性。Shen 解释为什么在具体词教学中双编码未显显著效果的理由:在具体词教学中,在只用一种语言码教学时,虽然没有呈现图像,由于具体词的具体性质,在学生的头脑中很可能已经唤起了早先存储的关于这些具体词的图像。在教学中,当学生看到某个词时,相应的心理具象就会被激活。比如说,看到"起床"这个词并了解了它的定义之后,个体过去存储的相关的一个人从床上起来的心理图像就会在头脑中激活。但是在学抽象词时,个体头脑中没有现成的心理图像,所以教学中出示视觉图像就会在很大程度上帮助对词进行意象编码。为什么该研究只发现双编码更有助于对词的形义的保持,而没有提到音呢？Shen 认为,汉语缺乏音形之间的联系,而该研究在用意象码的时候只用视觉意象而不是听觉意象,所以,我们看不到对字音保持的显著效果。这一点对我们很有用,在用双码进行字词教学时,尤其是介绍抽象词时,教师应该考虑到三点:第一点是教学除了用定义来解释词时,还应该提供关于词的图像或视觉动象。有时候,对于抽象词很难找出一个对应的图片,教师可以设计一些图表呈现给学生以帮助理解。第二点是为了帮助学生更好地加工字词的音,教学应该设计一些能增强听觉编码的活动,伴随其他编码方法以激活学生的听觉意象。因此,除了让学生读字词之外,应当鼓励运用根据声母、韵母或声调相同给字词分类,或在字词中寻找表声部首等教学活动。这些活动有助于学生注意到字词的音并进行有意义的练习。第三点是在教学新词时,教学活动不能只停留在对表征意义加工水平上,而是要引导学生达到联结意义水平上的加工。在完成表征意义水平加工后,教学活动应该指向能帮助学生建立新词与学过的相关的词的联系以及目的词与其他相关的概念系统和意象系统的联系。

4.2 Cognitive load theory 认知负荷理论

Cognitive load theory is an instructional theory initially proposed by Sweller (1988), which is based on Miller's limited capacity of short-term memory concept (Miller 1956). One of revolutionary human memory models is the Atkinson-Shiffrin Model proposed by Richard Atkinson and Richard Shiffrin (1968). This model proposed a three-stage human memory system; that is, information is processed by a memory system through three stages: The first is a sensory register for storing incoming information for a few seconds. This information is then transferred to the second stage, short-term memory, for encoding. As information is encoded in the short-term memory, short-term memory also is referred to as working memory. At this stage, information can be held for about 30 seconds without repetition. Once the encoding is completed, the information will be passed to the third stage, long-term memory, where information can be stored forever if given enough rehearsal. Cognitive load refers to instructional load (or knowledge load) placed in the memory system. The cognitive load theory studies the cognitive load placed in the working memory, because the capacity of working memory is limited; therefore, overloading the working memory will negatively affect learning.

认知负荷理论作为一种教学认知理论最初由 Sweller (1988) 提出。这一理论的基础是 Miller 的短时记忆容量有限性的概念 (Miller 1956)。Atkinson & Shiffrin (1968) 曾经提出过一个具有划时代意义的 Atkinson-Shiffrin 记忆模式。这个模式假设信息在人脑记忆系统中经过三个阶段的加工：第一阶段是感觉登记，这一阶段能储存新进来的信息大概几秒钟，之后信息被转到第二阶段——短时记忆系统进行编码。因为短时记忆是对信息进行编码的机制，所以短时记忆也被称作工作记忆。在这一阶段，如果不对信息进行复述的话，信息可以滞留大概30秒钟。当信息编码完成后，信息被继续转至长时记忆系统，在这一系统中，如果给予足够的复习，信息可以永久地保持下去。认知负荷，指的是加在记忆系统上的教学负荷 (或知识负荷)。认知负荷理论研究工作记忆中的认知负荷，因为工作记忆系统的容量很有限，因此，超负荷会影响工作记忆的效度。

Three types of cognitive loads could affect the efficiency of the working memory (Paas, Renkl, & Sweller 2003). The first type is intrinsic cognitive load. This refers to the amount of learning materials for a specific class. Reducing the amount of learning materials will reduce the intrinsic cognitive load. In addition, a well organized lesson with high element interactivity (elements of learning materials are interconnected) will also reduce the intrinsic cognitive load, compared with a poorly organized lesson, even if the amount of information is the same in the two lessons. In order to eliminate intrinsic cognitive load without sacrificing information volume in a given lesson, the instructor should make an effort to reorganize the lesson to increase its level of internal interactivity. The second type of cognitive load is the extraneous cognitive load. This type of load is caused by inappropriate ways of presenting teaching materials to students. Put simply, the instructor's use of inappropriate teaching methods or procedures makes the materials more difficult to learn or causes unnecessary learning. The third type of cognitive load is germane (effective) cognitive load. In contrast to the extraneous cognitive load, the germane cognitive load represents the pedagogically sound and well-designed instructional methods or procedures used during instruction. This type of cognitive load enhances learning.

有三种认知负荷能影响工作记忆的效度(Paas, Renkl, & Sweller 2003)。第一种是内在认知负荷,是指一堂课中要学的材料的数量。减少学习材料的量就能减少内在认知负荷。另外,一个组织有序的使内容之间产生有机联系的课文较之条理性差的课文,即使信息量不变,前者更能减低内在认知负荷。为了在不牺牲信息量的条件下减少内在认知负荷,教师应该在教学前对课文内容进行审查,确定课文是否体现材料内部的联系性和有序性。第二种认知负荷是外在认知负荷。这一类的负荷是由于教师不恰当地组织教学而人为地增加了材料的困难度,学生不得不花更大的努力去学习而造成的。第三种是有效认知负荷。与外在负荷相比,有效负荷是教学中教师采用合理方法和课堂组织形式最大程度提高学习效率的负荷。这种认知负荷促进教学效果。

Sweller (1994) pointed out that two critical learning mechanisms can be used to evaluate what is learned. One is schema acquisition and the other is the automaticity in the information process. A **schema** is a cognitive constructor organizing the elements of information according to an individual cognitive style. Human brain does not store information arbitrarily; rather, it is stored in an organized fashion. The knowledge stored in the brain just like the books stored in the library, which are well organized so that they can be retrieved easily when needed.

When a new book is acquired, the librarian will classify it into an existing category. If there is no existing category, then a new category will be created. The schema has the same structure of categories in our memory. To give an example, when a new word 同学 is introduced, we could put it under a school category, based on meaning classification; we could also put it under a noun category based on classification of part of speech; or we could put in another specified category based on each individual preference. The key to schema acquisition is to establish connections between new knowledge and existing knowledge, so that new knowledge can be stored in an organized way.

Sweller (1994) 指出,学习有效性可以用两个指标来衡量。一个指标是"图式"的习得,另一个是信息加工的"自动化"。图式是个体用来组织信息的一种个体化的认知结构。人的大脑不是随机地无组织地存储信息,而是以一种高度组织的方式存储信息。知识在大脑中的存储就像图书储存在图书馆一样,是有序的,所以信息提取就很方便。当图书馆收到一本新书后,图书馆员就会按事先的分类把它放到同类的图书中。如果现存的分类不适合新来的书,那么就会把新书归入一个新的类别。人脑中的图式也是根据相同的图书分类原理来组织知识的。举个例子来说,当新词"同学"被介绍给个体,个体可以根据意义联系把它放在心理词典的学校类中;也可以根据词的分类把它放在名词类;或根据个体其他的分类标准放在其他的类别中。图式习得的关键是建立新知识与旧知识之间的联系,所以新知识可以被有组织地存储起来。

Automaticity refers to processing of information automatically using learned knowledge without extra effort. After the word 同学 is learned, a learner is asked to read the sentence 生日晚会上,很多<u>同学</u>都来了,但是我的同桌没有来。How does the learner process the word 同学? One situation is the controlled process. The learner may search hard from the memory and try to recall the pronunciation and meaning of the word 同学. After several seconds of thinking, the learner recognizes the word and decodes its meaning. Another situation is automatic processing. The learner does not need to pay particular attention to the word 同学, he/she can effortlessly recognize this word. According to Sweller, effective instruction leads students toward schema acquisition and automatic processing of knowledge. Any instructional activity that deviates from schema acquisition and automatic processing is considered extraneous cognitive load and should be reduced.

自动化指是大脑不需要太多有意识的努力就能对信息进行自动加工。当理解了"同学"这一词后,如果让个体读"生日晚会上,很多<u>同学</u>都来了,但是我的同桌没有来"这个句子时,个体是如何加工"同学"这个词的呢?一种情况是控制型加工。个体会很努力地在头脑中寻找这个词,努力回想它的音和义。经过几秒钟的努力后,个体终于认出了这个词。另一种情况是自动加工。个体不需要对这个词加很多注意就能不费力地认出来。根据Sweller,有效的教学是这种教学的目的和过程是引导学生建立图式最后达到对信息进行自动加工。任何偏离建立图式和促进加工自动化的教学活动都是属于外在认知负荷,都应该减掉。

Pedagogical implications
教学应用

By applying the cognitive load theory to character/word instruction, classroom instruction should make efforts on the following aspects.

把认知负荷理论应用在字词教学上,意味着课堂教学必须在以下方面作出努力:

- Control the amount of vocabulary input to maintain a suitable intrinsic cognitive load
  控制生词输入的量以保持适量的内在认知负荷

Since the capacity of working memory is limited, students cannot process too many new words in a given period of time. What amount of vocabulary is suitable for students? There is no simply question to this answer as It depends on individual differences. However, the instructor can find out a baseline based on vocabulary quiz performance. If the mean accuracy rate reaches 90% or more on a vocabulary test, this means the current vocabulary input amount is suitable for the students. If the accuracy rate either increases or declines, then the instructor should consider increasing or reducing the amount of weekly vocabulary learning. Another way to do this is to set up separate requirements for word recognition and production for beginning level learners. For instance, we can test students for all new words in the lesson as recognition, but only part of the new words for production.

因为工作记忆的容量有限，学生无法在单位时间内加工太多的生词。那么一堂词汇课中学多少字词才是适量的？这个问题没有简单的答案，因为这取决于个体学生的接受能力。虽然如此，教师可以通过学生的字词测验成绩找到一个基本量。如果全班平均生词测验正确率在90%或以上，说明当前的生词教学量是适中的。如果平均正确率下降或上升，那么教师应该考虑增加或减少生词学习量。另一种办法是在初级阶段对生词的学习采取认读与默写分流。比如，我们可以要求学生认读课文中所有的生词，但是只要求能写出其中的一部分。

- Minimize extraneous cognitive load
  减少外在认知负荷

The cognitive load theory suggests that effective instructional materials (with high level of interactivity and cross referenced between the components) will lead to effective learning because it will direct learners' cognitive resources toward activities that are relevant to learning rather than toward preliminaries to learning (Sweller 1991). However, in some situations, the instructor may find that the lessons to be used in the class are poorly organized. Learners would have to put in great effort mentally to integrate the materials in order to comprehend the new words. To reduce the preliminary learning activities, the instructor should organize the learning materials into integrated formats so that they can be easily understood by learners. In a traditional classroom, the instructor introduces vocabulary according to the sequence that the vocabulary appears in the glossary and explains the words one by one. This type of method obviously increase extraneous cognitive load, as the new words are not well integrated, which may require memorization of new words in isolation. To minimize the extraneous cognitive load, we suggest that the words be grouped based on meaningful categorization before presenting them to students. The instructor may review all of the new words and decide how to group them. For example, if a lesson is about "travel," the teacher could group the words according the sequence of travel, such as prior to travel, during travel, and post travel. When introducing the word group "Prior to travel", the instructor could introduce the words based on a theme "things we need to do prior to travel." Therefore, students could use this theme as memory peg, to build interconnections among the words such as 地图, 旅行社, 航空公司, 订票, 售票员, 护照, 签证. There are many ways of integrating the new words for instruction, any creative way of integrate the new words for better comprehension from students should be encouraged.

　　认知负荷理论告诉我们,高效的教学材料应该具有高度的条理性以及材料内部的相互联系性,这样的材料才能有助于有效学习,因为这可以把学生的注意力直接导向学习材料内容的本身而不是那些学习的准备活动上(Sweller 1991)。但是有时候,教师会发现课文的内容不是那么有条理,学生先要花很大的力气通过一些教学准备活动来弄清楚材料之间的内部联系才能对材料进行理解。为了减少这些教学准备活动,教师应该在教学前对材料进行适当处理使它系统化,容易被学生接受。在传统的课堂上,教师根据生词在课后生词表中的列出的序列来一一介绍生词。这种方法很明显会增加外在认知负荷,因为生词的排列缺少内部联系,学生必须按序一一记忆生词。为了减少外在认知负荷,我们建议教师在呈现生词时先把生词分类。教师可以先看一下这些生词决定如何分类。例如,如果这篇课文的内容是"旅行",教师可以按旅行的顺序把生词分成三组,比如,旅行前、旅行中、旅行后。在介绍旅行前这一组生词时,教师可以根据主题"旅行前要做的事"这个顺序来介绍生词,这样,学生可以用"旅行前"作为记忆支点来记住地图、旅行社、航空公司、订票、售票员、护照、签证等词。我们有很多种方法对字词进行分组或分类,学生自己想出来的任何一种有新意的能帮助更好理解记忆生词的分类方法都应该受到鼓励。

- Focus on establishing schema
  注重图式的建立

In designing vocabulary learning activities, efforts can be made on the following things: 1. Connecting the target word with a previously learned word by finding connections to sound, shape, and meaning. 2. Connecting the target word with students' relevant life experiences.

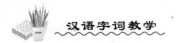

3. Connecting the target word with the other words in the same lesson; 4. Sorting the newly learned words into different categories based on the students own classification rules. 5. Presenting the target word in different linguistic contexts and then having the students discuss how the target word is used in different linguistic situations. 6. Providing real or simulated real-life situations for students to use target words in spoken and written communication.

在设计字词教学活动时,教师必须在下列方面作出努力:(1)使新字词与先前学过的字词在音、形或义上建立联系。(2)使新字词与学生的相关的个人生活经历发生联系。(3)使新词与同一篇课文中的其他字词建立联系。(4)让学生自己根据他们个人的需要和特点对新字词进行分类然后记忆。(5)使新字词在多种语境中呈现,引导学生讨论某个词在不同语境中的意思。(6)提供模拟或真实语言环境让学生通过说或写的形式来运用新字词。

- Strive for automaticity
  强调自动化

Newly learned words will not be transferred to long-term memory for later automatic recognition without frequent review and substantial practice. Therefore, the teacher should provide sufficient activity to allow students to practice newly introduced words in the classroom. After a group of words are introduced, review activities should follow prior to introducing the next group of new words. Towards the end of class, comprehensive review activities should be provided to allow students to review all of the words introduced in the class. In order to keep students motivated, the review activities should vary in their format and should progress from simple to comprehensive. Once a new lesson is completed, the teacher may purposefully design vocabulary activities for the next lesson that will allow students to use words learned from previous lesson when engaging in new learning activities.

如果没有频繁的复习与深入的练习,新近学到的字词就无法被转到长时记忆系统以备需要时自动提取。所以教师应该设计足够的教学活动让学生在课堂上练习新近介绍的字词。当每一组词介绍完以后,先要安排复习活动,之后再介绍新一组词。在下课前,教师应该提供综合性的复习活动使学生对该课介绍的新词有一个全面的复习。为了让学生积极地投入到复习活动中,复习活动应该变化多样并由简单到复杂。当一篇新课文学完后,在学下一篇课文时,教师要有意识地设计一些活动使学生在新课学习活动中能用到前一课的生词。

4.3 Level-of-processing theory 认知加工深度理论

Level-of-processing theory presents a memory model of how memory traces are passed through an information-process structure. Specifically, it is about how to process information in order to leave deep traces in the memory as deep processing will enhance memorization and facilitate retrieval. This model was initially proposed by Craik and Lockhart (1972). Rehearsal is well known to be the key that allows transfer of information from working memory. However, Craik and Lockhart hold that memory was enhanced more by depth of processing than by how long or how often the information was rehearsed. In other words, rehearsal is effective only when done in a deep and meaningful fashion. The theory suggests that memory occurs on a continuum from shallow to deep, with no limit on the number of different levels. However, it is distinguishable with regard to shallow, intermediate, and deep levels (Craik & Lockhart 1972).

认知加工深度理论呈现给我们一个信息加工过程中记忆痕迹是如何留下的这样一个记忆模式。具体地说，就是如何加工信息才能在记忆系统中留下比较深的痕迹，从而提高记忆效果进而有利于信息提取。这个模式最初由 Craik & Lockhart (1972) 提出。我们都知道复习是把信息从工作记忆存到长时记忆的关键。但是 Craik & Lockhart 认为，记忆能否加深取决于在复习过程中对信息的加工深度而不是复习的频度和时间长度。换句话来说，有效的复习是对知识进行有深度有意义的加工。这一理论提出了记忆加工是由浅到深的一种持续性过程，虽然不清楚到底有多少层次，但是至少能区分出三种水平的记忆加工：浅度加工、中度加工和深度加工。

Shallow level processing involves analysis of physical and sensory characteristics. At this level, the information is usually processed discretely and mainly by rote memorization. To give an example, for the word 政治 the learner may know its pronunciation zhèngzhì, but may not know the connection of the pronunciation with the radicals within the characters. The learner has memorized the definition of 政治: "Social relations involving intrigue to gain authority or power," but really do not understand what this means. The intermediate level of memory relates to recognition and labeling. Learners can recognize the word 政治 when it appears as an independent item or in a context. They can tell that a government is 政治组织, but a school does not fit the definition. The deep level is the storage of meaning and networks of association. At this level, learners understand 政治 as a phonetic-semantic compound, and they understand the role of phonetic and semantic radicals in those characters. They understand that 政治 can be combined with other words to express different meanings such as

讲政治,政治路线,政治斗争,政治情况; they understand 政治 in a concrete way and can give examples about how 政治 can have many connections with their own daily life; how a school as a nonpolitical organization could be heavily involved with politics; and how 政治 could be very good for people, but also could destroy people. Although learners may have not gained a fully developed schema related to the word 政治, they can understand this word based on their existing experience.

浅度加工是指对信息的物理属性和感知特征的分析。在这一个水平上,信息加工的方式是零碎的以机械记忆为主。举个例子,对"政治"这个词的加工,个体知道它的发音是 zhèngzhì,但是不知道这个发音与形成这个词的部首有什么关系。个体能背诵"政治"这个词的定义:"与权威或权力有关的各种社会关系",但是不理解这句话究竟是什么意思。

中度水平加工是指个体能对信息进行辨别和加标记。例如,个体能在不同语境中再认"政治"这个词。也能区别政府是一个政治组织,但是学校不是。深度水平的加工是对信息以一种意义网络关系的方式进行储存。在这一水平上,个体理解"政治"两个字都是形声字,知道声旁和形旁与汉字的关系。他们懂得政治可以和其他词结合表达不同的意思,比如,讲政治、政治路线、政治斗争、政治情况。个体能比较具体地理解这个词,能够给出例子,关于政治是怎样存在于他们日常生活的各方面;学校作为一个非政治组织可以被很深地卷入到政治中去;政治可以为民造福,也可以祸害于民。虽然,个体可能对"政治"这一概念的完整图式还没有建立,但是他们基于各自的现存的经验,理解了这个词。

From this discussion, we can tell that deeper processing involves meaningful processing. Meaningful processing arises when the target item is linked with learners' personal existing knowledge and experience. Target words "make sense" to learners. Meaningful processing is also an elaborated processing that makes the target information more distinctive and unique, thereby leaving a deeper impression on the learners' minds so that the information will not be easily forgotten.

从上述的讨论中,我们可以了解到深加工是一种有意义的加工。有意义的加工是那种把字词学习与学习者个体经验结合起来的加工,从而让学生感到目的词对他们来说是"有意义的"。有意义加工也是一种细致和复杂的加工,因为这种加工能使对目的词的加工具有独特性,从而在头脑中留下较深的印象,不容易忘记。

Pedagogical implications
教学应用

By applying the level-of-processing theory to word instruction, we can adopt the following means to enhance the level of information processing.

从认知加工深度理论在字词教学应用方面来说,我们可以采用下列措施来提高信息加工深度。

- Provide etymological and orthographic information for new characters
  向学生提供新字词的字源和正字学知识

The formation of Chinese characters is not random; rather, it is deeply rooted in Chinese culture. In chapter 1, we mentioned the four methods of creating Chinese characters. By tracing down its etymological origin, students will find that each character is loaded with fascinating cultural content. Thus, explaining etymological knowledge and analyzing orthographic structure of characters to give students a meaningful account of character formation is a way of helping deeper processing. Shen's study (2010) on radical knowledge development among beginning CFL learners reported a survey result on students' opinions of the most effective teaching methods in radical instruction. Students considered explanation of the etymology of the radicals (which also are simple characters), their origins, and their orthographical development as one of the four most effective methods. Some teachers may be concerned that this will take up too much class time. However, giving etymological account of characters not only facilitates deeper processing and stimulates students learning interest; it also helps students to find the orthographic pattern of character formation and semantic construction. By accumulating this type of knowledge, students can learn new characters by using learned orthographic knowledge. They will be more autonomous in character learning; therefore, "sharpening the axe won't interfere with the cutting of firewood."

汉字的形成不是随意的,它是有深厚的文化根基。在第一章中,我们提到过汉字造字的四种方法。通过了解字源知识学生会发现汉字承载着富有魅力的文化内涵。这种对汉字字源和正字知识的了解过程也是帮助学生进行深度加工的过程。Shen (2010b) 做了一个关于汉语二语学习者部首知识发展的研究,该研究运用了问卷调查,发现学生认为教师解释部首(也是独体字)的起源以及它们的形体发展变化是最有效的教学方法之一。有些老师担心解释字源会占用太多上课时间。但是教师们应该理解,字源知识能促进字词的深度加工并激发学生对学习汉字的兴趣,另外,也帮助学生获得正字知识。正

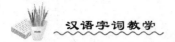

字知识的积累能让学生在学习新字词时自觉运用这一知识去发现部首与合体字的关系。这样在汉字学习中,学生就能掌握学习的主动权。所以学习字源和正字知识是"磨刀不误砍柴工"。

- Increase elaboration and effort level of encoding
  增加编码的复杂度和困难度

As mentioned earlier, the level-of-processing theory suggests that more elaborate processing leads to a deeper processing because elaborate processing involves making information more meaningful by means of visual imagery, by relating new material to known information, and by arranging information into a meaningful structure (Craik & Tulving 1975; Craik & Watkins 1973). How can we increase the level of elaboration? One way is to provide more detailed, vivid description during word encoding. For example, when introducing the word 挑战, the definition of 挑战 as a noun is "Something that by its nature or character serves as a serious test." The instructor can present a picture showing a mountain climber hanging onto a cliff and trying to climb up to the peak of the mountain. The teacher can ask the students to talk about their feelings and thoughts about the topic "if I am the climber…", and then ask the students to discuss a 挑战 situation based on their own personal experiences or others they are familiar with. Students can be asked to summarize what kind of tasks or situations can be considered as 具有挑战性. This type of activity will make the encoding process more meaningful.

前面我们提到,认知加工深度理论提示我们细致复杂的加工是一种有意义的加工,因为它包括了把信息形象化,让新信息与旧信息形成联系,或把信息组合成有意义的结构等途径来加工信息(Craik & Tulving 1975; Craik & Watkins 1973)。那么我们怎样才能在字词教学中提高信息加工的细致和复杂度? 一种方法是为字词提供具体生动的描述。譬如,在教学"挑战"这一词时,我们知道作为名词,它的定义是"一种事物从性质和特点上能成为对我们的一种考验"。教师可以出示图片,上面是登山运动员正奋力爬攀着一个悬崖。教师可以通过让学生讨论问题诸如:"如果我是这个登山者,我现在正感受到……"让学生体验一下这种爬攀经历;教师也可以让学生回顾生活中有没有过"挑战"这样的经历或回想一下他们的家庭成员和朋友们有没有这样的经历。最后,教师可以让学生总结一下什么样的活动或情况对他们来说是具有挑战性的。这一类与个体经验相联系的教学活动使学生对"挑战"的加工变得有意义。

Increased effort at the level of encoding processing is another way to create a long-lasting memory trace. One study in second language acquisition showed that learners who take more effort in processing materials have better memorization (Schneider, Healy, Borne, Jr. 2002). Laufer and Hulstijn (2001) proposed a task-induced involvement vocabulary instruction method, which is an excellent example of increasing the effort level of encoding. The involvement includes three components: need, search, and evaluation. Need is concerned with the need to achieve. Search is the attempt to find the meaning of a new L2 word or to find a L2 word to express an idea. Evaluation entails a comparison of a given word with other words, a specific meaning of a word with its other meanings, or combining the word with other words in order to assess whether a word does or does not fit its context (Laufer & Hulstijn 2001).

增加编码的困难度是加深记忆痕迹的另一种方法。二语词汇习得的研究显示,学生花较多的力气进行字词加工能导致比较有效的字词记忆(Schneider, Healy, Bourne 2002)。Laufer & Hulstijn (2001) 提出了一个任务导入型词汇教学方法。这是个很好的增加编码困难度的方法。这一任务导入型词汇教学方法包含三个因素:需要、寻找、鉴别。需要是指学生对字词的学习是出自为了解决问题的需要。寻找是指学生积极找寻有关的词来表达自己的想法或观点。鉴别是对字词进行比较找出哪个词适合或不适合某种语境。

Based on this idea, we propose a four-component method for task-based vocabulary instruction. The four components are need, search, discrimination, and evaluation. The need refers to students' need to learn new words to complete a task or to solve a problem. They are intrigued to learn. The search means that students search for the new words that they need to solve the problem. They actively find the sound and meaning to match the shape of the new words. Discrimination refers to finding the differences and similarities among related words and finding out the unique features of each new word under learning. Evaluation is assessment of the learning result and finding out whether they have learned the new words needed for task completion or problem solving. Below is an example to illustrate the use of this method in teaching Chinese words.

受这一任务导入型词汇教学方法的启示,我们在这里提出一个四因素任务型汉语二语词汇教学途径。这四因素分别是:需要、寻找、甄别、评价。需要是指学生需要学习新词是出于完成任务或解决问题的需要。受解决问题的诱导,学生有了学习新词的需要。寻找是学生寻找解决问题所需要的新词。或学生积极地寻找与目的词的形对应的音和义等。甄别是对相关的新词的相同点和不同点进行甄别,找出每个新词的各自的特征。评价是指学生评价自己的学习结果,譬如,是否成功地学会了运用新词,解决了问题或完成了任务。下面我们用一个教学示例,具体解释这一教学途径。

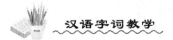

Teaching example 2: Four-component method for the Task-based vocabulary instruction
教学示例2 四因素任务型词汇教学途径

The title of lesson: Making a plan for Camping at a National Park
课题：制订去国家公园野营计划

Sheet 1. The word to be learned in the class
本课要学的生词表：

月、日、几点、集合、大峡谷、优山美胜(Yosemite)、火车、灰狗、黄石公园、汽车、校车、飞机、睡袋、船、手电筒、蜡烛、避蚊油、帐篷、爬、火柴、钓鱼、篝火晚会、出发、飞盘、看书、划船、野餐、星期、湖

Need 需要

To make students feel interested in learning new words and that they need new words to solve problems 让学生对学习本课生词发生兴趣，为了解决问题，他们需要学新词。

Step 1. Warm up. The instructor asks students to talk about whether they like camping and to share their camping experiences with the others. 热身运动。教师让学生说说他们是否喜欢野营，请他们把自己过去的野营经历与班上同学分享。

Step 2. Propose a task. Assume that the class is going to go camping at a state park next week. The students' task for this class is to make a camping plan. 提出任务。假设全班要去一个国家公园野营，学生的任务是制订一个野营计划。

Students all agreed to the proposal and feel that they want to learn the new words in order to solve the problem that interests them. 学生都同意这一提议，他们想要学会有关生词来制定野营计划。

Search 寻找

A task sheet (see below) is presented to the students. The instructor asks the students to form small groups to make a camping plan based on the questions provided in the task sheet. In this step, students need to find appropriate words and study them in order to complete the task.

教师呈现野营计划问题提纲(见下面)要求学生组成小组根据下面的问题提纲制订计划。学生必须从生词表上找出相应的词来完成这个任务。

Sheet 2. 野营计划 (camping plan)
- 什么时候去
- 去哪里　　(只选一个地点)
- 怎么去
- 带什么
- 做什么

Step 3. Students are required to sort out all the words from the word list into categories based on the questions listed in Sheet 2. Below is an example of a completed word sorting. 学生必须把生词表上的字词按问题提纲分组。下面是一个学生对生词进行分组的例子。

Sample sheet　　野营计划 (camping plan)
- 什么时候去　(星期　月　日　出发　几点　集合……)
- 去哪里　(大峡谷　优山美胜 (Yosemite)……)
- 怎么去　(火车　灰狗汽车　校车　飞机　船……)
- 带什么　(睡袋　手电筒　蜡烛　避蚊油　帐篷……)
- 做什么　(爬山　钓鱼　篝火晚会　飞盘　看书　划船　野餐　湖……)

Step 4. Students learn the words and make a plan. In addition, they can add their own words for answering the questions and add more questions to the list. 学生学习生词,制订计划。另外他们可以根据需要增加新词或增加问题。

Step 5. Each group shares their plan with the whole class and provides justification for their choice for each question (e.g., why choose to go to Yosemite or Grand Canyon) 每一组向全班呈现计划并说明理由(例如,为什么要选优山美胜或大峡谷)。

Discrimination　甄别

Guide students to understand the semantic differences of related words and how they are used in different contexts.

教师引导学生理解相关字词的语义上的不同以及它们在不同语境中的运用。

Step1. The instructor presents a group of words and asks students to point out the differences in these words and to give examples using them. 教师提出下面一组词让学生说出不同点并举例说明怎么用这些词。

比较: 1) 野营　野炊　野餐　　2) 野趣　野味　野生

Step 2. The teacher asks students to group into pairs and to pick a word from the list and search previously learned meaning-related words from their mental lexicon to form a question. Students can follow examples presented by the teacher, such as (比较：湖、海、河）

教师要求学生两个人一组从生词表上选一个词找一找以前学过的什么词与这个词有意义上关联。学生可以按照教师提供的例子 (比较：湖、海、河)来进行这一活动。

Step 3. Exchange the completed answers with another group and work on the answers for the questions which are not listed on the sheet, but raised by other groups.

学生各组交换上述问题的答案。并回答那些任务单上没有的由学生自己提出来的问题。

Step 4. Each group presents its camping plan to the whole class in an oral presentation 各组向全班口头报告他们的野营计划。

Evaluation　评价

To evaluate whether students have learned the new words from Sheet 1 and to what degree that have learned the new words.

评价学生是否已经学会生词表上词以及对每个词的掌握程度。

Step 1. One group chooses two questions from sheet 2 to ask other groups. The other groups have to answer questions both orally and in writing using the newly learned words. Groups take turn to work on this task until all groups have had a chance to ask and answer questions.

每一组从问题提纲中选两个问题，请其他组同学回答。回答问题组的同学必须用口头和书面两种形式用刚学到的字词来回答问题。各组轮流问答问题。

Step 2. Each group presents their written plan via the LMO to the whole class. The class members read the written plan and critique the accuracy of word use. Students are encouraged to find and correct mistakes made in the written responses of the other groups.

每组通过投影仪向全班展示他们的书面计划。其他同学评点是否用对了词语。教师鼓励学生相互找出错误，改正错误。

（Teaching example 2 is contributed by Helen H. Shen, the first author of this book）

- Encourage students' self-elaboration
鼓励学生进行自发性的复杂编码

Creating encoding uniqueness is another way to enhance a memory trace. A study (Kuo & Hooper 2004) compared different methods of mnemonics use among high school CFL learners learning Chinese words. One of these was student self-generated encoding. In this condition, students were encouraged to create their own memory aids by drawing a picture, writing a sentence, or inventing a story associated with characters. The result showed that the student-self-generated mnemonics group performed best in post vocabulary testing. Another study (Shen 2004) compared three encoding conditions in learning Chinese words among English-speaking intermediate college CFL learners. Condition 1 was self-generated elaboration in which students created a method for memorizing the sound, shape, and meaning of the words; condition 2 was instructor-guided elaboration in which the instructor explained the etymology of the words, if applicable, analyzed the radicals, and gave examples of word use in a context. Condition 3 was rote memorization in which students simply repeated the sound, shape, and meaning of words without elaboration. Both student self-generated elaboration and instructor guided elaboration significantly improved word retention, although instructor guided elaboration was superior to student self-generated elaboration. These studies provided evidence that in vocabulary instruction, in addition to instructor-guided elaboration, teachers should encourage students to make self-reference elaboration, because this type of elaboration directly related to the learner's own experiences and their own learning styles, which enhances memorization.

编码的独特性是加深记忆痕迹的又一种方法。Kuo & Hooper (2004) 比较了高中汉语二语学习者运用记忆术的方法学习汉字。其中一种记忆方法是学生自发性的复杂编码。也就是鼓励学生运用各种方式对字词编码使有利于记忆,比如给字词画图,写一个句子或创造一个故事。研究的结果表明,学生自发性的复杂编码组在实验后的字词测验中成绩优于其他组。Shen (2004) 比较了中级汉语课上字词教学的三种编码方式。方式一是让学生自发对字词进行复杂编码。学生自己创造一种方法来记忆字词的音、形、义;方式二是教师指导下的复杂编码,即解释字源知识和分析汉字的部首以及举例说明字词的用法;方式三是简单编码,即机械地记忆生词,只是不断重复字词的音、形、义,但是不做复杂编码。结果表明学生自发性复杂编码和教师指导下的复杂编码的字词学习效果显著地优于简单编码,教师指导下的复杂编码效果最优。这些研究向我们展示了在字词教学中,除了教师指导下的复杂编码,教师还应该鼓励学生进行自发性的复杂编码,因为这种编码是直接源于学生的生活和学习经验,符合个体的独特的学习风格,所以有助于记忆。

4.4 Multisystem account 多种通道理论

The multisystem refers to the human sensory system that uses multimodality to perceive events and objects. This sensory system includes visual, aural, tactual, taste sensation, feeling, and motor senses. The multisystem account proposed by Engelkamp (2001) is predicated on dual coding theory, but it provides detailed accounting of the role of the non-verbal system in language learning based on a series of empirical studies. Tulving (1972) proposed two types of memory systems: episodic memory and semantic memory. Episodic memory receives and stores information about temporally dated episodes or event, and the temporal-spatial relations among these events. Therefore, it is stored as an autobiographical form in the memory system. Semantic memory, on the other hand, is a system for storing information in schema form and uses language or other verbal symbols. It does not register perceptible properties or inputs but instead registers cognitive referents of input signals (Tulving 1972). For example, if a person is talking about his friend, he may describe his friend with words like friendly, helpful, and 'likes to play basketball' from his semantic memory. However, this person may also recall an image of his friend's smile when they first met, how his friend accompanied him to find the materials in the library that he needed, or a scene of his friend playing basketball on one occasion from episodic memory. The semantic and episodic memory systems can operate independently, but they also interdependent as they support and complement each other to provide full recall of events.

Engelkamp (2001) holds that the episodic memory consists of subsystems based on the human multiple sensory modals such as the motor system and the tactual system. Each system encodes information based on its unique sensory channel. Therefore, if we use multimodalities instead of a single modality to encode information, when we recall the information, each modal will contribute a unique cue to the recall of this information. The **multisystem account** pays special attention to the role of enactment in the encoding process. In a series of experimental studies, Engelkamp (2001) confirmed that enacted learning contributes to information retention.

多种通道理论中的多种通道指的是个体感知系统运用多种感官通道感知事件和事物。多种感官包括视觉、听觉、触觉、味觉、感情觉、运动觉。这一理论由 Engelkamp (2001) 提出，是建立在双编码理论上的一种编码理论，该理论在实证性研究的基础上对非语言系统在加工中的作用进行了详细阐述。在早期，Tulving (1972) 提出了两种记忆系统说，情节记忆和语义记忆。情节记忆是对事件或经历的时间性记忆，或者是事件的时空关系的记忆。因此它是把事物以一种照相式的形式存储在记忆系统。语义记忆,从另一方面来说,是用语言把信息加工成图式的方式存储在记忆中,它不是记录感觉特点而是记录对信息的一种认知结果 (Tulving 1972)。举例来说,一个人在提到她的男性朋友的时候,她会从语义记忆系统中提取"友好,会帮助人,喜欢打篮球"等词进行描述,这些是语义记忆的结果。同时,她也会回忆起她与他第一次见面时他笑时候的样子,他是怎样陪着她在图书馆帮她找到她所需要的材料,以及一次看他打球的情景,这些材料则是由情节记忆系统提供的。情节系统和语义系统操作互相独立但又是互相依赖的,因为它们相互补充提供对事物的完全的记忆。

Engelkamp (2001) holds that the episodic memory consists of subsystems based on the human multiple sensory modals such as the motor system and the tactual system. Each system encodes information based on its unique sensory channel. Therefore, if we use multimodalities instead of a single modality to encode information, when we recall the information, each modal will contribute a unique cue to the recall of this information. The multisystem account pays special attention to the role of enactment in the encoding process. In a series of experimental studies, Engelkamp (2001) confirmed that enacted learning contributes to information retention.

  Engelkamp (2001)认为,情节记忆是由人体多种感觉通道组成的多种子系统提供,比如动觉和触觉系统等来帮助对事物的记忆。每一系统根据它对事物的独特的感知渠道来对信息进行编码。因此,如果我们用多种感觉通道而不是一种通道对信息进行编码,我们在回忆该信息的时候,每一子系统都会提供一个独特的提醒线索从而提取信息。多种通道理论尤其重视运动觉在编码中的作用。在一系列的实验中,Engelkamp (2001)证实了运动觉对信息保持所起的作用。

The multisystem account suggests that we should take advantage of learners' episodic memory in vocabulary learning to achieve a maximum effect of retention and recall. Because it provides additional memory cues for the same object, it reduces the interference from other information as the multi-cues will support each other and strengthen the memory. It also helps with comprehension as the concept is supported by concrete evidence. More importantly, it also increases learning interest by involving enacted activities.

  多种通道理论提示我们在字词教学中应该利用学习者的情节记忆来提高记忆效果。因为情节记忆为同一信息提供了额外的提醒线索,这能减少由其他信息带来的干扰,因为多种提醒线索互相支持能强化记忆。情节记忆也有助于对字词的理解,因为它为语义概念提供了具体的事实。更重要的是,动觉活动能使学生对字词学习更感兴趣。

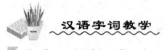

Pedagogical implications
教学应用

Based on the multisystem account, we should take the following methods into consideration during vocabulary instruction.

根据多种通道理论的精神,字词教学中,我们应该考虑采用以下的一些活动。

● Drawing　画画

Ask students to provide illustrations based on etymological knowledge for difficult words. This method is especially effective in the beginning level class because it helps students to understand the logographic nature of the Chinese characters. The illustration can be a concrete or symbolic sketch of the word. We can also ask students to draw the pictographic forms of the word. Afterwards, we can ask students to guess the target words based on each other's illustrations. As individual students have their own unique way of processing the character, personal drawing is an excellent way of letting students express their uniqueness in character encoding. In using this method, the instructor would need to set a time limit because some students may spend too much time on the quality of their sketches. The purpose of sketching the words is to comprehend and memorize the words, not to show how well a student can sketch.

教学中可请学生根据汉字字源知识为汉字画画。这一方法在初级教学阶段尤其有效,因为这能帮助学生了解汉字的象形字本质。汉字画可以是具体的也可以是符号式的速写。我们也可以要求学生直接为汉字画出相应的象形文字。然后,让学生根据互相的汉字画来猜测对应的汉字。因为每个学生都用他独特的方式感知汉字,学生的个人的汉字画是一种让学生表现他们对汉字独特感受和编码的很好机会。在使用这一方法时,教师应该规定活动时间,因为有些学生可能会花很多时间去提高他们画的质量。我们要让学生明白,画汉字画的目的是增强对字词的理解和记忆,而不是看某个学生画画水平有多高。

● Acting out　动作演示

Acting out the word is another way of using episodic memory. Acting out not only means using body action to act out the action words, but also means using all sensory modalities to sense the word. For example, when introduce the word 唱歌, we can have a student actually sing a song for a minute. When introduce the word 汽油, we can ask students to describe their feeling when smell 汽油.

用动作把字词表演出来是运用情节记忆系统的另一个方法。表演不仅仅是用动作表演动词，也包括用其他感官通道来感知字词。例如，介绍"唱歌"，我们可以用一分钟时间让学生学唱一段歌。在介绍"汽油"这个词，我们可以让学生描述闻到汽油的感觉等等。

- Role play　角色扮演

Students can take roles to perform a word in contexts such as 我喝醉了 and 我很快乐. We can also ask students to make semantic connections between words by making a short dialog or a skit; or to group the related words based on a theme such as a birthday party or dining in a restaurant.

学生可以在语境中分别选择角色表演词和句子，比如表演"我喝醉了"和"我很快乐"。教师可以让学生通过编对话和小品的形式建立新词之间的语义联系，或者用一个主题把词串起来，如"生日聚会"或"在餐馆吃饭"，然后进行表演。

Here, we must point out that the use of enacted instruction methods is time consuming, so instructors must consider the necessity of using this type of method and not to overuse them. Another thing the instructor should know is that episodic memory supplements semantic memory but not replace semantic memory. The ultimate goal of word instruction is to help learners to store the information in the semantic memory as schema format. Therefore, when using the enacted methods, we should always connect them with the semantic encoding and make sure students understand the word conceptually with the support from the episodic details.

我们需要指出的是，表演也是很费时间的教学活动，所以教师应该考虑到运用这种活动的必要性，不要过度使用这一方法。另一个需要注意的是情节记忆是对语义记忆的补充，而不能替代语义记忆。字词学习的最终目标是帮助学生在语义记忆系统建立图式。因此，在运用表演方法时，我们应该把它与语义编码结合起来，确保学生在情节编码的支持下能进行语义编码理解和记住字词的定义。

4.5 Competition theory 竞争理论

The competition theory proposed by Brian MacWhinney (1987, 2001) is a language acquisition theory, but is fully rooted in the retrieval-induced forgetting theory of cognitive science. The retrieval-induced forgetting theory, a classic theory initiated by MacGeoch. (1932, 1942), holds that forgetting is caused by two types of interference: proactive interference in which the previously learned events interfere with the memory of later-learned events, and retroactive interference in which the subsequently learned events interfere with the memory of previous learned events. These two types of interferences are caused by the competition among memory traces. Further studies revealed that the competition for memory traces could be caused by: 1. the memories associated with a common cue compete for access to conscious recall when that cue is presented. 2. The cued recall of an item will decrease as a function of increases in the strength of its competitor's association with this cue. 3. The act of retrieval is a learning event in the sense that it enhances subsequent recall of the retrieved item (Anderson, M. C., Bjork, R.A., & Bjork, E. 1994). The repeated retrieval of a given item will strengthen that item, causing loss of retrieval access to other related items.

竞争理论作为二语习得理论之一由MacWhinney (1987, 2001)提出。该理论的基点是认知科学遗忘理论的提取—导入说。提取—导入说是经典的遗忘理论之一,最初由MacGeoch (1932, 1942)创立。该理论的基本观点是遗忘是由两种干扰造成:前摄干扰和后摄干扰。前摄干扰是先前学习的材料干扰了对后来学习的材料的记忆;后摄干扰是后来学习的材料干扰对先前学习材料的记忆。这两种干扰的形成是信息提取过程中被激活的提醒线索之间的相互竞争。进一步的研究表明被激活的提醒线索的相互竞争可能由三种原因造成:(1)当目标提醒线索进入到意识水平时,与它相关的提醒线索也被激活与其竞争同时进入到意识水平。(2)目标提醒线索的强度会减弱,如果与其相关的非目标提醒线索强度增强。(3)对目标信息提取本身可以成为一个复习活动,能使后续的对同一目标信息的再提取变得容易(Anderson, M. C., Bjork, R.A., & Bjork, E. 1994)。也就是说,重复提取某种信息会强化该信息的提醒线索,由此而造成弱化其他相关信息的提取。

Based on the retrieval-induced forgetting theory, the competition theory assumes that the connection of lexical items in mental lexicon can vary in their degree of activation when they are retrieved. During lexical processing, items are in competition with one another in terms of their connections in phonology, orthography, and semantics. In each of these competitions, the item that wins out in a given competition is the one with the greatest activation. An item must dominate over its competitors for a sufficiently stronger and longer period in order to emerge as the winner. The theory proposed four factors that can raise or lower the activation of an item: cue support, completeness, domination, and previous activation (MacWhinney 1987). We will explain these four factors in detail with connecting them to vocabulary learning in Chinese.

基于提取—导入说的观点,竞争理论假设心理词汇系统中词之间的联结会随着提取的频率而发生变化。在目标词的提取过程中,与目标词相关的词在语音、词形、语义之间的联系上与目标词相互竞争。在竞争中获胜的词就会被激活。为了在竞争中取胜,一个词必须比其他词在提醒线索强度上和提取时间上占有优势。竞争理论揭示了四种因素会影响一个词被激活程度:线索支持效应、线索吻合度、线索主导性和先前激活效应(MacWhinney 1987)。下面我们从汉语字词学习的角度对四因素作详细描述。

Cue supporting effects: The connection between recall cues to the item to be retrieved. If a cue is strongly activated, it will have a strong connection to the item. For example, when the target word to be recognized is 打雷, if learners have strong recall cues such as a vivid images of lightning, and acoustic memory of thunderous sound connecting with the target word 打雷, then, 打雷 will be successfully recognized and it will not be recognized as 打擂.

线索支持效应指的是提醒线索与被提醒的字词之间联结的强度。如果一个提醒线索激活度很高,那么它与被激活的词的联结强度也高。假设被提取的目标词是"打雷"。如果学习者对目标词拥有很强的提醒线索,比如在头脑中有关"打雷"的生动的视觉意象和雷声的听觉意象,紧紧地与"打雷"这个词联系在一起,那么,目标词"打雷"就会被提取,而不会提取另一形似音似词"打擂"。

Completeness of match effects: The cues for a certain item have a complete match with the target items. If the cues do not provide as good an overall match of the targeted item as an alternative item, the alternative item may be retrieved. When see the word 打雷, if the learner has no ambiguousness about its pronunciation, dǎléi, and its meaning, to thunder, the recognition of 打雷 would be more successful than the situation in which the learner is not sure whether 雷 should be pronounced as léi or lèi, or if 雷 means *thunder or lightning*.

线索吻合度是指提醒线索与目标词相吻合的程度。如果提醒线索与目标词吻合度不高,那么另一个相似的词可能被提取。当看到"打雷"这一词时,学习者对它的发音dǎ léi,和它的意义"云层放电时发出的巨大响声"不存在模糊性,那么"打雷"被提取的可能性就大,反之,如果学习者不清楚"雷"应该是读成léi还是lèi;"雷"的意思应该是"巨大的声音"还是"闪电光",那么"打雷"被提取的可能性就小。

Dominant effects: The decision to go with one competitor over another is based on the extent to which that competitor dominates over the other competitors. If the target word to be recognized is 形势 other similar sounding words such as 形式, 刑事 may be activated from the memory during recognition. However, during the competition of these items, if the learner has better recalling cues for 形式 than 形势, or 刑事 then 形式 will be put in the dominant position. Once it is in the dominant position, the item starts to have a dominant effect on processing. Even though it is wrong, the learner tends to believe that the dominant competitor is the correct word. As a result, the wrong item 形式 will be retrieved.

主导效应是指最后决定提取哪个词是由某个词的主导地位决定的。如果非目标词在竞争中占了主导地位，那么该非目标词就会被提取。假如目标词是"形式"，另两个同音词"形势"和"刑事"在提取过程中参与竞争，它们也在大脑中被激活。在竞争过程中，如果学习者对"形势"的提醒线索优于"形式"或"刑事"，"形式"就会处于主导地位。一旦进入主导地位，该词就发生主导效应，尽管它不是目标词，但是受到主导效应的影响，学习者会相信这一主导地位的词是目标词，由此导致了错误提取。

Previous activation effects: If a similar item was previously activated, it will receive further activation in processing a similar target item. For example, if the words 电灯, 电话, 电线 are introduced and the learner knows that the three items are all related to 电, if 电灯 is frequently retrieved previously, then when 电线 is presented to the learner, the learner may read it as 电灯. The reason is that 电灯 has been activated previously and it becomes a stronger competitor in the completion of retrieval.

先前激活效应是指如果与目标词相似的词先前被激活过，那么在目标词提取时，它会再度被激活。例如，学生学了电灯、电话、电线三个词，他们知道这些词都与电有关，如果"电灯"是经常被提取的的词，当"电线"呈现在学生面前时，他可能会把它读成"电灯"，因为这一词先前被提取了多次，在相似词中成为一个较强的竞争者。

A study that analyzed English-speaking advanced CFL learners on lexical errors in reading Chinese text reported that students make three types of errors (陈绂 1996). These error types are excellent samples to explain the retrieval failure due to the four types of effects mentioned above. The errors are caused by the failure during competition between the target item and other sounds, shapes, and meanings of similar items. According to the author, one type of error is retrieval of the similar shape of words, for example students read 等位 as 第位, 动员 as 功员, 迈步 as 边步; the other type of error is retrieval of meaning similar words, such as reading 出售 as 出货, 阅览, as 读览, 不应, as 不该; Another type occurs when the target word is mixed with a synonymous word or meaning related word such as reading 参与 as 参加, 农业 as 农村, 外汇 as 外币.

陈绂(1996)在一个分析英语母语的汉语学习者用词错误的研究中报告了学生在阅读中文文本时常犯三类错误。第一类是学生提取形似字，例如把"等位"读成"第位"，"动员"读成"功员"，"迈步"读成"边步"；第二类是提取近义词，如把"出售"读成"出货"，"阅览"读成"读览"，"不应"读成"不该"；第三类错误是把目标词与近义词或意义有关联的词相混，如把"参与"读成"参加"，"农业"读成"农村"，"外汇"读成"外币"。这些错误类型是上述提到的四种因素而造成的提取失败的很好的例子。这三种错误都是由于目标词在提取时与音近、形近或义近词的竞争中失败所致。

Pedagogical implications
教学应用

With an understanding of competition theory in vocabulary instruction, we should consider students' errors in character recognition and lexical access are part of the normal learning process in lexical knowledge development. However, the retrieval-induced errors could be reduced if instructions can incorporate the following measures:

如果我们理解了竞争理论对字词教学的指导意义，那么我们应该把学生的汉字认读或词义提取中的错误看成是正常的，它是学生词汇发展过程中的伴生物。虽然如此，如果教学能注意下面提及的方法的话，由提醒线索误导的字词读写错误就会减少。

- Utilize multiple codes for encoding
  采用多种方式编码

The cue support effect hints that once a word is introduced, if the brain stores strong cues that associate with the target word, the recognition of the target word will be easier and faster. Therefore, our instruction should endeavor to provide multiple codes such as verbal, imagery, and enacted codes for encoding. This multiple coding would create multi-cues for recall. To cite an example, when introducing the word 困难, the verbal encoding method could explain the etymological formation of the characters 困 and 难, how each character contributes to the word meaning 困难, and how the word is used in the context. The imagery approach for 困难 could be photos of encountering difficulties, or recalling difficult life situations that students have encountered in the past. The enacted encoding of 困难 could ask student to hold their breath as long as they can and then express what kind of feeling they have if they encounter

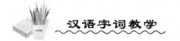

breathing difficulty. These multiple encoding methods will leave a deeper memory trace for better retrieval. If one cue is lost in the memory, additional cues can still be used for recall.

线索支持效应提示我们,当一个词被介绍给学生后,如果学生头脑中储存了与该词有关的很强的提醒线索,那么再认时就会变得快速、容易。因此,教学应该在为学生提供多种编码方法上做出努力,比如,同时运用语言码、意象码、动作码对新词进行编码。因为多码可以给同一词提供多种提醒线索使提取变得容易。举个例子说,当我们向学生介绍"困难"这一词时,语言码可以是向学生介绍汉字"困"和"难"这两个字是怎么形成的,这两个字各自的意思跟词"困难"的意思有什么联系,"困难"一词在句中是怎么使用的。意象码是向学生呈现遇见各种困难时的图片或请学生回忆生活中遇到困难时的场景。动作码可以是让学生试着屏住呼吸感知到呼吸的困难等。这种多种编码方法会在学生头脑中留下比较深的记忆痕迹,使提取变得容易。这样,如果一个线索失去,学习者还可以用其他线索进行提取。

- Pay attention to comparison and contrast
  运用比较和对比

On many occasions, the retrieval failure is not because the word is lost from our memory, but because there is interference by similar items. The target item often fails to be retrieved because a similar item is in a stronger position for competition. As a result, that similar item is retrieved. By understanding this point, our instruction should use comparison and contrast methods. In order to build schema, we need to relate the new target word with old words with similar sound, shape, and meaning so that the new item can be integrated into a schema system. However, at the same time, we also need to direct students' attention to the differences in those similar items to eliminate the confusion introduced by the sound, shape, and meaning similarities. In comparing the similarity and differences between the target word and learned similar words, we must not only compare the target word with related Chinese words, but also need to compare the semantic scope of the target Chinese word with its L1 equivalent. For example, the word 灿烂 can be translated into English as "brilliant." In Chinese, 灿烂 can be used to modify a person's smile, such as 灿烂的笑容, but in English, it is not conventional to say brilliant smile. In English, we can say he is brilliant, but we do not say 他很灿烂 because, in Chinese, 灿烂 does not have the specific meaning of "extremely smart," but it can be used to indicate outstanding in all aspects, such as 灿烂的一生. This kind of comparison can help reduce the confusion or interference from L1 on L2 word study.

在很多情况下,提取失败并不是因为个体对目标词的遗忘,而是因为其他相近的非目标词的干扰。目标词没被提取的原因是另一个相似的非目标词在竞争中处于优势地位,所以导致目标词提取失败。理解了这一点,教学中,我们要多采用比较和对比的方法。为了建立图式,我们需要让新词与有关的在音形义上的相似的词建立联系,新词就可以被结合到图式中去。但是,在这样做的同时,我们也要把学生的注意力引导到注意相似词之间的不同点,尤其是细微的差别以减少由于相似而带来的混淆。我们不仅仅要让学生比较汉语的相似词,而且还要注意比较目标词在语义上与学生第一语言中对应词的差异。举个例子,"灿烂"可以翻译成"brilliant"。在汉语中,"灿烂"可以用来形容人的笑容,如"灿烂的笑容",但是英文中,几乎没有人说 brilliant smile。在英文里,我们可以说"he is brilliant"(他极其聪明),但是直接翻译成中文是"他很灿烂"。这不是中文的表达式,因为"灿烂"没有"极其聪明"的意思,但是"灿烂"可以形容一个人在各方面都很出色,例如"灿烂的一生"。这一类的比较会帮助减少由母语带来的混淆和干扰,使学生对词的语义色彩有清楚的了解。

- Schedule systematic review
  安排系统的复习

Previous activation effects imply that retrieval of old words having sound, shape, or meaning connections with the target word will frequently affect the retrieval of the target word. Therefore, increasing the opportunity of practicing and using newly introduced words is critical for reducing the interference from frequently retrieved old words. For planning a review, we should take advantage of two cognitive effects: spacing effect and variation effect (Jahnke & Nowaczyk 1998).

先前激活效应告诉我们先前经常提取的词对目标词在音形义上有相似之处的话,会影响对目标词的提取。因此,创造各种机会让学生对新学的字词进行复习和运用是很重要的。在制定复习计划的时候,教师应该充分利用两种认知效应:间隔效应和变化效应(Jahnke & Nowaczyk 1998).

The spacing effect refers to arranging a review in a spaced or distributed fashion. Consider that we review 30 words in a 30-minute class. We should not ask students for repeated reading of one word for one minute and then move to the next word. A much better way is to read words 1-30 and then start over again with a different order. Spaced practice is much more effective than massive practice. The reason is simple. When a word initially appears, the brain will process it as a new stimulus that requires attention and effort for processing. If the word is repeated massively in a single time slot, the learner will treat each subsequent repetition as a rest opportunity and use no effort and pay less attention to the target item because the target item has already been recognized (Dempster 1987).

间隔效应是指复习活动应该是间歇性的而不是集中性的。我们来考虑一下如何在30分钟内复习三十个词。一种方法是让学生在一分钟内重复复习同一个词,而在下一分钟内复习另一个词,但这不是一个好方法。较好的方法是,让学生把30个词从头到尾读一遍,然后把词的次序打乱再从头到尾地读。因为间隔复习比集中复习要有效得多。理由很简单,当一个词最初呈现时,大脑把它当作一个新刺激,需要调动注意力对它进行加工。如果一个词在同一时间中大量重复,学习者就会把重复看成是休息的机会,因为目标词已被认读,大脑不需要对其进行再次加工。

The variation effect means that during the review process, the instruction should use different methods to review the same set of words, in order to make each review unique for the purpose of drawing learners' attention. Below is an example of variation in methods for learning the same set of words.

变化效应指的是在复习过程中,应该使用不同的方法来复习同一组词,这样做是为了让每一次复习对学习者来说都是一次独特的经历,以吸引他们的注意力。下面举的是使用变化的方法来学习同一组词的一个例子。

Teaching example 3: Variation in methods for learning the same set of words
教学示例 3 用不同方法学同一组词

Method 1: Picture – word match. Ask students to determine the corresponding words by looking at the pictures. 方法 1. 图片与词匹配。请学生看图找出对应的词。

Method 2: Pick three cards and test your classmates. Ask each student to choose three cards from the list of vocabulary cards and then walk around the classroom to ask other students each to choose one card to read and explain its meaning. 方法 2. 找三张字卡考你的同学。请每位学生从自己事先做的生词卡中抽出三张,在教室里分别找到三位学生让他们解释字词的意思。

Method 3: Find the words from the sentences. The teacher either speaks the word or presents it in a written a sentence and asks the students to point out which words in the sentence are the target words. 方法 3. 从句中找词。教师用口头或书面呈现句子,让学生指出其中哪些词是新学的。

Method 4: Draw a word net. The teacher asks students to create a few categories and then to sort words from the cards to create character networks based on their meaning connections for each category. For example, a category of eating food will allow students to classify any food and eating related words into that category. 方法 4. 字词网络图。教师要求学生提出几个意义分类的标准，让学生根据标准把字卡分类。例如，如果其中一类是"吃食物"，那么学生就把食物以及与吃有关的词分到那一类去。

Method 5: Tell a story using words from the list. Students can create a story based on the theme provided, using a number of the target words. 方法 5. 讲故事。学生需要根据所给的主题用上新词编一个故事。

Method 6: Information gap. Divide the words into two groups and write them on sheet A and B. Have the students work in pairs. Student A holds sheet A and B holds sheet B. Student A can ask student B to guess a word from sheet A based on information he/she provides to Student B. For example, student A ask student B, 一个星期里，什么时候不用上班? student B will guess the word 周末。方法 6. 信息差。把词分成两组，分别写在生词单 A 和生词单 B 两张纸上。学生两人一组。学生 A 拿好生词单 A，学生 B 拿好生词单 B。学生 AB 根据对方描述的信息猜对方生词单上的词。例如，学生 A 问学生 B，一个星期里，什么时候不用上班？学生 B 就猜出那个词是"周末"。

(Teaching example 3 is contributed by Helen H. Shen)

References 参考文献

陈绂 (1996) 谈对欧美留学生的字词教学,《语言教学与研究》第 4 期。

沈禾玲 (2008) 认知理论及其在汉语作为二语的字词教学中的应用,《中国文字研究》第 1 期, 149-158。

Anderson, M. C., Bjork, R.A., & Bjork, E. (1994) Remembering can cause forgetting: Retrieval dynamics in long-term memory. *Journal of Experimental Psychology: Learning, Memory, and Cognition*, 20, (5), 1063-1087.

Atkinson, R.C., & Shiffrin, R.M. (1968) Human memory: A proposed system and its control processes. In K. W. Spence and J.T. Spence (Eds.), *The Psychology of Learning and Motivation: Advances in Research and Theory*, Vol. 2, pp. 89-195. New York: Academic Press.

Craik, F.I.M., & Lockhart, R. S. (1972) Level of processing: A framework for memory research. *Journal of Verbal Learning and Verbal Behavior,* 11, 671-684.

Craik, F.I.M., & Tulving, E. (1975) Depth of processing and the retention of words in episodic memory. *Journal of Experimental Psychology: General,* 104, 268-294.

Craik, F.I.M. & Watkins, M. J. (1973) The role of rehearsal in short-term memory. *Journal of Verbal Learning and Verbal Behavior,* 12, 450-461.

Dempster, F. N. (1987) Effects of variable encoding and spaced presentations on vocabulary learning. *Journal of Educational Psychology,* 79, 162-170.

Engelkamp, J. (2001) Action memory: A system-oriented approach, in H.D. Zimmer, R.L. Cohen, M.J. Guynn, J. Engelkamp, R. Kormi-Nouri, & M.A. Foley (Eds.), *Memory for action: A Distinct Form of Episodic Memory,* pp. 49-96. New York: Oxford University Press, Inc.

Engelkamp, J. Jahn, P. (2003) Lexical, conceptual and motor information in memory for action phrases: a multi-system account. *Acta Psychologica,* 113, 147-165.

Jahnke, J. C. & Nowaczyk, R. H. (1998) *Cognition.* Upper Saddle River, NJ: Prentice Hall.

Jocoby, L. L., & Craik, F. I. M. (1979) Effects of elaboration of processing at encoding and retrieval: Trace distinctiveness and recovery of initial context. In L.S. Cermak & F. I. M. Craik (Eds.), *Level of Processing in Human Memory.* New York: Lawrence Erlbaum Associates.

Kuo, M-L. A., & Hooper, S. (2004) The effects of visual and verbal coding mnemonics on learning Chinese characters in computer-based instruction, *Educational Technology Research and Development,* 52, (3), 23-38.

Laufer, B., & Hulstijn, J. (2001) Incidental vocabulary acquisition in second language: The construct of task-induced involvement. *Applied Linguistics,* 22, (1), 1-26.

MacWhinney, B. (1987) The competition model, in B. Macwhinney (Ed.), *Mechanisms of Language Acquisition,* pp. 249-308. Hillsdale, N.J.: Lawrence Erlbaum Associates, Inc.

MacWhinney, B. (2001) The competition model: the input, the context, and the brain, in P. Robinson (Ed.) *Cognition and Second Language Instruction,* pp. 69-90. Cambridge, UK: Cambridge University Press.

MacGeoch, J. A. (1932) Forgetting and the law of disuse. *Psychological Review,* 38, 352-370.

MacGeoch, J.A. (1942) *The psychology of human learning.* New York: Longmans.

Miller, G. A. (1956) The magical number seven, plus or minus two: Some limits on our capacity for processing information. *Psychological Review,* 63, 81-97.

Paivio, A. (1969) Mental imagery in associative learning and memory. *Psychological Review,* 76, 241-263.

Paivio, A. (1986) *Mental representations: A dual coding approach.* New York: Oxford University Press.

Paivio, A. (2007) *Mind and its evolution: A dual coding theoretical approach.* Mahwah, New Jersey: Lawrence Erlbaum Associates, Publishers.

Paas, F., Renkl, A., & Sweller, J. (2003) Cognitive load theory and instructional design: Recent developments. *Educational Psychologist,* 38, (1), 1-4.

Schneider, V. I., Healy, A.F., & Bourne, Jr. L. E. (2002) What is learned under difficult condition is hard to forget: Contextual interference effects on foreign vocabulary acquisition, retention, transfer. *Journal of*

Memory and Language, 46, 419-440.

Shen, H. H. (2004) Level of cognitive processing: Effects on character learning among non-native learners of Chinese as a foreign language. *Language and Education,* 18, (2), 167-181.

Shen, H. H. (2010a) Imagery and verbal coding approaches in Chinese vocabulary instruction. *Language Teaching Research,* 14, 485-499.

Shen, H. H. (2010b) Analysis of radical knowledge development among beginning CFL learners. In M.E. Everson & H. H. Shen (Eds.) *Research among Learners of Chinese as a Foreign Language,* pp. 45-65. Honolulu: University of Hawaii, National Foreign Language Resource Center.

Sweller, J. (1988) Cognitive load during problem solving: Effects on learning. *Cognitive Science,* 12, 257-285.

Sweller, J. (1991) Cognitive load theory and the format of instruction. *Cognition and Instruction,* 8, (4), 293-332.

Sweller, J. (1994) Cognitive load theory, learning difficulty, and instructional design. *Learning and Instruction,* 4, pp. 295-312.

Tulving, E. (1972) Episodic and semantic memory. In E. Tulving & W. Donaldson (Eds.), *Organization of Memory,* pp. 381-402. New York: Academic Press.

Chapter 5 第五章
Character learning strategies and training

汉语二语字词学习策略及训练

5.1 Vocabulary learning strategies: concept and scope
汉语字词学习策略：定义和内涵

In the *Modern Chinese Word Dictionary* 现代汉语词典（2005: 138），strategy is defined as guiding principles for action and format of combat. In English, *strategy* comes from the ancient Greek term *strategia,* meaning generalship or the art of war (Oxford, 1990: 7). Therefore, strategy is related to the ways and means of winning a battle or combat. By extending this definition to classroom learning, learning strategies are actions, methods, or mental processes that learners employ during learning to acquire knowledge. Chinese vocabulary learning strategies are part of the learning strategies that learners utilize for learning characters and words. In this section, the terms vocabulary learning strategies and vocabulary learning methods are considered to be interchangeable.

在《现代汉语词典》(2005:138)中，策略的定义是"根据形势发展而制定的行动方针和斗争方式"。在英文里，策略这一词源于古希腊的 *strategia*。它的意思是斗争方式或战争的技艺(Oxford 1990: 7)。所以，策略是关于打赢战争的方式和方法。把这一概念引申到课堂学习，学习策略是指个体为获得知识而采取的行动、方法或思维方式。字词学习策略是汉语学习策略的一部分，是个体用它来学习字词的方法、方式。在这一章中，学习策略与学习方法是可以互相替代的。

Vocabulary learning strategies are created and utilized by learners. Although each strategy is different, strategy-induced learning shares some common features. First, it is goal-directed learning. Learners adopt or create certain strategies for the purpose of solving a certain vocabulary-learning problem. For example, in order to memorize the word 兴奋 (*exciting*) a student created a story in which a farmer sees a big field, so he is very excited (Wei 2010). Second, it is self-regulated learning. Students themselves decide which strategy to use, how to use it, and when to use it in order to learn particular words. Third, it is individualized learning. Due to the differences in cognitive styles and learning behaviors, each student may have a set of preferred learning strategies. One strategy that is effective for one learner may not work for another learner. Here is a story from the first author of this book:

> Asking students to make and use vocabulary cards to learn words is a common strategy; so I asked students to make vocabulary cards themselves and brought them to the class for vocabulary learning activities. However, a student once told me that he made these cards just to fulfill the class requirement, but he never used them after the class because it worked better for him to read words from the list in order to memorize them rather than to flip vocabulary cards.

Some students prefer listening to music when learning vocabulary, others do not. Therefore, we can recommend that students use certain vocabulary learning strategies, but cannot force them to accept or discard certain strategies if they do not feel comfortable in doing so.

字词学习策略是由学习者创造并使用的。虽然每种策略都不一样,但是策略导入的学习却有其共性。首先,它是一种目标指引的学习。学习者创造或采用某种策略都是为了解决字词学习问题。例如,为了记住"兴奋"这一词,一个学生编了一个记忆方法——一个农民看见一块很大的田地,他很兴奋 (Wei 2010)。其次,这是一种自律性的学习。为了学习或练习某些字词,学生自己决定用什么策略,怎么用,什么时候用。再次,这是个体化的学习。由于个体的认知风格和学习行为各异,每个学生可能有自己偏爱的学习策略。一种策略对某个学生来说可能很有用,对另一个学生可能不适用。下面是 Helen H. Shen 举的一个例子:

> 学生用字卡来学习生词是一种常用的方法,所以我要求学生自做生字卡,上课时带来让学生从事各种以字卡为工具的字词活动。但是有一次一个学生对我说,他做字卡是为了完成老师的要求,他下课后从来都不用字卡学汉字,因为对他来说,看一串字词比翻卡容易记住字词。

有些学生喜欢边学习字词边听音乐,有些则不喜欢。所以,我们可以向学生推荐使用被实践证明是有效的学习策略,但是我们不能强迫某学生接受或放弃某种学习策略,如果他们不愿意的话。

Learning strategies have been studied for decades, but we still lack adequate criteria to establishing a standard taxonomy. Nonetheless, scholars tend to agree to classify the learning strategies into four general categories: cognitive strategies, metacognitve strategies, social strategies, and affective strategies (Takač 2008). **Cognitive strategies** are direct learning strategies that relate to purposeful mental action or activity of processing learning materials such as encoding, comprehension, memorization, and application. **Metacognitive strategies** are indirect learning strategies that do not directly involve knowledge processing, but they facilitate execution of cognitive strategies such as setting up goals, planning learning steps, and evaluating learning results. Three types of knowledge are required for creation of metacognitive strategies (Wenden 1998): personal knowledge, task knowledge, and strategic knowledge. Personal knowledge is how the learners know themselves as a learner, such as knowledge of personal language proficiency, learning habits, interests, behavior, and motivation. Task knowledge is learners' knowledge about the purpose of a task and how it will serve their language learning needs. For example, the learner knows how many vocabulary words they should learn for a particular lesson, how many of them require recognition and production, and whether they are required to use the words in new contexts. Strategic knowledge refers to knowledge of available strategies the learner can use and how to use them to reach the goal based on the learner's personal learning habits and style. **Social strategies** are the strategies related to the way that individual learners learn through cooperation or interaction with others, such as interacting with teachers, classmates, friends, and native speakers. **Affective strategies** are the strategies used by learners to motivate themselves to learn, to eliminate distractions caused by emotional fluctuations, and to control their feelings when they are in a bad mood.

　　对学习策略的研究虽然已经进行了几十年，但是我们仍然没有一个学术界公认的理论框架用来指导建立标准的策略分类表。虽然如此，学者们大都倾向于把学习策略分成四大类：认知策略、元认知策略、社交策略和情感策略(Takač 2008)。认知策略是直接学习策略，指的是大脑直接用于对学习材料进行认知加工的策略，例如解码、理解、记忆、应用等策略。元认知策略是间接学习策略。那些策略没有直接参与对材料的认知加工，但是它们促进对认知策略的使用，例如，制定学习目标、计划学习进度、评价学习结果等。元认知策略的运用需要三种知识 (Wenden 1998)：个体知识、任务知识和策略知识。个体知识是学生对自己作为一个学习者的了解，比如，学生本人的二语语言水平、学习习惯、学习兴趣、学习行为及学习动机。任务知识是学习者对学习任务的了解，如学习目标及这一目标与他们学习需要的关系。具体地说，学习者清楚对于特定的课文，有哪些字词需要学习。哪些需要认读，哪些需要会默写，哪些需要会运用。策略知识是学生知道他们可以运用哪些策略和如何运用某种策略来根据个人的学习习惯和风格去达到学习的目标。社交策略是指学习者如何通过与别人的交往，比如与教师、同学、朋友和汉语母语者进行交往来学习字词。情感策略是个体用来如何鼓励自己学习，减少那些因为感情变化而带来的学习干扰，在心情恶劣的情况下控制自己的情绪的策略。

Since vocabulary learning strategies are part of learning strategies, in general, the above discussed four types of strategies can be applied to vocabulary learning. However, vocabulary learning is different from other learning tasks such as grammar, reading, and writing; therefore, individuals may adopt specific strategies that more precisely fit with vocabulary learning. For example, a social strategy might be to have a native language partner as a conversation partner to improve oral proficiency. Asking the language partner to point out the errors in word use or pronunciation during the communication is a strategy for improving vocabulary knowledge.

因为字词学习策略是学习策略的一部分,一般来说,上述提到的四种类别的学习策略也适用于字词学习策略分类。但是,字词学习与其他语法、阅读、写作等学习是不同的,字词学习策略是指学习者可能采用那些专门适合于字词学习的策略。例如,社交策略可以是与一个汉语母语者结成语言伙伴进行交流以增强口语的流利度。其中,请语言伙伴指出自己在用词或某字发音错误则是字词学习策略。

5.2 Studies on Chinese vocabulary learning strategies
汉语二语字词学习策略的研究

The first empirical study on character learning strategy in a classroom environment among CFL learners was conducted by McGinnis (1995). In total, 29 participants were asked to self-report about their character-learning strategies during a five-week summer immersion program. Rote repetition was the most frequently used strategy and the next was creation of idiosyncratic stories about the characters. Another study by Ke (1998) investigated English-speaking beginning college CFL students' perceptions on the relative effectiveness of various types of character learning strategies. The 223 students participating in the study were asked whether they agreed or disagreed with 11 statements predesigned by the author. The majority of participants agreed that learning character components (radical and phonetic components) was more effective than learning stroke order or creating their own stories about what characters look like to them. A small-scale study by 曾金金 (2000) investigated character learning strategies among German-speaking college CFL learners from beginning to advanced levels. This study also adopted a self-report data collection method. According to the author, students reported 15 types of learning strategies that they used in their character learning. The most common ones were: repeatedly writing the characters, using vocabulary cards, and using radical knowledge.

在美国从事第一个汉语二语实证性字词学习策略研究的当推 McGinnis 教授 (1995)。他要求29名英语母语学习者对他们在为期五个星期的暑期沉浸式汉字词学习中所用的策略进行自我报告。从中发现,机械重复是学生最经常使用的方法。次常用方法是自己编关于字词的小故事。Ke (1998) 调查了英语母语的汉语学习者对字词学习策略相对有效性的看法。参与此项研究的223个学生被要求对事先设定的11项学习策略进行比较。结果表明,大部分学生同意学习汉字的部首(声旁和形旁)比学习笔顺或自己给汉字编小故事更有效。另一个小规模的研究(曾金金 2000)调查了母语德语的从初级到高级的大学汉语学习者的字词学习策略。这一研究也是让学生对自己所用的汉语字词策略进行自我报告。根据学生共报告了15种学习策略。其中常见的策略有:重复抄写字词,用字卡以及利用部首知识学字词。

A more comprehensive study on character learning strategies of nonnative beginning college CFL learners was conducted by 江新、赵果 (2001). The 138 participants with different foreign language backgrounds who were studying in a target language speaking environment were asked to rate strategies listed in the survey form based on a five-point Likert scale indicating one as "never do it," and five as "always do it." Of the 36 commonly used strategies, 31 were cognitive strategies and 5 were noncognitive strategies. Factor analysis revealed that the 31 commonly used strategies could be grouped into 6 groups: group 1. 笔画策略, stroke strategies - studying stroke order and write characters according to the correct order; group 2. 音义策略 sound-meaning strategies—paying attention to sound and meaning of characters; group 3. 字形策略 shape strategies—paying attention to the physical shape of the characters and repeated writing them; group 4. 归纳策略 inductive strategies--revealing the similarity of characters in sound and in shape and by analyzing phonetic-semantic radicals; group 5. 复习策略 reviewing strategies, to review the learned characters; group 6. 应用策略 application strategies—using learned words in reading and writing for metacognitive strategies, two groups of strategies were identified, Group one was monitoring 监控, finding and analyzing the errors made by students themselves during the learning process. Group two was planning 计划, making a plan for character learning based on goals. In a subsequent study (赵果、江新 2002), the researchers further investigated the correlation between the six identified groups of cognitive strategies and vocabulary learning performance. The application strategies had positive correlations with the character production performance. The radical strategies had positive correlation with the retention of meanings of characters. The study showed that strategies were more helpful in learning phonetic-semantic compounds than non-phonetic-semantic compounds.

江新、赵果(2001)对大学初级非母语汉语学习者在目的语环境下的字词学习进行了研究。138名在目的语环境中学习的母语为不同语种的学生参与了该研究。参与者被要求用五分点的利氏量表对一组学习策略进行比较。该量表以1为"从来不用",5为"总是用"来区分策略的使用频度。共找出36种常用策略,其中31种是认知策略,5种是元认知策略。通过因素分析方法,31种认知策略可以被分为6组：一组是笔画策略,学生学习字词笔顺并按照笔顺来书写汉字；二组是音义策略,学生注重对汉字词的音义的学习；三组是字形策略,学生很注意字词的间架结构并重复抄写字词；四组是归纳策略,通过分析部首,学生归纳出字词中的同音或同形的特征；五组是复习策略,学生复习学过的字词；六组是应用策略,学生运用新学的字词进行写作和阅读。对于元认知策略,作者把它们分成两组,一组是监控,对自己在学习过程中的书写错误进行分析。另一组是计划,根据学习目标制订学习计划。在稍后的一个研究中(赵果、江新 2002),两位研究者进一步对六组认知学习策略与汉字学习效果之间的相关性进行了调查。结果表明,学习策略的使用与学习结果呈正相关。分析部首的策略与汉字的保持呈正相关。研究还表明,较之非形声字,这些学习策略对学习形声字更有效。

Another comprehensive study on character learning strategies conducted in a non-native language learning environment (Shen 2005) involved 95 college CFL learners from beginning, intermediate, and advanced levels. The study adopted a three-step data collection procedure that used three questionnaires. A statistical procedure of factor analysis was used to classify the identified strategies into groups based on underlying commonalities of factors. The study identified 30 commonly used character-learning strategies. Among these, 24 were cognitive strategies, five were metacognitive strategies, and one was a social strategy, as presented in Table 1.

　　另一研究是在非目的语环境中进行(Shen 2005)。该研究的参与者是95名英语为母语的大学初级到高级的汉语学习者。该研究采用三个问卷调查分三步收集数据。从问卷中识别了30种常用字词学习策略。其中24种为认知策略,5种为元认知策略,1种是社交策略,请参见表1。

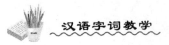

Table 1 30 Commonly Used Character Learning Strategies
表1 30种常用字词学习策略

Strategy Item 策略条目	Category 分类
1. Repeats the sound when the character is first introduced. 字词第一次呈现后重复地读。	C 认知
2. Pays attention to the tone and associates it with Pinyin. 注意声调并与拼音的联系。	C 认知
3. Previews the new words before class. 课前预习生词。	M 元认知
5. Finds an equivalent word from the native language. 从母语中找到相应的词。	C 认知
6. Previews the new words the night before class. 学生词的头天晚上预习生词。	M 元认知
7. Reviews newly learned words by writing them many times. 通过反复写来复习生词。	C 认知
8. Visualizes the character. 在头脑中呈现字词的视像。	C 认知
9. Pays attention to how the character is used in context. 关注字词在句中如何使用。	C 认知
10. Checks reference sources for a character's meaning. 在有关资料中查找字词的意思。	C 认知
11. Reviews words by going over notes, example sentences. 在复习时看课堂笔记和例句。	C 认知
12. Determines if one character in a new compound word has been learned before. 想想复合词中的汉字以前是否学过。	C 认知
13. Quizzes oneself. 自我测验。	M 元认知
14. Looks at strokes and associates them with a similar character already learned. 注意笔顺,把这个字与以前学过的相似的字联系起来。	C 认知
15. Says the character and visualizes it. 说字词并在头脑中建立视觉意象。	C 认知
16. Listens carefully when the new character is first introduced. 字词第一次呈现时,仔细地听字词的发音。	C 认知

17. Recognizes radicals which have been learned. 　　辨别字词中以前学过的部首。	C 认知
18. Pays attention to stroke order. 注意字词的笔顺。	C 认知
20. Uses the new character orally in a sentence. 　　在口语中使用新学的字词。	C 认知
21. Reads the new character out loud and associates its sound with the meaning and 　　shape. 大声读字词并把音与形和义联系起来。	C 认知
22. Says the character when writing it. 　　写汉字的时候同时读汉字的音。	C 认知
23. Finds out the meaning of the radical in the character. 　　找出汉字中部首的义。	C 认知
24. Finds the connection between the new character and previously learned radicals 　　in terms of sound, meaning, and shape. 找出新字与新字所包含的以前学过的 　　部首的音、形、义之间的联系。	C 认知
25. Asks others how they use a particular character in sentences. 　　问问其他人，他们是怎么在句子中运用新字词的。	S 社交
26. Reviews newly learned words before class and quizzes, and on weekends. 　　在课前，字词测验前及周末复习字词。	M 元认知
27. Memorizes the sound first, then the meaning and shape. 　　先记住音，再记义和形。	C 认知
28. Associates the sound of a character with its meaning and shape. 　　建立音与义、形之间的联系。	C 认知
29. Does homework first before memorizing the new characters. 　　在记忆新字词时先做作业。	M 元认知
30. Listens to conversation by native speakers. 　　听汉语母语者对话。	C 认知

Note: C = Cognitive strategies, M = Metacognitive strategies, S = Social strategies. C=认知策略

A factor analysis revealed that these 30 commonly used strategies could be classified into 8 groups based on their commonalities. Among the eight groups, groups 1-7 were cognitive strategies: Group 1, cognitive strategies relating to learning characters by using orthographic knowledge, such as paying attention to graphic structures, making connections with previously learned similar characters, visualizing the graphic structure of the character, and making use of phonetic and semantic information in radicals; Group 2, cognitive strategies dealt with learning new words by understanding their meanings in different written and spoken contexts. Group 3, Cognitive strategies relating to learning behaviors of memorizing and retaining newly learned characters effectively such as making mental linkages among sound, shape, and meaning with a character and relating the new words to its context in both oral and written methods. Group 4, cognitive strategies relating to receiving new character information at the initial stage from the instructor, such as listening carefully to the pronunciation and tone, observing stroke order carefully and trying to write the new character when it was first introduced. Group 5, were cognitive strategies of memorization that emphasized the use of the sound of the character as a cue for making connections to the meaning and shape. Group 6, cognitive strategies related to seeking reference for understanding the new characters, such as relating new characters to the first language and asking how they are used in context. Group 7, cognitive strategies used an aural approach to improving retention of new characters that had already been introduced, such as listening to native speakers and saying the word to oneself. Group 8, metacognitive strategies such as structured review before and after class. The study revealed that students considered group 1 orthographic knowledge based learning strategies and group 8 structure review were most helpful in preparing their vocabulary quizzes.

作者运用因素分析法揭示了30种常用策略根据其内在的共同特征可以被分成8组。其中1-7组是认知策略。第1组是运用正字知识来学习字词的策略，比如，注意字形的间架结构，与以前学过的音形义相似汉字建立联系，建立汉字的视觉意象，利用声旁和形旁学习。第2组是通过不同的口头和书面语境来理解字词意义的策略。第3组是关于有效记忆与保持的策略，比如如何在头脑中建立音形义三者的联系并用口头或书面方法把生词放在句子中来记忆。第4组是关于生词最初呈现时如何感知它们的策略，比如仔细地听音节与声调，仔细观察笔顺并把字词写下来。第5组是关于如何利用音作为记忆支点把它与形和义联系起来记住字词的策略。第6组是寻找其他方法理解字词，例如，把新字词与第一语言联系起来，搞清楚怎么用字词来造句。第7组是用听的方法来加强记忆，比如仔细听汉语母语者对词的发音，把字词大声说出来给自己听。第8组是元认知策略,比如有计划地在课前进行预习,在课后进行复习。这一研究表明,在这8组学习策略中,学生认为第1组以正字知识为基础的学习策略和第八组有计划地预习与复习对准备字词测验最有效。

A further study investigated the effects of metacognitive beliefs and strategies on character learning performance. In that study, the metacognitive beliefs refer to students' beliefs of their own learning and their positive expectations for their learning performance and value of success. Data on 45 English-speaking beginning college Chinese learners' metacognitive beliefs, metacognitive strategies, and their character learning performance were analyzed. A positive correlation was found among the three; that is, students who were confident about their ability to learn the language and understand their responsibility in planning their learning did well in their character tests.

还有一个研究是关于元认知的态度取向与策略对汉字学习的影响(Wang, Spencer, & Xing 2009)。元认知态度取向是指学生对自己学习成绩和成功价值的积极期望。这一研究分析了45位母语英语的大学汉语学习者的原认知态度取向与元认知策略的使用。结果表明学习成绩与元认知态度取向,元认知策略使用呈正相关。也就是说,那些对自己学习能力比较自信并知道如何对自己学习进行计划的学生,他们的字词测验成绩也较优。

The above study shows that CFL learners used a wide variety of cognitive strategies in their vocabulary learning, but they paid less attention in the use of metacognitive strategies, social strategies, and affective strategies. The learning reality is that metacognitive strategies sometimes play important roles in character learning. Here is a story from the first author of the book:

A student came to my office and told me that he wanted to drop his Chinese class. The reason was that he had a busy schedule and could not find time each day to work on Chinese characters. I asked him to show me his daily schedule book. I went over his schedule and pointed out to him that there were a few time slots that he could use for vocabulary learning each day. After this meeting, the student decided not to drop the class, as he was convinced that he actually had time to study characters on daily basis.

This story showed us that many students do poorly in vocabulary learning not because they have problems in using cognitive strategies, but because they lack strategies in metacognition and do not know how to monitor their own learning.

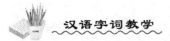

上述提到的研究显示,学生们在字词学习中使用各种各样的认知策略,但是他们对元认知、社交策略、情感策略等的使用不怎么重视。但是现实的情况是有时候元认知策略对字词学习起十分重要的作用。下面是 Helen H. Shen 举的一个例子:

一个学生到我的办公室来,告诉我他不想继续修中文课,理由是他每天的学习日程很紧,没有时间学汉字。我就让他把他的每星期日程计划表拿出来让我看看。我看他的日程表后,给他指出来,从他的表上看,每天他可以有几个几分钟的时间段学字词。自从这一次谈话后,那个学生决定不休课,继续他的中文学习,因为他已经被说服,他事实上每天可以抽出一点时间学字词。

这件事告诉我们,很多学生字词学习的成绩不理想不是因为他们不会使用认知策略,而是因为他们缺乏元认知策略,不知道怎么去监控他们自己的学习。

In summary, vocabulary strategy research is still an evolving field. Although the number of existing studies on CFL character learning strategies is limited, these studies have convinced us that students use a wide range of learning strategies in their character learning and that good learning strategies play a positive role in character acquisition.

综上所述,对汉语二语字词学习策略的研究仍然是一个正在展开的领域,虽然研究的数量还不太多,但是已有的研究已经可以向我们证实学生们在字词学习中确实运用多种学习策略,而且良好的学习策略的在字词学习中起着积极作用。

5.3 Identifying and training on vocabulary learning strategies
识别和训练字词学习策略

In the previous section, we concluded that character-learning strategies have a positive effect on character learning. Therefore, pedagogically, it is necessary for classroom instructors to help students to identify character-learning strategies as well as to provide strategy training so that students can learn using good character-learning strategies. A study (柳燕梅 2009) on the necessity, teachability, and effectiveness of strategy training for Chinese character learning among CFL learners conducted at the Beijing Language and Culture University has concluded that: 1. participants considered that strategy training was necessary in helping their learning characters; 2. Students who participated in the strategy training courses showed that they use more strategies in their daily character learning than the control group. This means that the training increased students' conscious awareness of using strategies; and 3. students in the experimental group purposefully used a number of strategies that significantly reduced the extent of character writing time during the memorization process compared with the control group. This study provided a positive note that strategy training is beneficial to students. In the next section, we will discuss how to identify useful word learning strategies that students are using and how to organize an effective character strategy training workshop.

在上一节,我们得出了结论,学习策略对汉语字词学习有积极作用。因此,从教学法的角度看,教师在教学中帮助学生识别优良的学习策略或提供学习策略的培训使学生能在字词学习中运用优良的策略是十分必要的。柳燕梅(2009)在北京语言大学进行的关于字词学习策略培训的必要性、可教性和有效性的研究得出的结论是:(1)参试者认为策略培训对帮助他们学字词是有必要的。(2)经过培训后的学生比没参加培训的学生在学习中运用更多的字词学习策略。这说明培训增强了学生策略运用意识。(3)跟控制组相比,参与策略培训的学生能有目的的使用策略记忆汉字从而减少了对汉字反复抄写的次数。这一研究肯定了策略训练能促进学生的字词学习。在下面的段落中,我们将讨论怎样帮助学生识别有用的字词学习策略以及如何有效地组织学习策略培训。

5.3.1 Identifying effective character-learning strategies used by your students
识别有效的字词学习策略

Experienced instructors often collect good character-learning strategies from their students. They may wish to introduce those strategies to new students. However, learning is personal and individual. Strategies that fit previous students may not entirely fit the current students. Therefore, it is the best that instructors identify what strategies their current students are using prior to introducing any other strategies to students, because students' self-developed strategies may fit their own cognitive style and learning habit better. It is necessary, every year, that instructors help students to identify their character strategies and determine which are effective. Instructors may adopt the following methods to help students identify effective character-learning strategies:

有经验的教师常常收集学生们的优良的字词学习策略,因为他们可以把好的策略介绍给其他学生。但是学习是个别化的个体行为,那些对适用于以前的学生的策略不一定也适用于当前的学生。所以教师最好在向学生介绍优良的学习策略之前,先帮助他们识别他们正在使用的字词学习策略。因为学生自己琢磨出来的学习策略更能适应他们自己的认知风格和学习习惯。因此,教师有必要每年都帮助学生找出他们在运用的字词学习策略中哪些是有效的。教师可以采取下面提到的一些措施来识别有效字词学习策略:

汉语字词教学

1. Classroom observation. During the class, the instructor should give students the opportunity to demonstrate how they use strategies in learning characters. The instructor can give each student a few new words and ask them do a self-study. The instructor can then walk around and observe how the students learn those new words, such as how they learn the sound, shape, and meaning of each word. Afterwards, the instructor could ask each student to report their learning results or give a mini-quiz to evaluate their learning results. This will help students to determine the effectiveness of the method they used for learning new words.

课堂观察。在课堂上,教师应该提供机会让学生演示他们用什么方法学字词。教师可以分给每位学生几个生词让他们自学。在这期间,教师巡视并观察学生的学习方法,比如他们是怎么学字词的音形义的。之后,可以让学生报告一下学习结果或给一个小测验评价学习效果。这样做可以让学生自己判断他们所用的学习方法的有效性。

2. Student self-reporting. The instructor asks students to think introspectively about what kind of strategies they use in vocabulary learning based on the established categories. For example, the instructor can first give the students the definition of cognitive, metacognitive, social, and affective strategies, and then ask students to name the strategies they use and to classify them into the four categories. Students then can share their learning strategies with each other.

学生自我报告。教师可以根据我们前面提到的四类学习策略为线索,请学生自我反思一下,他们平时是用什么方法来学习字词的。例如,教师先告诉学生认知、元认知、社交、情感策略的定义,然后让学生说说他们用的是什么策略,是属于哪种类别的。然后学生可以互相交流一下他们各自所采用的学习方法。

3. Questionnaire. On some occasions, some students may not be aware of the strategies they are using for character learning. The instructor can provide a list of strategies observed in the classroom or self-reported by previous and current students and can construct a structured questionnaire that asks the students to rate the frequency of each strategy listed in the questionnaire on a five-point Likert scale. Completion of the survey would provide students with an idea of the kind of strategies they are using. The Likert scale was invented by the American psychologist Rensis Likert. The five-point scale for the current example would be a scale with 5 choices from 1-5, as follows: 1. Never or almost never true of me; 2.Generally not true of me 3.

Somewhat true of me; 4. Generally true of me; 5. Always or almost always true of me. Students would be asked to mark only one statement from the five based on their true feelings for each of the strategies listed in the questionnaire. For example, if the strategy item is "I pay attention to the tone and try to associate the sound with Pinyin" (Shen 2005), and the student feels that he/she seldom uses that strategy, then, the number "1" should be marked. Once students have marked their choices for all strategy items in the questionnaire, then they can sort out the strategy use from the list, based on the number from high to low. A high number indicates a more frequently used strategy. After identifying the strategies that students are using in their character/word learning, the next step is to ask students to evaluate which strategies they think are most helpful with regard to memorizing either sound, shape, and meaning of characters as well as their vocabulary tests, again by applying a 5-point Likert scale. After students have finished evaluating the strategies, they should be asked to sort out the strategies from more useful to least useful based on their own ratings. Then students should then have a good picture about their strategy use.

调查表。有时候,有些学生自己可能没有意识到他们在用什么方法学字词。教师可以设计一个调查表,在表上列出那些教师在课上观察到和其他学生报告的学习方法让学生对这些方法用一个5分点的利氏量表进行使用频度评定。在这过程中,学生会注意到哪些方法是他们正在使用的。5分点利氏量表是由美国心理学家 Rensis Likert 发明的。在评定字词学习策略中,5分点是指由1到5的五项选择:(1) 代表从来都不是真实的;(2) 代表一般来说不真实;(3) 代表有时候是真实的;(4) 代表一般来说是真实的;(5) 代表总是真实的。老师让学生根据自己的情况对所列的每项学习策略按这5个等级进行评定。例如,如果调查表上列出的一个学习策略是"我注意字词的声调并把字词的音与拼音联系起来"(Shen 2005),答卷的学生认为他/她几乎不用这个策略,那么就应当在5分点量表上选(1) 从来都不是真实的。

5.3.2. Training on vocabulary learning strategies
字词学习策略训练

Strategy training includes two aspects of preparation: one is to compile a strategy taxonomy and the other is to make a training plan to outline the training procedures. We will discuss these two in detail below.

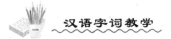

策略训练的准备包括两个方面:一是制定一个学习策略分类表,确定要介绍哪些策略;二是制定出一个策略训练的计划包括训练的步骤。下面我们详细探讨这两个方面。

Compiling a strategy taxonomy
制定学习策略分类表

Helping students to identify their effective vocabulary learning strategy can direct students' attention to how they learn and also encourage them to discover and create learning strategies that fit their own learning styles. However, creating and discovering an effective learning strategy by the students themselves alone would take a long time, as students are not able to judge the effectiveness of a strategy until it has been used many times. If instructors have identified good strategies that have been proved effective from learning practice, they should introduce these strategies to students and train them in to how to use the strategies, so that students will be able to use many more strategies in their learning. Training on vocabulary learning strategy is a fast way to have students gain quality learning strategies in a short period of time. Prior to strategy training, the instructor would need to compile a strategy taxonomy which includes the four types of strategies already discussed. When compiling the taxonomy, for choosing cognitive strategies, teachers may pay attention to the following aspects:

帮助学生识别他们正在使用的有效的字词学习策略固然能让学生注意到他们是怎么学字词的,同时也能鼓励他们发现并创造适合于他们自己学习风格的字词学习方法,但是,让学生自己来发现和创造有效的学习方法不是一朝一夕就能做到的,因为学生无法判断一个方法是否有效除非这个方法被用了很多次。如果教师已经识别出一些学习策略并在过去的实践中证明是有效的,他们应该把那些策略介绍给学生,对学生进行字词学习策略的训练,学习策略训练是一种让学生在短时间内积累较多好的学习方法的捷径。但是在训练之前,教师首先要做的事是制定一个包含四个类别的学习策略的分类表。在制表的时候,对于认知学习策略的选择,考虑选择以下的策略:

1. Strategies helping conceptualization. These are strategies used to understand the sound, shape, and meaning of the target words through analysis of radical components within the target words, analysis of morphological structure of the word, and comparison of words with other similar words to establish a clear concept of the target word. An example would be understanding that the word 打 is a phonetic-semantic compound by identifying phonetic radical, 丁, semantic radical,

扌, and number of perceptual radicals (a total of two). If the word is a bisyllabic word, such as 打击, after analyzing the individual characters 打 and 击, students would learn the strategies to figure out the morphological structure of this word. They should know that this is a coordinate word as 打 and 击 both are verbs and the semantic importance of each word is equal. Students should know the meaning of word 打击 as a whole and should know how it differs from 打架 by judging the word meaning and word structure (verb-object).

能帮助概念化的策略。概念化的策略是指那些通过对汉字的部首的分析,构词法的分析,通过与近似词(音近、形近、义近)比较后在头脑中形成对目的词的清晰的概念一类的策略。举个例子来说,在学"打"字时,学生理解"打"是一个形声字,声旁是"丁",形旁是"扌"。如果要学的字是双音节词"打击",对"打"和"击"分别作了分析以后,学生应该学习有关分析词的构造的方法,他们应该知道这是一个联合词,"打"和"击"都是动词,每个字的语义在这个词中都是同等重要。学生不仅仅知道"打击"的构词结构,还应该知道用什么方法鉴别它与"打架"在语义和构词法上的不同。

2. Strategies helping to establish association. This includes two types of strategies. One is creating mental linkages among sounds, shapes, and meanings within the character and word, such as reading out loud the words, visualizing its shape, using a finger to write it in the air several times, and attaching a meaning to the sound and shape. The second type of strategy is to associate one word with another word. Strategies of this type can include using a story or dialog to integrate a series of target words, or associating either sound or meaning to the first language to find a memory peg, such as using the English word "bar," which has a similar sound with the character 吧, and the English meaning of "bar" as a "counter for selling wine or drinks," which is directly related to 酒吧. So the connection between "Bar" and 酒吧 helps memorize 酒吧. Grouping words based on themes is another way of making association between words, such as using a "hospital" as theme to group the words 医生、病人、心脏病、吃药、打针 together.

能帮助建立联结的策略。这一类的策略包括两小类。一类是能帮助建立字词内部因素之间的联结。如音形义三者的联系,每个汉字与组成的词的意义联系。那些策略包括大声朗读字词,建立词的视觉意象,用手指空写,把字义与其音形相联系等。另一小类是把一个词与另一词联系起来。所用的策略可包括用一个故事或对话把一系列的生词联系起来,把字词的音、义与相关的第一语言的词联系起来建立记忆的支点。比如,英语中的"bar"与汉语的"吧"音似,义近,bar 的其中一个意思是卖酒的柜台,如果让 bar 与酒吧建立某种联结,那么记住"酒吧"就很容易。把词根据主题进行分组是另一种建立联结的方法。比如,可用"医院"为主题,建立医生、病人、心脏病、吃药、打针等词之间的相互联系。

3. Strategies helping to make Connection. This means to connect the words with personal life experiences or previously learned words, and to find the synonyms and antonyms for the target words. For example, for the word 酒吧, students can ask themselves whether they have seen or have been in 酒吧 in their own country. What experience have they gained about 酒吧? If they have never been to a 酒吧, do they know any person, either their friends or their family members, who have been in a 酒吧? They can also make some connections between this word with previously learned word about such as 九 which has the same pronunciation and other previously learned words, 酒瓶、酒杯、and 喝酒, which can be seen in 酒吧. If a target word is 思念, students can connect this word with a learned synonymous word 想念 to help remember the meaning of the word.

　　能帮助建立关系的策略。这类策略是让词与个人生活,与以前学过的词产生联系,找出近(同)义词反义词等。以"酒吧"为例,学生可以问问自己他们在自己的国家里有没有见过酒吧,有没有去过酒吧。关于酒吧他们经历了一些什么? 如果他们从来没去过酒吧,他们所认识的人,朋友或家庭成员有没有去过酒吧? 学生还可以把"酒吧"中的"酒"与以前学过的同音词比如"九"发生联系以帮助记忆字音。另外让"酒吧"与在酒吧中经常看到的以前学过的酒瓶、酒杯、喝酒等事物发生联系。如果要学的目的词是"思念",学生可以把这一词与学过的同义词"想念"联系起来,从而记住"思念"的意思。

4. Strategies of using Imagination. This type of strategy helps to create mental image of the words. For example, when the word 英雄 is introduced, students can visualize a hero or heroic behaviors, which is stored in their mind. When they learn the phrase 山雨欲来风满楼, students can create a mental picture of this scene.

　　能帮助唤起视觉意象的策略。这种类型的策略能使学生在头脑中建立词的视觉形象。例如,当介绍了"英雄"这个词后,学生头脑中英雄人物的意象或生动的英雄行为能呼之欲出。当学习了"山雨欲来风满楼"时能创造出这一场面的视觉景象。

5. Strategies of using animation. This type of strategy involves using physical action, such as acting out a word with a gesture or an action, including drawing.

　　能运用动作的策略。这类策略包括体态动作,比如用某种姿势或动作表现词,包括用画画的方式来表现词。

6. Strategies for application. This type of strategy involves using the target words either in a simulated or authentic language situation to complete communication tasks.

　　能帮助字词应用的策略。这类的策略包括如何能在模拟和真实语言情境中运用所学的词来完成交际任务。

For metacognitive strategies to be included in the training, the instructor can consider the following aspects:

关于元认知策略,教师可以考虑包括下面提到的一些方面:

1. Time planning. This refers to strategies used for planning where, when, and how to study vocabulary. This type of strategy involves working out a weekly or monthly written plan, and putting the plan in a noticeable or easy to find place as a reminder; finding and using all possible discrete times, such as 5 or 10 minutes, to study vocabulary.

　　时间规划。指的是用来计划在哪儿,什么时间,怎么学字词。这类策略包括制定每周或每月学习计划,把计划放在醒目或容易找到的地方以提醒自己。找出能够利用的一些零碎的时间,比如五分钟或十分钟来学习字词。

2. Enforcing a schedule. Once students have their schedules worked out, if the plan is not enforced, the learning will not happen. Strategies such as staying with the plan on a daily basis, changing the plan if it does not work, or asking others (roommates or friends) to give a reminder can help make sure that the scheduled time is used for vocabulary study.

　　实施计划。计划制定了以后如不实行,那么学习就无法进行。促使自己实行计划策略可包括如何每天按计划行事,修改计划如果计划不切实际,或请别人(室友或朋友)提醒自己保证能把计划的时间用于字词学习。

3. Monitoring strategy use. This refers to determining what strategies the learner is using and in what way the learner uses it, and whether a certain strategy is helpful. For

example, if a student gets a good or bad vocabulary test result, the student may wish to reflect on what kind of learning strategies are useful for preparing for this particular kind of test.

  监测策略的使用。指学习者决定应该用什么策略怎样用,策略是否对自己有用。例如果某学生在一次字词测验中成绩很好或不好,他/她也许应该反思一下什么样的学习策略对准备字词测验是有用的。

Since social strategies are related to learning words by communicating with others, these could include pair or group work in the classroom and language practice with others outside of class. The training may focus on strategies of finding opportunities for socialization and strategies of how to communicate with others with limited target words and how to work cooperatively with others. We often observed that some students were quite outgoing and they often dropped into the instructor's office to practice oral Chinese and to try to use newly leaned words. Some students are reluctant to practice the target language with others, even inside the classroom. Therefore, we should encourage students to use strategies to find opportunities such as living with a roommate who speaks Chinese, or living with a Chinese family, finding a language partner on campus, making friends with a native speaker, pairing with classmates after class to work on Chinese, signing up for on-line chatting, and blogging and email exchanges for the purpose of learning and using vocabulary.

  社交策略是关于通过与他人的交流来学习字词的策略。这些策略包括课堂内的两人或多人小组的活动及课外与其他人一起练习字词的活动。策略训练的内容应注重于怎样找机会与他人交流,怎样利用有限的目的语字词进行交流,怎样与同伴合作完成交流等。我们经常观察到,有些学生非常外向,经常到老师的办公室来运用新学的字词跟教师练习口语。有些学生不大愿意与别人交流即使在上课时候也是如此。因此,我们应该鼓励学生找机会与人交流,比如,找说汉语的同学为室友,住到中国人家庭里,在校园里找语言伙伴,与汉语母语者交朋友,与同班同学结对在课后进行练习,在线谈话,通过博客和电子邮件的交流来学习字词等。

Affective strategies are related to building students' confidence, increasing their self-motivation, and controlling anxiety and frustration during learning. Young college students, especially in the beginning level classes, are just starting their college lives, which is very different from high school life. They need to learn to be more independent and self-regulated. Sometime they have difficult in controlling their own emotions in adverse situations such as feeling that they are falling behind in the class due to personal, health, or family matters. The training on affective strategies may focus on two aspects: one is how to solve a problem on one's own; for example, how to handle the situation when doing poorly in an exam, or to handle feelings of falling behind in the class, or having difficulty in using words or understanding a conversation partner's wording, how to reduce anxiety by thinking and doing something positive. The other aspect is to how to find a place to talk about the problem; for example, talking to teachers, classmates, parents, and friends to seek advice.

情感策略是关于在学习过程中树立学习信心，增加自信心和进行自我鼓励，控制焦虑和绝望情绪等。那些年幼的大学生，尤其是新生们刚开始他们的大学生活，需要学会独立生活和自律。有时候，他们在逆境中无法控制自己的感情，往往因为个人的私事、身体情况或家庭因素等造成了学习落后局面。这方面的策略训练应该包括两个方面：一是如何依靠自己解决困难，比如，怎么对付考试没考好或在班上成绩落后时自己的消极情绪，怎么处理与对方进行交流时找不到词或听不懂词时的尴尬，怎样通过想或做一些积极的事来摆脱焦虑感。另一个方面是怎么找到一个合适的场合谈自己的问题寻求帮助。例如，如何向老师、同学、父母和朋友咨询来解决问题。

Steps for strategy training
策略训练步骤

Once the strategy taxonomy is compiled and the instructor knows what strategies the students should learn, the next step is to run training workshops that can include the following steps:

制定好了策略分类表，教师知道了应该训练学生哪些字词学习策略，下一步是怎么办学习策略培训班。下面是参考步骤：

Planning. The instructor needs to work out a schedule for training, such as time, duration, and number of strategies to learn for each training session. The instructor should also make sure that each session introduces only a number of strategies and does not overload students.

计划。教师需要制订出一个培训计划，包括什么时间进行、训练的阶段、每个阶段应该学习哪些策略。教师应该记住每个阶段只集中于几种策略的训练，不要让学生超负荷。

Demonstrating. After each strategy is introduced, if possible, the instructor should demonstrate how to use it in different learning situations to reach a certain goal. Some cognitive strategies are not visible, so the instructor needs to use think-aloud methods to demonstrate strategies. For example, when learning the character 春, the instructor would demonstrate that memorization f this character can be done by thinking about three persons embracing the sun in the springtime.

  示范。介绍完每一个策略,如果有可能,教师应该示范如何在不同学习情况下使用这一策略以达到学习目的。有些认知策略是内隐的,不容易观察,教师可以用出声思维的方法来示范策略。例如,学习汉字"春",教师可以把心里想的如何记住这一生词的想法:"三个人在春天里拥抱着一个太阳"说出来。

Practicing. In order to have maximum outcome from strategy training, the training should not be just a matter of introducing strategies to students, but also a matter to make sure that students actually will use the strategy in their own learning. Thus, enough time should be allocated to have students practice the strategy use on site. The practice could be individual or in a small group.

  练习。为了使培训取得最大的效益,策略训练不能停留在只向学生介绍策略,而是要让学生付诸实践。因此,教师要提供足够的时间,在介绍完一组策略后,在课堂上让学生当场练习使用某组策略。练习可以是个别的,也可以以小组的方式。

Feedback. Once students gain confidence and feel comfortable about using newly learned strategies, the instructor may ask the students to report, either in oral or in written form, on their experience learning and using strategies, such as which strategy is easy to lean and to use, which strategies do not work for them, and what problems they encountered while using the newly learned strategies. The instructor can then make adjustments in strategy training, based on the students' feedback.

  反馈。等学生有了足够的信心使用新学的策略并最后能得心应手地使用时,教师可以让学生用口头或书面的形式报告一下他们学习和使用这些策略的经验和体会。比如,哪些策略容易学,容易用,哪些对他们不适用,在学习和使用过程中遇到了哪些困难。教师可以根据学生的反馈对策略训练计划进行调整。

Evaluating. It is possible that some students do not see effects of strategy use because a particular strategy may not fit into their cognitive style. It is also possible that students may not use a strategy appropriately. Therefore, the instructor should ask students to do self-evaluations of strategy use after a certain period of practice. The evaluation can be qualitative, provided by verbal comments, or quantitative, provided by rating the strategies on a scale. This will give students an idea regarding how well the newly learned strategies actually work.

评估。有些策略对某些学生并不起作用很有可能是因为它们不适合那些学生的认知风格。也有可能是因为学生使用不当引起的。因此,经过一段时间策略的使用实践后,教师应该让学生进行自我评估。评估可以是定性的分析,如提供文字说明,也可以是定量的,让学生对策略用量表进行评定。评估的结果,能让学生衡量出新学的策略可行性。

Sharing. Sometimes one strategy works well for one student, but not for another student. The problem is not the strategy itself, but could due to inappropriate use of the strategy. For example, some students may report that radicals are not useful in helping to learn compound characters. These students probably do not know that radical strategy helps only for semantic and phonetically transparent compound words, not for opaque words. Therefore, they should not apply this strategy to every character. During strategy practice, students may have a creative way of using a certain strategy or have created a new strategy for learning a particular word. Instructors should provide opportunities to let students share their ways of using strategies.

分享。有时候,一种策略对某个学生有效但对另一个学生无效。问题可能不是策略的本身,而是由于不当的使用引起的。例如,有些学生可能认为部首知识对学习合体字没有作用。那些学生可能不知道,部首知识对学那些部首形义透明度高的合体字有用而对形义不透明的合体字不起什么作用。因此,他们不能对所有的合体字都用部首分析法这类策略。教师应该提供机会让学生相互交流。

During the training, the instructor should bear in mind that vocabulary learning strategies could be idiosyncratic. It is important that we respect individual differences and do not force students to use strategies that they do not feel comfortable learning and using.

在培训期间,教师应该记住的是:字词学习策略可以是很个性化的。重要的是,我们要尊重个别性的存在,不能强制学生学习和使用那些他们认为对自己不适合的策略。

The effectiveness of vocabulary strategy training is affected by a number of factors (Chamot & Rubin 1994): One is students' language proficiency level. Usually high proficiency students use more strategies and also learn more quickly. The other is the difficulty level of the language tasks. For example, strategies used for recognition of characters may be easier to learn than strategies used to producing target words in written form. Another factor is the difference in language modality. Mastering a word means hearing a word by understanding its meaning, speaking the word using one's own language, reading and understanding the meaning of the word in different contexts, and writing the word using one's own language. In general, reading and listening as receptive activities are easier than speaking and writing. In addition, motivation is also a factor affecting strategy training. Students who are highly motivated and who have positive learning attitudes toward strategy learning may learn better than students who are not interested in strategy learning or who do not believe that strategies are helpful in their learning.

策略训练的有效性受几种因素制约(Chamot & Rubin 1994)：一是学生的目的语水平。一般来说，目的语水平高的学生对新策略的接受也相应快。二是语言学习任务的难度。譬如，字词认读策略可能比字词默写策略容易掌握。三是语言表现的形式。掌握一个词，意味着听到这个词能知其义，能用这个词来口头表达自己的想法，当该词在不同文本中出现时能知其义，能用这个词书面表达自己看法。一般来说，读和听作为接受性学习策略接受起来比说和写的产出性策略要容易。另外，学习动机也是影响策略训练的一个因素。对策略学习抱有积极性态度的学生要比那些抱消极态度或怀疑态度的学生学得好。

As mentioned earlier, strategy learning is individualized. Some strategy that works well for one group of students may not work for another group of students due to their cognitive differences. Therefore, it is best that we do not set up strategy training as a required course. It may work better to make it an elective course or a workshop. Participation in this type of training is not mandatory.

正如我们前面提到的，策略学习是个体化的。由于学生认知过程的不同，有些策略对某组学生适用，但对其他组学生可能不适用，因此，策略训练课最好不要设为必修课，而是设为选修课。学生参与训练应该是自愿的而不是强迫的。

References 参考文献

柳燕梅(2009)汉字策略训练的必要性、可教性和有效性的试验研究,《世界汉语教学》第4期,280-288页。

江新、赵果(2001)初级阶段外国留学生汉字学习策略的研究调查,《语言教学与研究》第4期,10-16页。

曾金金(2000)德国学生学习汉字的情况及其学习策略,《语言研究》增刊,327-331页。

赵果、江新(2002)什么样的汉字学习策略最有效?《语言文字应用》第2期,79-85页。

中国社会科学院语言研究所词典编辑室编(2005)现代汉语词典(第五版),北京:商务印书馆。

Chamot, A. U., & Rubin, J. (1994) Comments on Janie Rees-Miller's "A critical appraisal of learner training: Theoretical base and teaching implications." *TESOL Quarterly*, 28, 771-776.

Manzo, U. C., & Manzo, A.V. (2008) Teaching vocabulary-learning strategies: Word consciousness, word connection, and word prediction. In A. E. Farstrup & S. J. Samules, *What Research has to Say about Vocabulary Instruction*, pp. 80-105. Newark, DE: International Reading Association.

McGinnis, S. (1995) Students' goals and approaches. In M. Chu (Ed.). *Mapping the Course of the Chinese Language Field: Chinese Language Teachers Association Monograph Series*, vol. III. (pp. 151-168). Kalamazoo, Michigan: Chinese Language Teachers Association, Inc.

Ke, C. (1998) Effects of strategies on the learning of Chinese characters among foreign language students. *Journal of Chinese Language Teachers Association,* 33, 93-112.

Oxford, R. L. (1990) *Language learning strategies.* Boston; Heinle & Heinle Publishers.

Schmitt, N. (1997) Vocabulary learning strategies. In N. Schmitt & M. McCarthy (Eds.), *Vocabulary: Description, Acquisition and Pedagogy*, pp. 199-227. Cambridge, UK: Cambridge University Press.

Shen, H. H. (2005) An investigation of Chinese-character learning strategies among non-native speakers of Chinese. *System*, 33, 49-68.

Takač, V.P. (2008) *Vocabulary learning strategies and foreign language acquisition.* Tonawanda, NY: Multilingual Matters, LTD.

Wang, J., Spencer, K, & Xing, Min (2009) Metacognitive belief and strategies in learning Chinese as a foreign language. *System*, 37, 46-56.

Wenden, A. L. (1998) Metacognitive knowledge and language learning. *Applied Linguistics*, 19, (4), 515-537.

Wei, J-C. (2010) *An investigation on methods and techniques in beginning Chinese vocabulary instruction.* Unpublished MA thesis, The University of Iowa.

Chapter 6 第六章
A framework for CFL vocabulary instruction

汉语二语字词教学模式

In the previous chapters, we discussed how the unique orthographic features of Chinese language poses challenges to CFL learners in vocabulary learning, how learners' first language causes negative transfer to Chinese vocabulary acquisition, how learners cognitively process Chinese words, how instruction should apply cognitive theories to maximize instructional effect in vocabulary instruction, and how we identify and train effective vocabulary learning strategies. In this chapter, we propose a framework for CFL vocabulary instruction based on the discussions from the previous chapters. This framework consists of three dimensions. The first dimension is fostering meaningful vocabulary learning from a cognitive processing perspective. The second dimension is promoting skill integration from a linguistic perspective. The third dimension is adoption of a three-tiered instructional approach from a pedagogical perspective. Copious teaching examples are provided at the end of the chapter to illustrate the three-tiered instructional approach. We believe that effective vocabulary instruction is an art of seamlessly interweaving the knowledge of the three dimensions to a perfect balance among the three. We will present this model in the following sections.

在前面的章节中,我们讨论了汉语独特的缀字特征如何给汉语二语学习者带来字词学习上的困难,学习者的第一语言是如何给汉语字词习得造成负迁移,学习者如何对字词进行认知加工,教学应该如何应用认知理论来最大程度提高字词学习的效益,我们应该如何识别及训练字词学习策略。基于这些讨论,在这一章中我们提出一个汉语二语字词教学模式。这个模式由三个维度构成。第一个维度是从认知加工的角度进行有意义的字词学习,第二个维度是从语言学的角度训练综合技能,第三个维度是从教学法的角度采用三层次教学途径。在本章的末尾,我们提供详实的教学示例来具体说明三层次教学途径。我们相信高效的字词教学是三个维度知识的天衣无缝的交织,并取得三者之间完美的平衡。我们将在下面具体讨论这一模式。

6.1 Fostering meaningful word learning
培植有意义的字词学习

Definition for meaningful learning. Meaningful learning, initially proposed by Ausubel (1963), is the opposite of rote learning. Rote learning refers to memorizing materials without full understanding and the new information being learned is not integrated into the learners' existing knowledge system. In a meaningful learning condition, in contrast, the learning materials are fully comprehended by the learners and they know how to incorporate the newly learned material into their existing knowledge system. Ausubel (1977) explained two conditions that must be met for meaningful learning to happen. One is that learners need to relate the new learning task nonarbitrarily and substantively to what they already know and the other is that the learning task must be potentially meaningful to the learners. In other words, it relates to the learners' structure of knowledge on a nonarbitrary basis. Meaningful learning can be receptive as long as the learning material is subsumable and learners actively relate the materials to their own cognitive structure (Ausubel 1962). In Chapter 4, we introduced the concept, *schema,* which is a cognitive construct developed by learners to organize knowledge in a meaningful way within their brains. Meaningful learning is a type of learning that facilitates schema acquisition. Based on this discussion, meaningful vocabulary learning is defined as making connections between newly learned words and existing cognitive schema, refining and expanding existing schemata, or constructing new schemata.

有意义学习最初由 Ausubel (1963) 提出，它与机械学习水火不相容。机械学习是指对新材料的记忆没有建立在理解基础上，新的知识没有被结合到现存的个体的知识体系中。在有意义学习的条件下，学习材料完全被个体理解，个体知道如何把新材料融合到自己的知识体系中。Ausubel (1977) 解释了有意义学习的两个必须条件。一个是学习者必须把新材料与已有的知识建立一种非随意性的、实质性的联系。另一个条件是学习材料对学习者来说有潜在意义。也就是说，它与学习者现存的知识结构的联系是有机的。有意义的学习可以是接受性的假如学习材料是能够被接受的而学习者能积极地把学习材料结合到他们的认知结构中去(Ausubel 1962)。在第四章中，我们引入了"图式"这个概念。它是个体为在大脑中把新材料有意义地组织起来而发展的一种认知结构。有意义的学习是一种促进图式习得的学习。基于这个观点，我们把有意义的字词学习定义为把新学的字词有机地结合到现存的认知图式中并提炼和发展现有图式或建立新图式的一种学习。

Stages of meaningful word learning. Since the initial proposal of meaningful learning by Ausubel, this topic has been substantially investigated, including the application of this theory in vocabulary learning. Stahl (1983) proposed that meaningful vocabulary learning occurs when learners acquire both definitional word knowledge and contextual word knowledge. According to Stahl (1985), definitional knowledge is defined as the knowledge of the relationships between a word and other known words. Contextual knowledge is defined as knowledge of a core concept and how that concept is realized in different contexts. Shuell (1990) held that meaningful cognitive learning is an active, constructive, and cumulative process in which learning is characterized by both qualitative and quantitative changes. Shuell (1990) further proposed that learning goes through initial, intermediate, and terminal phases. In the initial stage, the learner memorizes facts and uses a preexisting schema to interpret the isolated pieces of data. The information acquired during this phase is concrete rather than abstract and is bound to the specific context in which it occurs. In the intermediate phase, the learner begins to see similarities and relationships among these conceptually isolated pieces of information. New schemata that provide the learner with more conceptual structures are formed, but do not allow the learner to function on a fully autonomous basis. In the terminal phase, the knowledge structures and schemata formed become better integrated and function more autonomously. The characteristic of this phase is performance rather than learning. Knowledge has been transformed into skills. Predicated on this general framework, we propose a three-stage meaningful word learning model for CFL. The three stages consist of comprehension, internalization, and integration. The key point of meaningful word learning is that students are actively and constructively involved in all stages of learning. The characteristics of meaningful learning in each of the three stages are illustrated below.

有意义字词学习的阶段。自从Ausubel提出有意义学习的理论后,学者们对这一理论进行了广泛的实证研究包括把这一理论应用到词汇学习中。Stahl (1983) 认为,有意义的词汇学习是学习者习得词的定义知识和上下文知识。根据Stahl (1985),定义知识是指一个词与其他词之间的关系的知识。上下文知识,是指词的核心概念知识以及这一核心概念在不同上下文中的体现。Shuell (1990) 认为,有意义的认知学习是积极的、建设性的、积累性的过程,在这一过程中学习会发生量和质的变化。Shuell (1990) 进一步提出,有意义学习由初级、中级和最终三个阶段组成。在初级阶段,学习者记忆事实并用现存的图式来解释个别的信息。在这一阶段,学习者获得的信息是与具体情境相联系的还没有上升到抽象水平。在中级阶段,学习者开始意识到个别信息之间的相似性和关系,展示这种关系的新的图式逐渐形成,但是学习者不能自动地运用这些图式。在最终阶段,客观知识体系与主观图式结构已经建立很好的联系,学习者能运用图式自动获得新知识。这一阶段的特点是知识已经被转化为技能技巧,学习者能自如运用学到的知识。借鉴这一三阶段意义学习模式的精神,我们提出一个三阶段汉语二语有意义字词学习模式。这三阶段分别为理解阶段、内化阶段、整合阶段。有意义字词学习的关键点是学生自始至终积极地、建设性地投入到学习中。下面我们阐述每一阶段的学习特征。

Stage 1. Comprehension. In this stage, students learn the definition of new words and try to make sense of the new words through various drills. Using the word 意思 as an example, learning is characterized by a number of observations: 1. being able to analyze the orthographic structure of individual characters such as that 意思 both have heart radicals; 意 has three radicals, and 思 has two radicals; 2. being able to recognize the word when it is seen; 3. being able to reproduce the word after hearing it; 4. being able to understand core meanings of the word (see the list below); and 5. being able to produce a sentence using the word according to provided model sentences illustrated in the parentheses below:

阶段1:理解。在这一阶段,学生学习字词的定义,通过各种操练来理解字词的意思。以学习"意思"这一词为例,这一阶段的学习特征是:(1)能够分析汉字的结构,比如指出"意思"都有"心"部,"意"有三个视觉部件,"思"有两个部件;(2)看到这个词能认读;(3)听到这个词能写出来;(4)能理解该词的核心概念(见下所列);(5)能模仿提供的范例(见下面括号内)造句。

1. 意思可以指语言文字代表的"内容"(信任的意思就是相信你。)
2. 意思可以代表"意见"或"愿望"(我的意思是我暑假去一趟中国。)
3. 意思可以代表"心意"(这双鞋你就收下吧,这是我的一点小意思。)
4. 意思可以指一种趋向(看起来,他没有要跟我和好的意思。)
5. 意思可以指一种情趣(电子游戏真是太有意思了。)

However, meaningful learning will not take place if the instructor just asks students to look up new words in the dictionary or glossary and use each word in a sentence (Thelen 1986), if students are not actively and constructively motivated to explore new words. At this stage, instructors should try to boost the enthusiasm of learning and motivate students to explore the words by themselves and make new word learning a personal experience. Activities such as showing pictures to students and asking them to find corresponding words for the pictures; grouping students into pairs to ask each other questions based on the target words, asking students to pick a few their favorite words to learn by themselves and then to teach the words to other students; or asking students to categorize new words based on their own classification rules and then to explain to the class how they categorized the new words are all helpful in stimulating students' learning interests.

但是有意义的学习不会发生,如果教师只是让学生查字典或读课后的生词表列出的对词的解释,或者让学生用词造句(Thelen 1986),如果学生并没有积极地建设性地去探索关于新字词的知识。在这一阶段,教师应该尽量激发学生的学习热情,鼓励学生自己去探索字词学习的方法使学习成为个体的一种体验。各种教学活动比如让学生根据图片找词;两人小组互相就新字词提问;让学生找出他们最喜欢的词自学然后教给其他同学;让学生根据自己设定的标准对字词分类,然后向全班解释分类的理由等,都能够激发学生学习的兴趣。

Stage 2. Internalization. After initial comprehension, the learners try to memorize the words by finding the connections between the newly learned words with other existing words in their mental lexicon. The learning at this stage is characterized by changes in existing schema. The changes include expanding the existing schema due to incorporation of new knowledge, and forming new schemata caused by inconsistencies between new knowledge and existing knowledge. For example, the learner gradually realizes that in addition to the core meanings, the word 意思 possesses other different meanings, as in the following sentences:

阶段2:内化。经过第一阶段的理解,在这一阶段学生试图通过找出新词与先前学过的储存在他们心理词典中的字词之间的联系。这一阶段的学习的特征表现为现存的图式的改变。这种改变包括图式的扩展由于结合进了新的内容;新图式的建立由于原有的图式与新知识之间不存在包容性。譬如,学习者逐渐意识到除了核心概念之外,"意思"还有别的解释,如下:

1. 不好意思,我先走了。
2. 这两个年轻人整天形影不离,好像有点意思。
3. 你这个人真有意思,连这么点面子也不给。
4. 你没看到昨天这个场面吧,那可是太有意思了,谁都不让谁。

Therefore, the learner may conclude that the meaning of 意思 in a particular sentence depends on the particular context. The word meaning 意思 in the two sentences 你这个人真有意思,连这么点面子也不给 and 你这个人真有意思,连周末都不休息,真是个工作狂 are totally different. The former expressed unsatisfactory feelings of the speaker toward the person referenced in the sentence, but the latter expressed the speaker's respectful feeling toward the person referenced in the sentence.

因此，学习者可能得出结论，"意思"这个词在不同上下文中的确切意义是由特定的上下文决定的。"意思"在"你这个人真有意思，连这么点面子也不给"与"你这个人真有意思，连周末都不休息，真是个工作狂"句中的解释是完全不同的。前者表达了说话者不满意的情绪，后者表达了说话者对句中的人的尊敬的感情。

The learner also understands that 意思 has certain degree of overlap with words such as 内容、意见、愿望、心意、趋向、情趣, but they are not equal and cannot be substituted for each other in many contexts, as illustrated below:

学习者还明白了"意思"与"内容、意见、愿望、心意、趋向、情趣"等词在意义上有一定程度的交叉，但不是相等的，他们在许多语境中不能互相替代，例如：
1. 这件事你做得不对，我对你有意见。（"意见"不能用"意思"代替）
2. 这篇文章的内容与形式不太一致。（"内容"不能用"意思"代替）
3. 您的心意我领了，但是您的钱我绝不能收下。（"心意"不能用"意思"代替）

At this stage, different forms of practicing of the target words in different linguistic contexts are critical in order to aid internalization. To make practice meaningful, the exercises should be thoughtfully designed. The content should invoke the learners' interests; it can be related to learners' existing world knowledge and real life situations. The content should also be challenging, but within the learners' reach under instructors' guidance. The content should cover a wide range of linguistic contexts in which learners understand how the words are used in different contexts. The format of exercises should vary to attract students' attention. At this stage, instruction should give more weight to task-based and problem-solving type exercises over discrete non-contextual drills.

在这一阶段，在不同语境中用多种形式"有意义"地练习新字词对促进内化是至关重要的。有效练习的设计应该考虑这些因素：活动的内容能激发学生学习兴趣，能与学生现有背景知识和他们的生活相联系，内容还应该具有挑战性，但学生是能够在教师的指引下达到目标的，内容还应该包含各种语境，从而学生能懂得新字词在各种语境中如何运用。练习的形式应该是多样的以吸引学生注意。在这一阶段，教学活动的重心应该偏向任务解决型而不再是着重非语境化的单项操练。

Stage 3. Integration. Toward the end of this stage, the newly learned target words are assimilated and integrated into the learners' knowledge system and they can use target words with ease to create their own sentences and express ideas either in speaking and writing. The characteristics of learning at this stage indicate that the learner can use the target word in their daily life communication on the topics that are congruent with their proficiency level; the learner is able to judge the appropriateness of using the word in a context from syntactic and pragmatic perspectives. The newly restructured schemata are relatively stable and they function appropriately, until a discrepancy occurs at the time when a new linguistic situation cannot be explained by the existing schemata relating to the assimilated target words. At this stage, the instruction is focused on students' application of target words in their daily life communication. Vocabulary learning tasks for this stage can include the following activities: interviewing with native speakers or other Chinese speaking friends to get information, expressing opinion on certain topics, watching TV programs, listening to radio broadcasts on selected topics, writing journals or other theme-based short essays, and reading selected online or offline materials to get information; and classroom presentations to report their interviewing or reading results. In designing these activities, the instructor should bear in mind that the focus of these activities is vocabulary application and should purposefully highlight words to be used in those activities that are helpful to increase students' conscious level of using vocabulary.

阶段3:整合。在这一阶段的后期,新学到的字词已经同化和融合到学习者的现存的知识体系中,他们能够得心应手地用新字词创造句子,通过口头和书面形式来表达自己的观点。这一阶段的学习特征表现为学习者能用新字词来解决那些他们汉语水平所及的日常生活中的问题。学习者能够从语法和语用方面来判断用词的正确与否。那些新近重组的图式相对稳定并能正常地运作,除非碰到了不能用现有的图式来解释那些新字词的情况。在这一阶段,教学应该注重让学生在他们的日常生活中运用学到的新字词。合适的字词学习活动可以包括:通过采访汉语母语者得到新信息,表达对某种事物的看法;有选择地看电视、听广播,写日记或写指定主题的小短文;读经过筛选的在线或线下的阅读材料获取新信息;通过课堂报告形式报告他们采访和阅读的结果。在设计这些活动时,教师应该记住的是这些活动的重点是字词应用,所以教师应该强调哪些字词应该在活动中运用,以增强学生的对目标字词的运用意识。

Factors affecting meaningful word learning
影响有意义学习的因素

The progress of meaningful learning from stage 1 to 3 is a developmental continuum of learners' word knowledge from receptive to productive status. It is a change of exercise formats from controlled drill practice to uncontrolled task completion and purposeful application. During this process, a numbers of factors could cause barriers to meaningful learning. These factors include cognitive, linguistic, cultural, and communication factors.

有意义字词学习的三个阶段是学生的字词知识从接受到产出的一个持续发展的过程，也是练习的形式从控制型的单项操练转化到开放型的任务完成和有目的的应用过程。在这个过程中，有几个因素决定着有意义学习的成效。这些因素包括认知、语言学、文化和交际等方面。

Cognitive factor. In chapter 3, we introduced **Cognitive load theory.** This theory states that the working memory of the human brain is limited and can only process a certain amount of information within a limited time period. In vocabulary instruction, we cannot introduce excessive numbers of new words in a single time slot as students cannot process all of the words introduced no matter how meaningful the encoding process might be. Cognitive load is determined by a couple of factors. One is students' target language proficiency level. Beginning level students may take a much longer time to learn a new word than advanced students, as they have not established a well structured Chinese word encoding and processing system in their brains. The other is students' linguistic background. Students who previously have learned other foreign languages may have accumulated more experience regarding how to learn L2 words than those who have never been exposed to a foreign language.

1. 认知因素。在第四章中，我们介绍了认知负荷理论。这一理论认为个体的工作记忆容量有限，在单位时间内只能加工有限的信息。因此，在字词教学中，我们不能在一个时间单位内超负荷地介绍新词，无论编码的过程是多么有意义。认知负荷由两个因素决定。一个是学生现有的目的语的水平。初级汉语水平的学生对同等量的新词的学习花的时间要比高级水平的学生多，因为他们大脑中对于汉语字词的编码和加工的机制还没有完全建立。另一个决定因素是学生的语言学习背景知识。那些以前学过其他外语的学生可能比没学过外语的学生多积累了一些学习外语词汇的经验。

Cultural factors. During vocabulary learning, barriers may be created if a certain amount of cultural knowledge is required, but is not explicitly and adequately explained in order for accurate comprehension of the meaning of a target word by the learner (Meyer 2000). Some words are common which are easy for students to understand, such as 面包, 水果. Some are unique and are observed only in certain cultural settings, as depicted in a story from the first author of this book:

2. 文化因素。 字词学习期间,如果为理解目的词所需要的某种文化知识没有被讲清楚、讲透,就会造成字词理解的障碍(Meyer 2000)。有些词很普通,学生很容易理解,比如面包、水果,但是有些词就比较独特,只有在某种文化背景下产生的,就像本书第一作者 Helen H.Shen 以下所举的一些例子:

> When I introduced the character 米, I told students that 米饭 was a main dish on the dining table in China. Southern Chinese eat a lot of cooked plain rice. Students were puzzled. When I asked them how they prepared the rice for a meal, they told me that they seldom ate rice; rice was always considered a side dish. They never ate plain rice. They often added milk to rice. One student (who is about 50 years old) mentioned that when he told his female Chinese doctor that he drank 牛奶 a lot every day, the Chinese doctor laughed after hearing this. He was puzzled. The doctor explained to him that in China, we considered 牛奶 to be baby food, so she was amused that a man in fifties was eating baby food. This cultural barrier could often be observed in the classroom. For example, some abstract words such as 孝道, 妇道 may be understood by students as their literal meaning, but the students have greater difficulty in comprehending the implied and inferred meanings due to lack the knowledge of Chinese culture.

> 当我向学生介绍汉字"米"的时候,我对学生说,在中国"米饭"是主食,中国的南方人吃很多白米饭。学生感到很困惑。当我问他们在他们的餐桌上米饭是做成什么样的,他们告诉我,他们很少吃米饭。米饭是副食不是主食。他们从来都不吃白米饭。他们有时候把牛奶放在米饭里。一个学生(大概五十岁左右)提到当他跟一个中国的女医生说他每天喝很多牛奶时,那位医生就笑了起来,他感到纳闷。那位医生解释到,在中国,我们觉得牛奶是婴儿食品,所以一个五十多岁的男人还吃婴儿食品让她觉得好笑。在教室里这种文化上的差异经常可以被观察到。例如,有些抽象词,像"孝道"、"妇道",学生能了解表层的意思,但是由于缺少有关文化方面的知识,对于其中的深层的含义理解就有困难。

This story tells us that it is not easy for students to integrate the meaning of the target words into their existing schema due to the differences introduced by a new culture.

这些例子告诉我们,由于对一种新文化的不了解,要把新字词融合到学生现存的图式中不容易。

Linguistic factors. If certain linguistic knowledge (such as orthography, morphology, grammar) required to comprehend the target words is not explicitly or adequately explained, it causes difficulty in word comprehension. For example, students are often confused by the grammatical function of Chinese function words. Even advanced learners may still not feel confident to use participle 了 in their writing. They are not sure where they should use it and where they should not use it.

3. 语言因素。如果理解新词需要学生有关的语言学知识(如缀字知识、构词知识、语法),但是学生对这些知识缺乏清楚的、足够的了解,那么就会造成理解困难。例如,学生经常会对虚词的语法作用感到困惑。即使是高级班的学生,他们可能仍然对在写作中怎么使用"了"缺乏信心。他们不能确定什么地方要用,什么地方不用。

Communication factors. Meaningful learning requires multi-level communication between the instructor and learners and between learners. Communication factors refer to the time and quality of the instructor and students using the target language in the class during their communication. There are two levels of communication that directly affect meaningful vocabulary learning. One level is teacher-student communication. The following is another story from the first author of this book:

4. 交际因素。有意义学习要求课堂上师生之间和学生之间的多层面交流。交际因素指的是用目的语进行这种交流的质和量。课堂交流分两种层面,一是教师与学生的交流。另一层面是学生之间的交流,下面是本书第一作者 Helen H.Shen 的故事:

Once I attended a beginning level Chinese class. The teacher spoke English most of the class time. After class, I asked why. The teacher answered, "If I speak Chinese, students would not understand, so I have to speak English." I told her that the problem was that by speaking in English most of class time, the students would have little chance to hear and speak Chinese words in the class.

有一次我去听一节初级汉语课。教师在课堂上大部分时间都用英语。下课后,我问这位教师为什么用那么多时间说英语。那位教师说,"如果我说中文,学生都听不懂,所以我只好说英文"。我对她说,如果你大部分的时间都说英文,学生就很少有机会听和说汉语字词,他们当然听不懂了。

With very limited practice, how can they learn words? On the other hand, if the instructor speaks Chinese, which students could not understand, students would get lost in the class, and learning will become meaningless. The other level of communication that affects vocabulary learning is student-student communication. In a big classroom setting, paired student or small group work may provide more opportunities for students to practice words;

however, it may be difficult for the instructor to monitor individual students' learning quality and provide appropriate guidance and feedback. In order to reduce ineffectiveness during classroom communication, the instructor should try to speak in Chinese at a level comprehensible to the students and should provide enough opportunities for students to speak using previously and newly learned words at a mutual understanding level, which, in turn, would facilitate meaningful learning.

如果学生课堂练习目的字词的机会很少,那他们怎么能学会字词呢?从另一方面说,如果教师说的中文学生听不懂,学生就会感到困惑,学习对他们来说就变得没有意义。 另一层次的交流是学生之间的交流。在一个大教学班上,学生两人小组交流可以增加交流机会,但是教师很难对每组的每个学生的学习质量进行监控,给予学生必要的反馈。为了减少无效交流,教师应该努力用一种简单的汉语,使学生能够理解的方式与学生交流。另外提供足够的机会让学生能运用以前或新学的字词在互相能够理解的水平上进行交流,从而促进有意义学习。

How can classroom instructors identify or eliminate the negative effects of these four factors to ensure meaningful vocabulary learning? For the cognitive factor, the teacher could use surveys, interviews, and class observation methods to find appropriate cognitive loads for students in a given class. This will equip instructors with the knowledge of how many words should be introduced per week and the appropriate level of extra class assignments. For communication effectiveness, the instructor can use pictures, gestures, actions, and PowerPoint Slides to assist verbal expression to help the students to understand the target language. In addition, new instructors may observe experienced instructors' classes and learn how to use simple target language to communicate with students and get their message across.

教师在教学中如何能减少以上四因素对有意义学习的负面影响呢?就控制认知负荷来说,教师可以通过问卷调查、谈话、课堂观察等方法确定一堂课中学生合适的认知负荷量。这样教师就能确定每星期应该教多少生词,给多少课外练习。关于提高交流效度方面,教师可以用图像、手势、体态语言、投影片等来辅助语言表达帮助学生听懂目的语。另外,新教师可以观摩有经验的教师的课,学习如何用简单的目的语与学生进行交流达到交流目的。

For the linguistic and cultural factors, although it is impossible for instructors to predict all possible problems that students may encounter in learning new words in a particular class, preparation to provide "organizers" to help students in linking new words with their existing knowledge is an effective way to facilitate meaningful learning. The concept "organizer" was proposed by Ausubel (1977) and refers to special introductory materials that take account of the relevant background knowledge already established in a learner's cognitive structure to provide anchoring ideas for the new materials to be learned. As Ausubel stated "the principal function of the organizer is to bridge the gap between what the learner already knows and what he needs to know before he can successfully learn the task at hand" (Ausubel 1977: 168). The organizer usually is introduced in advance of the new learning task; therefore, it is also called an *advance organizer*. To give an example, 国营企业 is a word phrase that is not familiar to students in the U.S. and may cause a comprehension problem. Prior to introducing 国营企业, the instructor designed some warm-up activities to serve as an advance organizer for introducing 国营企业. The instructor first asked students to name a few things owned by the U.S. federal government. Students then named post offices, interstate highways, etc. The instructor then asked students to discuss the advantages and disadvantages of Federal government ownership of these things. After that, the instructor asked the students to think about what would happen if all private companies were owned by the government. With all of this foreshadowing, the instructor then presented them with the word 国营企业 and asked students to explain the meaning of the word and to discuss possible benefits and problems of 国营企业 that may occur in China. With those "advanced organizers," students did not have a problem to comprehend 国营企业.

至于语言学习背景和文化方面的知识，虽然在某堂课中，教师事先无法预测学生由于缺乏这两方面的知识可能会遇到什么样的困难，但是教师可以准备提供"先行组织者"来帮助学生把新字词与他们的现存知识结构联系起来理解新字词。先行组织者的概念由 Ausubel (1977) 提出，指的是教师特别准备的材料在学生的现存知识与将要学习的新字词之间起一个桥梁作用。就像 Ausubel 所说的，"'组织者'的主要作用是用来填补学生已知知识与正要学的知识之间的沟壑" (Ausubel 1977: 168)。组织者一般是在介绍新材料之前先介绍给学生，所以我们称它为"先行组织者"。举个例子来说，"国营企业"是一个高年级学生将要学习的新词组，因为美国的高度私有化，教师觉得学生对这一词的深层理解可能有困难，所以在介绍这一词之前，教师设计了一些热身活动作为先行组织者。教师先让学生说说美国政府拥有和管理哪些服务性企业。学生回答，邮局、州际公路等。然后教师让学生讨论一下美国政府拥有和管理这些企业的优缺点。讨论完了，教师让学生想一想，如果美国的所有企业都让美国政府拥有和管理，情况会怎么样？等讨论完了这些后，教师把"国营企业"这一词组提出来，让学生自己来解释这个词组，然后组织讨论关于中国的国营企业可能会带来的有利和不利因素。有了"先行组织者"，学生对"国营企业"的理解就水到渠成了。

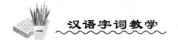

6.2 Promoting skill automatization
促进技能自动化

In chapter 1, we explained that full word knowledge including the four aspects of knowledge: definitional, syntactical, pragmatic, and network knowledge. Therefore, to learn word knowledge is to learn the four aspects of knowledge. However, traditionally, in the area of Chinese as the first language, knowing a word is defined as "四会" 会认 is recognizing the word, 会说 is using it in speech, 会写 is using it in writing, and 会用 is using the word in context (张田若、陈良璜、李卫民 2003). The 四会 criteria impose mastering word knowledge more from the procedural knowledge perspective than from the declarative knowledge.

在第一章中,我们解释了全面的字词知识包括四个方面的知识:字词定义知识、字词的句法知识、字词的语用知识、字词的网络知识。学习字词就意味着学习这四方面知识。但是传统上,在汉语作为母语的教学中,掌握一个词是以"四会"为标准。那就是会认、会说、会写、会用(张田若、陈良璜、李卫民 2003)。这四会标准对字词知识的掌握不仅仅是从陈述性知识的角度,更多地是从程序性知识的角度来定义的。

The discussion of declarative knowledge and procedural knowledge initially emerged in Ryle's work (1949). In his book of *The Concept of Mind,* Ryle distinguished two types of mental activities: knowledge remembering and knowledge executing. The former is considered to be declarative knowledge; the latter belongs to procedural knowledge (Anderson 1982, 2005). From CFL vocabulary learning perspective, **declarative knowledge** is about the facts of words- the definitional, syntactical, pragmatic, and network knowledge of the words that can be memorized and stored in the mind. **Procedural knowledge** is the knowledge of how to use the stored four aspects of word knowledge to complete language tasks. If a learner can automatically use declarative knowledge to solve real-life tasks, then the learner has acquired procedural knowledge. That is, the knowledge has been converted into skills. Since the ultimate goal of CFL vocabulary instruction is to help students to transform their vocabulary knowledge into skills, then, pedagogically, instruction should take into consideration the integration of word knowledge learning and four skill training at each stage of vocabulary learning. In the initial stage, instruction may pay more attention to speaking and listening skills over reading and writing, due to limited vocabulary knowledge. In real life, students need all four skills to handle daily life and job related communications; therefore, a balanced training on the four skills will lead to better vocabulary acquisition. Another important fact of the four-skill training is that learning will be more effective if multi-modalities participate in vocabulary learning. This is because listening, speaking, reading, and writing require cooperation of different physical and mental modalities that also facilitate declarative knowledge learning.

关于陈述性与程序性知识的讨论始于 Ryle 的著作(1949)。在他的《思想的概念》一书中,Ryle 区分了大脑两种思维活动:知识的记忆与知识的应用。前者被称为陈述性知识,后者被称为程序性知识 (Anderson 1982, 2005)。从汉语二语字词学习的角度看,陈述性知识是关于字词的事实知识—字词定义知识、字词的句法知识、字词的语用知识、字词网络的知识,那些可以在大脑中被记忆被储存的知识。程序性知识是怎么运用四方面的知识来完成交际任务的知识。如果个体能运用陈述性字词知识解决生活中的问题,那么,个体已经习得了程序性知识。也就是说,知识已经被转化为技能。既然字词学习的最终目标是把字词知识转化为技能技巧,那么,从教学角度来看,在每一字词学习阶段,教师应该考虑如何把字词知识学习与听说读写四种技能训练结合起来。在初始阶段,由于学生字词知识很有限,教学上可能需要多注重字词的听说能力。但是在实际生活中,学生需要听说读写四方面的技能来对付日常生活或工作中需要的交际活动,因此,注意听说读写四方面技能的平衡训练能导向更有效的字词习得。另一个坚持听说读写四方面平衡训练的理由是这样做能使得多种感官参与字词学习,从而取得更好学习效果,听说读写活动相互转换需要多种感官之间的相互合作,这会促进程序性知识的习得。

How can instruction help students to learn declarative knowledge and meanwhile to develop their procedural knowledge? At the beginning stage of vocabulary learning, information transformation is an effective method to help integrate word knowledge acquisition and skill development. "Information transformation" refers to transformation of one type of information into another type, such as transforming visual information into acoustic information. This method allows students to practice vocabulary with different modalities, while at same time keeping students interested in the learning activities due to the variation in methods. Please see Teaching example 3 for detail。

教学怎样让学生在习得陈述性知识的同时也获得程序性知识呢?在初级阶段学习时,"信息转换"是一种使知识习得与技能训练结合起来的有效的方法。信息转换指的是把一种信息形式转换成另一种信息形式,比如,把视觉信息转换成听觉信息。这种方法可以使多种感官参与字词学习,由于方法方式上的变换,也能激发学生学习的兴趣。具体的操作,请参看教学示例3。

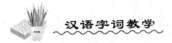

Teaching example 3. Information transformation
教学示例3 信息转换

Task 任务：
Introduce a friend (Pair work) 介绍一位朋友（两人一组）
Target words to be learned 下列是要求学会的字词：

> 高、矮、喜欢、开朗、内向、害羞、好吃懒做、胆小怕事、活泼可爱、普通、心地善良、风趣、幽默、爱管闲事、体贴温柔、聪明好学、诚实坦白、脾气、暴躁、小心谨慎、追求刺激、热心助人

Requirement 要求：
Please use as many words as you can from the above list to describe a friend of yours. 请从以上生词表中选用尽可能多的词汇来描述你的一位朋友。

Step 1. Role A and Role B take turns introducing one of their friends to each other. They take notes when the other party is speaking.
步骤1：角色A和B轮流向对方介绍自己的一位朋友。一方介绍时，另一方做笔记。

Step 2. Roles A and B write a paragraph about each other's friend based on the notes.
步骤2：角色A和B根据所作笔记写一段话描述对方的朋友。

Step 3. Roles A and B take turns reading their own writing to the other party. While each person is reading, the other party can ask question for clarification or can comment on the correctness of the description. Necessary revision is then made based on feedback.
步骤3：双方分别向对方读出自己所写的内容，听者可以提问或指出不当之处。根据反馈，双方再做进一步修改。

Step 4. Roles A and B exchange their writing. Each reads the other party's writing. During reading, they mark how many words from the list are used in the writing and also mark any error in the writing.
步骤4：双方交换稿子，朗读对方所写的内容，同时标出对方使用的生词表上的字词和所犯的错误。

Step 5. Role A and Role B exchange their opinions on each other's writing.
步骤5：双方点评彼此的写作。

(Note: This activity requires information transformation between speaking, listening, reading, and writing.)
（说明：该活动要求信息在听说读写四个方面之间的转换）

(Teaching example 3 is contributed by Helen H. Shen, the first author of this book)

After having accumulated a certain amount of vocabulary, simulated real life tasks such as theme-based activity is another approach for promoting skill acquisition. This approach could be used in the classroom as well as beyond the classroom. For example, if the lesson is about hospital information and students have learned a certain amount of vocabulary about hospitals, after class, the instructor can give a task to ask students to collect information about a Chinese hospital using their learned vocabulary. This task requires students to read certain articles on Chinese hospitals or to interview people who have visited a Chinese hospital. Based on the information gathered, the student would need to write up a report about what he/she knows about a Chinese hospital using the learned target words.

等积累了一定数量的字词后，教师应该设计一些模拟真实生活的语言任务，例如主题型活动是另一种训练技能的有效教学活动。这种活动课内课外都适用。例如，如果课文内容是跟医院有关，学生已经学了关于医院方面的一些词汇，那么，教师就给学生一个课外任务，让学生用所学字词收集有关中国医院的信息。这个任务需要学生读一些关于中国医院的材料或访问那些去过中国的医院的人。基于这些信息，请学生用所学的词写一个关于中国医院的报告。

6.3 Adopting a three-tiered instructional approach
采用三层次教学途径

In a classroom learning situation, meaningful learning cannot be realized without effective instructional approaches. In order to guide meaningful learning progress from comprehension stage to integration stage, the design of the instructional method should be in line with the cognitive process of meaningful learning. We propose a three-tiered instructional approach to realize meaningful learning. The first tier is a decontextualized approach; the second tier is a semi-contextualized approach, and the third tier is a contextualized approach. The decontextualized approach refers to the instruction methods and activities designed to teach target words detached from their communicative and linguistic contexts. The semi-contextualized approach refers to teaching target words with incomplete communicative and linguistic contexts. The language materials are excerpts from a full linguistic context or a real-life communication. The contextualized approach refers to teaching vocabulary using simulated or real-life communicative contexts or full linguistic context (Oxford & Crookall 1990).

在课堂学习情况下,如果没有有效的教学途径,有意义的学习就无法实现。为了引导有意义字词学习从理解阶段走向整合阶段,课堂教学的设计应该与有意义学习的认知过程相吻合。在这里我们提出三层次教学途径来实现有意义学习。第一层次是非语境化途径;第二层次是半语境化途径;第三层次是语境化途径。非语境化途径是指字词教学方法和活动不在语境中进行,而是与语境分离,学习字词不是为了完成交际任务。半语境化途径是指字词教学在不完全的语境中进行,语言材料是从语境中或真实语料中节选的。语境化途径是指字词学习是在模拟和真实生活交际活动中进行,学习的结果不仅仅是学会字词,也完成交际任务。

6.3.1 The decontextualized approach
非语境化途径

The purpose of using a decontextualized approach is to direct students' attention to the target words and make the target a focal point at the initial stage of learning. Thus, students can concentrate on the form, meaning, and sound of the target words without being distracted or confused by other information carried from linguistic contexts. This approach will help 1) establish internal connections among sound-shape-meaning of the target words; 2) establish a connection between the character and the radical within. It must be pointed out that "decontextual" means to extract the target words from a meaningful communicative linguistic context. It does not mean to teach every individual word without using any linguistic segments or context such as a word, a phrase, or a sentence. However, the focus of introducing target items by relating them to a word or a sentence is to help in understanding the target words. Therefore, the linguistic contexts provided for the target words should be familiar to students except for the target word. For example, we introduce the character 喝 by presenting students the word 喝水。水 should be a learned character so that it will be easy for students to connect the new word 喝 with the known word 水。The decontextualized approach is more suitable for gaining definitional knowledge of target words. Teaching examples 4-13 illustrate how this approach is used in instruction for beginning CFL learners.

采用非语境化教学途径的目的是在初始教学阶段让学生的注意力很好地集中到目

的字词,让它们成为注意的焦点。这样学生可以全力以赴学习单个字词的音形义而不受语境中的其他语言因素干扰。非语境化途径能够帮助学生(1)建立每个字词内部的音形义之间的联系。(2)建立部首与所含该部首的合体字之间的联系。我们需要指出的是这里的"非语境"指的是把字词与有意义的语言交际环境中分离开来。这不是指在教字词的时候不使用相应的多音节词、词组、句子。在教生字词时把它们与相关的多音节词、词组、句子联系起来的目的是为了帮助理解目的字词,所以所提供的支持该目的词的语言材料应该对学生来说是熟悉的。例如,我们介绍汉字"喝"的时候,向学生呈现"喝水"这一词,因为要学的字是"喝",因此,"水"对学生来说必须是一个已知的汉字,这样容易让学生理解"喝"的意思。非语境化途径比较适合于帮助学生学习生字词的定义知识。教学示例4到13向老师们具体展示这一途径在初级教学阶段的运用。

Teaching example 4. Illustrate the Character
教学示例4 画汉字:建立形 — 义联系

The goal of this activity is to encourage students to think deeply about a character's form and meaning. I have each student select a few new characters from the lesson to illustrate. They must turn the character into a picture that relates the form of the character to its meaning.

  该活动的主要目的是引导学生深入思考汉字形与义的关系。老师要求学生从课文中选取部分汉字,用一幅图画来表现该汉字字形与字义之间的联系。

In the first example (see the pictures at the end of this method) 喝 (to drink), the student has combined the meaning of the radicals within the character, and her own creative interpretation of the shape -, to create a story about what the character means. In her picture, the sun 日 is shining down on a man 人 in a field 勹, which is making him thirsty, so he drinks with his mouth 口. By making this story, she has come up with a way to remember which radicals are in this character, as well as the part of the character whose component radicals she has not yet learned 勹. In the second example, rather than telling a story that combines elements of the character, the student has simply turned the foot radical 足 into an image of a walking man.

  在第一个例子中(见下页),学生结合汉字"喝"的部首和自己对于"勹"富有创意的诠释,编了一个故事来阐述该汉字的义。图中,太阳照耀着在田地"勹"中劳作的人。他感到口渴,于是用"口"来喝水。通过编这个故事,该学生找到了一种既可以记住该汉字的部首,又可以记住其中没学过的部件"勹"的方法。在图的右侧,学生不是把汉字中的各个部件串成一个故事,而是把"足"这个这个字直观地用一个行走中的人表现出来。

For this activity, I require that students trace the character in a thick dark color, so the character is highlighted within the illustration. Second, the illustration must be very detailed or in color, which requires that students pay attention to the detail of the radicals, and the role of the radicals in the compound character. Finally, students must include the meaning and pronunciation of the character at the bottom of the picture to help establish the connection among sound-shape-meaning.

在这个活动中,老师要求学生用深色勾勒汉字的笔画,使其在图画中凸显出来。此外,由于画汉字需要注意细节和色彩,学生得仔细观察部首的细节之处及其在该汉字中的作用。最后,要求学生在图画下方标注该汉字的发音和意义的做法可以帮助他们建立汉字的音-形-义的联系。

Teaching example 5. Make a story about the character
教学示例5 编故事:意义记忆

For this activity, students are divided into groups. Each group can be 2-4 members. Students will need to develop memory-aid stories that relate the meaning and the form of the character. For example, one group of students took the character 忙 (busy) and described it as a man with two arms 忄 at a desk with a lamp 亡 who is very busy doing homework. Obviously, this is a student idiosyncratic story that is quite different from the common knowledge of thinking it is a phonetic-semantic compound and 忄 is heart radical meaning a person's heart is engaged when he/she is busy, while 亡 (wáng) hints at the pronunciation of the character 忙 (máng). However, if students think their personalized story can help memorize the character better than other explanations, it should be encouraged. However, in introducing more orthographic knowledge, students will voluntarily use the radical knowledge in their personalized character stories.

在这一活动中,学生每2到4人为一组,每组编写一个能把字形与字义联系起来,帮助记忆的故事。例如,拿到"忙"字的学生组将其表现为一个正忙于完成家庭作业的男生。他双臂(忄)倚桌,桌上有一盏台灯(亡)。这类故事带有明显的学生个人的特质。因为通常来说,形声字"忙"字会被解释为声旁"亡"(wáng)和形旁"忄"的组合,表现了一个人正全心投入于一件事,所以忙。但如果学生认为自编的故事比传统的解释更能帮助记忆,我们就应该予以鼓励。我们不用担心学生会误解部首意义,当他们进一步学习了部首知识后会自发地将部首的有关知识融入到自编的故事里。

I usually ask students to come up with stories for five to ten characters. After ten minutes, I have each group choose their best stories. One student representative from each group comes up and tells one of their group's stories to the entire class. I encourage students to do a quick sketch of their character and story on the board to clarify their ideas. After each group has had a turn to tell one story, the group representatives go back to their seats and a new set of representatives come up to share another set of stories.

在字词课上,我一般要求学生花十分钟时间给五到十个汉字编故事。然后各组自选一个故事,派代表向全班介绍他们的故事。在讲故事的同时,老师也鼓励这些代表在黑板上简要勾画出所描述的汉字和故事情节的联系。每组轮流讲完一个故事以后,代表们回到座位上,然后新一轮代表上台来讲新的故事。

Students work in groups for several reasons. First, multiple students can come up with more stories than a single student working alone. Second, when group members listen to a memory-aid story, they evaluate and improve it before presenting it to the class. This process of evaluating a story encourages students to think more deeply about the character and its meaning, and so it helps students memorize the character. Finally, shy students are more likely to share their stories with small groups than with the entire class.

让学生分组学习基于以下理由。首先,比起单个学生,多个学生能编写出更多的故事。其次,在选择故事给全班做展示之前,组员们要聆听、评判和改进彼此的故事。这个过程有助学生更好地理解汉字的字形和意义,深化记忆。最后,比起对全班同学讲述,较为内向的学生更容易做到在小组内分享他们的故事。

This activity can be conducted as an informal competition to increase student involvement. I never announce a winner, compare the quality of stories, or offer criticism, so it is not a real competition. However, when generating stories, the idea that they could come up with the most original or entertaining memory aid helps to motivate the students. During

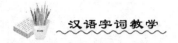

presentations, the students quietly judge each group's stories, and so they pay greater attention to the presenter and his/her ideas.

　　这个活动可以作为一个非正式的比赛活动以调动学习积极性,但老师并不宣布胜出者,也不比较故事的优劣或是提出批评,因此它并不是真正意义上的比赛。尽管如此,比赛性质的活动在构思故事阶段,会让学生变得更为主动来想出最具独创性的故事和最有意思的助记方式。而在演示故事阶段,因为学生会在心里评判每个组的故事优劣,所以在听故事时,他们的注意力会更集中。

Teaching example 6.　Find your partner
教学示例6　找朋友:建立词的概念

This activity helps students recognize the characters in disyllabic words. For each disyllabic word in a lesson, I make two flash cards – the first character on one card and the second character on another card. I mix all of the cards together and then hand them out to the class, so that each student holds one character. The goal of this game is for each student to find their partner – the student who is holding the second character of their word. So if one student is holding 友, they look for the student holding 朋, to make the word 朋友. To complete this activity, students must recognize the character in their hand, recall which word contains that character, and find their partner. Students usually seek out their partner by calling out the entire vocabulary word as they wander about the room. After every student has found their partner, I have all the students stand in a circle with their partners beside them. Each pair shows their cards together and says their word aloud. This way, every student gets a chance to see the characters and hear every disyllabic word from that lesson.

　　该活动帮助学生识别双音节词中的汉字。老师把每课的双音节词拆分成两组字卡,每张卡上有一个隶属于一个词的汉字,然后打乱顺序发给全班,人手一张。该活动要求学生找到与自己手上字卡搭配成词的另一张字卡。例如,一个学生手上的字卡是"友"字,那么他就需要找到有"朋"这张字卡的学生来凑成"朋友"这个词。为了完成任务,学生必须先识别出手上的字卡,回忆出哪个词包含该汉字,再去找另一张字卡。为了找到搭配的字卡,学生们一般是一边在教室里到处走,一边在嘴里念着那个词的完整形式。所有学生找到搭配的字卡后,老师让一部分学生站成一个圆圈,他们字卡的搭配方则站在他们的身后。每组都要展示他们的字卡并大声读出该词。这样,每个学生都有机会看到该课的字词并听到每个双音节词的发音。

Teaching example 7. Word relay race
教学示例7 听词找词:建立词的概念

For this activity, I use the same set of cards I used in the 找朋友 activity. The characters from a disyllabic word are written on two cards, the first character on one card, and the second character on a second card. I affix magnets to the back of the cards, so that I can stick the cards onto the whiteboard. Then I hang all of the first-syllable characters on the left side of the board, and all of the second-syllable characters on the right side of the board. In the middle of the board, I draw two squares, one for the first syllable, and one for the second syllable.

　　该活动使用的是和"找朋友"相同的一套卡片。每个双音节词的两个汉字被写在两张独立的带磁条的卡片上。老师将这两组卡片分别贴在白板的两边,中间画出两个正方形,分别用于放置每个词的首字和尾字。

I divide the class into two teams. One team is responsible for the first syllables. They sit on the left. The other team is responsible for the second syllables. They sit on the right. One representative comes up from each group. These two students stand behind a starting line, like runners in a race. They take action immediately after I call out a word such as 电话. The student on the left races to find the 电 card and put it in the box I have drawn in the center of the board. They want to put their card in the box before the student on the right side finds the 话 card. The student who puts the correct character in the box first wins a point for their team. Their team members can call out clues, such as "It's on the top right!" or "It's the one with the speech radical!", but they cannot get out of their seats to help. After each member of the group has had a chance to compete, I have the groups switch sides, and we play another round. I do this because it is generally easier to find the first character of a disyllabic word than the second character, so that each team has a fair shot at scoring points.

　　全班分为两组,站在左边的一组负责找每个词的首字,右边的一组找与之搭配的尾字。每轮活动,各组派出一名代表。就像赛跑选手一样,两人站在起点线后。每当老师念出一个词,他们开始行动。比如老师念"电话",左边组的学生代表找到"电"字卡放入白板中间对应的正方形内。如果他的速度快于右边组代表放"话"字卡的速度,左边组就得一分。其他组员可以给出提示,比如"在右上角","是有言字旁的那个字"等等,但不能起身帮忙。每个组员都完成一次任务后,两组换边重新再来。因为识别双音节词的尾字通常比识别首字耗时要长,换边对双方来说比较公平。

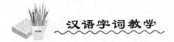

Teaching example 8.　Review race: character grabbing
教学示例8　抢汉字竞赛

This is a review activity for midterms, finals, or after returning from a long break. For this activity, I select a 50-70 characters the students have learned. I collect note cards in four colors - white, yellow, orange, and pink. I select the common or simple characters, such as 我, and write these on the white cards. The more complex or uncommon characters I write on the yellow cards (i.e., 岁). The characters that are even more rare or difficult I write on orange cards (i.e., 做菜). I write the hardest characters of all on the pink cards (i.e., 跳舞). I stick a magnet to the back of each card, and then hang all the cards on the board. Two to three students come to the white board. They have 30 seconds to grab all the characters that they recognize. They have to move quickly because the other student is grabbing characters too. After time is up, the students read the cards to me in Chinese. Each white card (easy) character they recognize is worth one point. Yellow card characters are two points, orange three, and pink four. We add all their points together. Whichever of the two students earns the most points wins. If a student grabs a card and then reads it wrong, or can't remember the pronunciation, then they lose points. If they read character wrong they lose points accordingly. By taking points off for wrongly read characters, I ensure that students will not just run up, and grab all of the cards indiscriminately.

该活动适合用于期中、期末或者长假后的字词复习课。老师选择学生已学过的50-70个词,并准备四色的卡片:白色、黄色、橙色和粉色。白色卡片用于写最常见最简单的如"我"这样的汉字,黄色的用于写较为复杂或少见的如"岁"这类汉字,而橙色的用于写更难的字词如"做菜",最难的字如"跳舞"则写在粉色卡片上。每张卡片都在背面贴上磁条,置于白板上。每次,两至三名学生来到白板前,花30秒时间取下所有他们可以识别的汉字。他们必须尽量迅速,以超过同时行动的对手。时间一到,学生们就向老师念出他们抢到的卡片。一张白色卡片(最简单级别)得一分,黄色卡片两分,橙色卡片三分,粉色卡片四分。分数累计后,得分最高的两名学生获胜。如果学生读音有误或是忘记了所抢卡片的发音,将被倒扣分。这样避免了学生仅仅为获得更多卡片而盲目争抢。

Teaching example 9.　Information gap
教学示例9　信息差:配对听写字词

This is a pair-work activity to help students practice both reading and writing characters. I divide students into pairs. One student in the pair is 甲. The 甲 students get a sheet 甲: The second student in the pair is 乙 who gets the sheet 乙:

该活动两人一组，帮助学生练习汉字的读写。学生分为两组。一组为甲组，另一组为乙组，分别得到如下甲、乙任务单：

甲			
1. _____	2. _____	3. _____	4. _____
5. 开会	6. 帮	7. 时候	8. 练习

乙			
1. 方便	2. 考试	3. 有事	4. 等
5. _____	6. _____	7. _____	8. _____

Students first take a minute to read the characters that are written on their page. If they need to, they can write the Pinyin above the character. They can also look up the character in their books. Next, 甲 asks 乙 "第一个词是什么？" (What is number 1?) 乙 reads 1-4 to 甲 in Chinese, and 甲 writes the characters in the blanks next to numbers 1-4 on their page. If they can't remember how to write the character, I have them write the word in Pinyin, and then look it up in their books after the activity is done. Then 甲 reads 5-8 to 乙, who records the characters in the blanks next to numbers 5-8. After the activity is completed, both partners compare their sheets, to check if they have written the characters correctly. This activity is the traditional 听写 dictation, except the teacher does not have to do the reading.

学生先花一分钟读出他们任务单上已写出的词。如有必要，他们也可以标出汉字的拼音，或查阅课本。然后，甲组学生问乙组学生"第一个词是什么？"乙组学生则读出字词1-4。甲组学生便依次填写任务单1-4的空白处。如果不知道怎么写某个汉字，他们也可以先记下拼音，活动结束后查阅课本。之后换成甲组学生读出5-8的字词，乙组学生填空。活动完成后，双方比较各自的任务单，查看是否正确写出了所有字词。该活动类似于传统的听写活动，但不是由教师读字词。

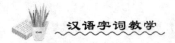

Teaching example 10.　Analyze the Characters in the table
教学示例 10　汉字分析表

I have students do at home is to fill in a character analysis table as illustrated below:

这一活动是一个课外作业。让学生填写汉字分析表（见下表）：

汉字分析表

	A	B	C	D	E
	Word	Word Meaning	Highlighted Character	Character meaning	Radical(s) and/or phonetics
E*	píngfēn 评分	To grade	píng 评	Judge, appraise	讠 speech 平 (píng)
1	qǐchuáng 起床		qǐ 起		
2	shēnghuó 生活		huó 活		
4	hǎibiān 海边		hǎi 海		
5	hǎibiān 海边		biān 边		
6	měitiān 每天		měi 每		
7	xiánzhe méi shì 闲着没事		xián 闲		

E* = example

The words 1 到 7 are target words I have preselected from one lesson. Students will complete the following as homework: First, students write the meaning of the whole word (词) in column B. Then students use an online dictionary to learn the meaning of individual characters (字) within the word. They write the meaning of the (字) in column D. The dictionary www.mdbg.net works best for this activity. Students further analyze the character (字) into its component radicals and phonetics to fill in column E. The next day, in class, the students discuss how the meanings of individual characters (字) within the word relate to the meaning of the entire word. For example, in the example 评分 - "to grade", the first character 评 means "to judge or appraise". 分 means "points" or "scores." Giving an A grade (评分) is a form of judgment (评). Next, we discuss as a class how the radicals within the individual character relate to that character's meaning. For example, in the example 评 - "judge" - the radical is speech 讠 and judgments are issued in speech. 分 is to use a knife 刀 to divide an object equally which hints points are equally distributed. In this activity, rather than simply hearing from the teacher what each character and radical means, the students have to hunt them down and record them on their own. The action of hunting, recording, and discussing requires that students more devote mental effort and time, which leads to deeper learning.

表上1到7的词语由老师从某课生词中选出。学生需完成以下任务:第一,在B栏写出词义;第二,利用网上词典查找出某个单字在该词中的意思;第三,在D栏写下该单字的意思。网上词典www.mdbg.net可以有效辅助该活动。学生最后在E栏标出该汉字如何拆分成部首以及其声旁的发音。第二天课堂上,学生们首先就单字的义和其所构成词语的义之间的联系进行讨论。例如,表中列出的例子"评分"的意思是"给出分数"。首字"评"的意思是"给出判断或评价",尾字"分"的意思是"分数"或"成绩"。而给出成绩"A等"就是评判的一种。然后,全班再集体讨论汉字的部首和整个汉字的意义之间的联系。以"评"字为例,"评"字是以"讠"为部首的,意思是"说话",而评价就往往是以言语的形式来表达的。而"分"字是指用"刀"来均匀切分物品,也正好喻示了分数的分布是均匀的。活动中,学生不仅仅是听老师的讲解,而是要自己动手去寻找、记录这些偏旁部首的含义。这个寻找、记录和讨论的过程需要学生投入更多的思考和时间,也就促进了学习的深度。

Teaching example 11. Find the right one
教学示例11 找对象:字形辨析

For this activity I choose a character, such as 风. Then, I find three characters that are similar to that character, such as 凤, 冈, and 网. I then mix the characters together and have the students select the correct character based on the English meaning on the right. Students circle the character that matches the English meaning, and then give the Pinyin with tone for that character. I usually do this for 5 to 10 characters. For beginners who only know a few characters, recognition of a character demands only that they recall the general shape. If you only know 你 and 好, it is easy to tell the two apart. However, to write the character, the student must recall every detail of strokes for a character. This differentiation activity requires that students focus on the details, which will help them later when they need to write the character. It also exposes students to a variety of characters, so that they can begin to build a subconscious understanding of character structure.

在这一活动中,老师先选择一个汉字,例如"风",然后将其与字形相近的汉字混在一起,如:Wind—凤 冈 网 风,让学生依据右边的英文解释选出正确的汉字。学生必须圈出和英文解释吻合的汉字,并给出拼音与声调。每轮活动控制在五到十个汉字。对于识字甚少的初学者,字形的识别只是要求他们记住大概的结构。如果仅仅知道"你"字和"好"字,区别两者不是难事,但是要写出汉字,学生就得回忆起每个汉字笔画的细节。这种字形辨析活动引导学生注重笔画细节,为他们以后的汉字正确书写奠定基础。同时,这一活动能让学生接触许多不同的形似汉字,能帮助他们潜意识里认知汉字的结构。

Teaching example 12. Complete the Character
教学示例12 找遗补缺:完成汉字

This activity is a "complete the character" exercise to encourage students to learn the details within a character. I give students a partially written character, as illustrated below, and ask them to fill in missing components.

这一"找遗补缺"活动的目的是鼓励学生了解汉字的笔画细节。老师提供给学生未完成的汉字如下,学生将其补全成完整的汉字。

Búcuò 不钅日   shuìjiào 睡冗

Teaching example 13. Correct the character errors
教学示例13 找出坏人:改错字

This activity helps students remember details within a character. First, I write several sentences. The sentences are all grammatically correct, but many characters within the sentence have errors which I observed from students' writing. Below is an example:

该活动帮助学生记忆汉字内部的笔画细节。首先,老师写下几个句子。这些句子在语法上是正确的,但在汉字拼写上有着学生作业中常见的错误。如下例:

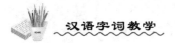
Wǒ yǒu mèimei, méiyǒu dìdi.   (7 errors)

Next, students must find and correct the errors. For example, the character 有 yǒu above has been written with an extra stroke. It looks as if the writer has confused 有 with 看 kàn. To correct the error, students cross off the extra stroke. Beginners have a hard time reading characters, even if they are all correct. If I give them this set of characters with errors, they probably could not guess what characters I "meant" to write. I provide them with Pinyin at the bottom, so they will know which words I mean. Having the Pinyin also allows students to look up the word in their dictionary, something they could not do with a flawed character alone. I also always provide how many errors the sentence contains at the end of each sentence, so students will know when they have finished finding the errors.

然后,由学生找出并改正错误之处。比如,例句中的"有"字有多余的笔画。书写者似乎把"有"字和"看"字混淆。学生就得去掉其多余的笔画来改正错误。对于初学者来说,有时候认读书写正确的汉字,也有困难。如果所给的汉字有错误,学生就更难分辨出要写的正确汉字是什么,所以,老师要在汉字的下方给出拼音以帮助识别。学生也可以利用该拼音,在词典中查找汉字。这是添加拼音的另一个目的。同时,老师还在句末标出每个句子所包含的错误的数量,让学生知道要纠多少错。

(Teaching examples 4-13 are contributed by Ms Catherine M. Fillebrown, Instructor of the Bergen County Technical schools at Paramus, New Jersey, USA)

6.3.2 Semi-contextual approach
半语境化途径

The semi-contextual approach helps students to understand how words are used in a simple linguistic context, and to understand the relationship between words, phrases, and sentences to acquire syntactic and network knowledge of target words. The instructional efforts are made to direct students to pay attention to how the words are used in the linguistic contexts and what kinds of semantic and syntactic relationships exist between the target words and other words. In order to make our readers understand this approach in a concrete way, here, we introduce three teaching methods under the category of the semi-contextual approach. They are word grouping, using corpus, and using concept mapping. We will discuss each of them in detail below.

半语境化途径帮助学生理解字词是怎样在简单的语句中运用的。了解词、词组、句子之间的联系并掌握字词的句法和字词的网络知识。教学应该在让学生注意目的字词是怎样在语句中运用及该目的字词在特定句子中与其他相关词在语义和句法上的关系方面做出努力。在这里,我们介绍属于半语境化途径的三种教学方法,使大家对半语境化途径有一个具体的了解。这三种方法分别是字词分组、运用语料库、概念图。

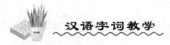

- Word grouping

字词分组

Each lesson has a list of new vocabulary for students to learn. Word grouping refers to classifying the list of the words into small groups according to their attributes. Grouping makes vocabulary learning easier because meaningful relationship will be established between words in the same group, which facilitates incorporation of the target words into existing schemata. Grouping can based on linguistic features, such as parts of speech, based on semantic connections such as meanings of similar or dissimilar words, and based on language functions such as words used for greetings, asking for directions or requesting, and based on themes such as playing a sports game, or mailing a letter at the post office. Word grouping should also take consideration the content of the lesson, so that the word study will facilitate subsequent lesson learning. At the initial stage, the instructor may provide models for grouping words. After an initial period of practice, the instructor can ask students to do groupings by providing grouping guidelines. Once students have fully understood the rationales and methods of grouping, the instructor can let students do their word grouping activity creatively. Please see Teaching examples 14-16 for using the word grouping methods.

一般来说,教材中每篇课文都列出该课的生词。字词分组是根据字词的某种特点对所列的生词进行分类,每类为一组。分组能让字词学习变得容易,因为它能让每组字词之间建立有意义的联系。这种联系有利于把新字词融合到个体现存的图式中去。分组可以是根据语言学的特征,例如按词类来分;也可以根据语义联系来分,例如把意义相近或相反分在一类;也可以按功能分类,比如打招呼,问路或提要求各成一组;也可以根据话题分类,比如体育运动或在邮局寄信等话题来分组。字词分组应该考虑课文的内容,从而促进稍后的课文学习。在初始阶段,教师可以提供分组的示例,让学生照样进行分组练习。之后,教师可以提供一些分组的指导提纲,让学生按提纲自己分组。等学生对分组的意图和方法有了确切的了解后,教师可以让学生自己想办法进行有创意字词分组活动。请参照教学示例14-16的不同字词分组方法。

Teaching example 14. Word grouping: find the key word
教学示例14 字词分组:找出关键词

Words are grouped together 生词组:

电器、电视机、电冰箱、洗衣机、电灯、电话

In this group, 电灯、电话 are learned words, but 电器、电视机、电冰箱、洗衣机 are new words. The purpose of this grouping is three-fold. One is to connect new words with learned words based on their similarities. The other is to find out inclusive（隶属）relationships between 电器 and the others words so that a new schema of this relationship can be established in the learners' minds. The third is to use 电器 as memory peg to link other words.

在这一组字词中,"电灯"和"电话"是已学词汇,而"电器、电视机、电冰箱、洗衣机"是生词。字词如此分组有三个目的。一是将生词和已学词通过相似点建立联系,另一方面是找出它们共同隶属的类别"电器",使学习者在脑海中建立起有关它们的新的图式。此外,了解"电器"这一类别还可以帮助学生记忆和该类别有关的其他字词。

Teaching example 15.　Word grouping: Landlord's story
教学示例 15　字词分组:房东的故事

Words are grouped together 生词组：

　　房东、出租、套、公寓、卫生间、厨房、卧房、客厅、楼

Grouping these words together is to establish meaningful connections among the list of words by creating a story line. The story could be 把这些生词放在一组,是为了串成故事来建立起它们之间的联系,帮助记忆。故事可以是:

　　"房东要出租一套公寓。那套公寓有两个卫生间,一个厨房,三个卧房,还有一个客厅。公寓在东大街的98号楼。"

Teaching example 16.　Word grouping: Looking for similarities
教学示例 16　字词分组:找出相同点

Words are grouped together 生词组：

　　跳、唱、打、谈

These four words are grouped for two reasons: 1. The words are all phonetic-semantic compounds. Students can explore the roles of phonetic and semantic radicals in terms of cuing the sound and meaning for the compound characters and to generalize rules whereby the phonetic radical is placed on the right within the compound character and semantic radicals are placed on the left. 2. These words are all action words. Students can act out these words to enhance their memorization. 3. The teacher can ask students to give more examples of these types of words by recalling previously learned characters with similar attributes.

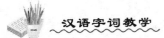

这四个生词归为一组的理由有三。首先,它们都是形声字。学生能认识到形旁和声旁的不同功用,并归纳出形旁在左,声旁在右的规律。其二,这些生词都是有关动作的词。学生可以逐一演示,帮助记忆。其三,老师可以要求学生以此类推,给出更多类似的已学字词。

(Teaching examples 14-16 are contributed by Helen H. Shen).

● Using corpus
利用语料库

Using corpus can help students develop a depth of vocabulary knowledge such as understanding the syntactical, semantic requirements, restrictions, and collocation for a target word to be used in a sentential context. The corpus provides comprehensive information about the word usage, which provides great convenience to instructors for preparing vocabulary instruction. It should be pointed out that meaningful learning occurs when the instructor guides students to analyze and synthesize the underlining rules of the target word usage, rather than when the instructor presents the rules to students and asks students to memorize them. In addition, using corpus means students are required to read certain numbers of sentences extracted from various corpuses. This requires students to have already accumulated a certain amount of vocabulary. Therefore, this method is more suitable for advanced students (please see Teaching example 17 for how to use corpus in vocabulary instruction).

利用语料库可以加深学生对新字词的理解深度,比如理解字词如何在句中受句法和语义的制约、词语搭配的限制。语料库可以提供字词使用的综合性的知识,这对教师准备字词教学带了很大的便利。应该指出的是,有意义的学习是学生在教师的指导下自己分析、综合字词使用的规则,而不是由教师直接把规则呈现给学生让学生去背诵。另外,使用语料库要求学生阅读各种从语料库选择出来的句子,这需要学生已经积累一定量的字词知识,因此,这一方法对高级班的学生比较合适(请见教学示例17,了解如何在字词教学中使用语料库)。

Teaching example 17. Using corpus for semantic differentiation between words
教学示例17 利用语料库区分语义

Instructional purpose: Understand the semantic scopes for words 抛弃、离开、丢掉
教学目的:理解"抛弃、离开、丢掉"的语义范畴

Step 1. The instructor presents the target word 抛弃 in a sentence and asks students to discuss the meaning of this sentence in small group of 3-4 persons.

步骤1：老师用 S1 句子展示生词"抛弃"，然后要求学生每3-4人为一组讨论该句子的意思。

S1. 为了留在美国他居然抛弃了自己的妻子和儿女。

Step 2. The instructor presents another two previously learned words 离开、丢掉 which have similar meaning of 抛弃, but are not identical (see S2, S3). The instructor asks the students to compare the similarities and differences of three words 抛弃、离开、and 丢掉. The instructor then asks the students to discuss whether S2 and S3 are correct and to give reasons for their judgment. Lastly, the instructor asks each group leader to present a group opinion based on their discussion. In the original case, the groups were not able to reach a consensus.

步骤2：老师给出两个分别含有"离开"和"丢掉"的类似的句子(见 S2,S3)。这两个词，学生已经学过，而它们和"抛弃"的意思相近却不相同。老师要求学生先来比较这三个词的异同，然后判断例句2和例句3是否正确，并给出理由。最后由各组组长报告本组的讨论结果。在真实的教学中，学生们没能就这一问题达成共识。

S1. 为了留在美国他居然抛弃了自己的妻子和儿女。

S2. 为了留在美国他居然离开了自己的妻子和儿女。

S3. 为了留在美国他居然丢掉了自己的妻子和儿女。

Step 3. The instructor presents the following three groups of words (please see Sentence groups 1-3) and asks students to group as pairs to explore the differences and similarities of using the 抛弃、离开、丢掉 in context. (Note: the sentence samples are retrieved from http://ccl.pku.edu.cn/Yuliao_Contents.Asp 北京大学汉语语言研究中心语料库 with some modifications.)

步骤3：老师给出以下三组句子。学生每两人一组，探讨"抛弃、离开、丢掉"在语境中使用的异同。(例句均来源于北京大学汉语语言研究中心语料库 http://ccl.pku.edu.cn/Yuliao_Contents.Asp，为了使难度适合学生的水平，在原句上略做了删改)

Sentence group 1.
- 朱德抛弃高官厚禄,寻求救国救民之真理。
- 其实大家从来就没有产生过抛弃小五的念头。
- 周恩来抛弃了军国主义可以救中国的想法。
- 人们终于在20世纪初抛弃了原子不可分割的陈旧观念。

Sentence group 2.
- 人们吃芹菜习惯把叶丢掉非常可惜,因为叶子很有营养。
- 我担心失去机会,不抓呀,看到的机会就丢掉了,时间一晃就过去了呀。
- 由于去年年底在英美车队丢掉了饭碗,威廉姆斯只得无奈地选择退役。
- 在伊拉克发生的事显示出布什在未来的大选中会付出丢掉总统宝座的代价。

Sentence group 3.
- 你看,我出生在北京我就没离开这个海淀区。
- 我其实也舍不得离开她,见她极力挽留我,便留了下来。
- 我很快地离开了那家地下招待所。
- 我还不想这么早离开人世。

Step 4. Under the instructor's guidance, the class summarizes their understanding of the three words:

步骤4:在老师的指导下,全班一起总结出对于这三个词的理解。
- 抛弃 (用于抛弃人、地位、思想观念、行为方式,是因为不喜欢,不合适,过时)
- 丢掉 (用于丢掉东西、工作,是因为不喜欢,过时,不小心,某种原因)
- 离开 (用于离开人、地方,是由于某种原因)

Step 5. The instructor asks students to work in pairs and complete the following exercise. Each group reports their work and gives the reason for their choice.

步骤5:学生每两人一组完成以下练习。每组报告他们的答案并给出选词理由。

抛弃、丢掉、离开
- 这本书很旧,已经没有用,我把它 ____ 了.
- 昨天安利找不到车钥匙(yàoshi),他不知道是什么时候 ____ 的。
- 我们应该 ____ 像"男尊女卑"那样的旧观念。
- 在2007年5月,我 ____ 了爱荷华,去了芝加哥。
- 因为我要去中国,我只好 ____ 我的父母亲。

(Teaching example 17 is contributed by Helen H. Shen)

- **构建概念(语义)图**
  Create concept (semantic) map

Concept mapping as an instructional theory was developed based on Ausubel's meaningful learning theory. Initially, this was developed by Novak's research program in 1972 and used in science education (Novak & Musonda 1991). Now it is widely used in language instruction. The concept maps are graphical tools for organizing and representing an invisible cognitive map that shows the pathways that the learner uses to connect meanings of concepts to form a cognitive schema in their brain (Novak & Gowin 1984). Concept maps can be presented either in concept or in propositions. Concept refers to a perceived regularity in events or objects, or records of events or objects, designated by a words or symbols. Propositions contain two or more connected concepts to form a meaningful statement. Propositions are therefore statements about an object or event, which can be called semantic units (Novak & Cañas 2008). For this reason, the concept map is also called the semantic map.

概念图构建作为一种教学理论的提出是基于 Ausubel 有意义学习的理论的精神之上。概念图构建的说法最早出现在 Novak 1972 的一个关于科学教育的研究项目中(Novak & Musonda 1991)。现在，这一理论已被普遍地使用在语言教学中。概念图是把个体头脑中的内隐的认知图用图表的形式使其变成看得见的外显图形，它反映出个体是怎样在头脑中建立概念联系组成图式(Novak & Gowin 1984)。概念图可以以概念的形式呈现，也可以是命题的形式呈现。概念指的是用语言或符号反映对观察到的事物或事件的规律性的总结或是对事物、事件的记录。命题则包含两个或两个以上的有联系的概念组成的对事物、事件的一个有意义的陈述，也被称为语义单位(Novak & Cañas 2008)。由于这一原因，概念图也称为语义图。

Concept maps used in vocabulary instruction bear several characteristics. First, the concept or proposition represented by words or sentences in the graphic is in an organized fashion with a focused theme. Second, the concepts presented in the map usually demonstrate three types of relationships between concepts or propositions. Type 1 map indicates hierarchical/parallel relationship. For the hierarchical one, the most inclusive or general concepts are placed at the top of the map and more specific, less general concepts in a lower position of the map or vice versa; for parallel one, it indicates either coordinative, mutual overlapping, or exclusive relationships between concepts (please see Figure 3 for a Type 1 map). The Type 2 map is organized chronologically based on an event or plot development (see Figure 4). The Type 3 map presents spatial relationships between concepts. The arrangement of concepts is based on physical location or spatial movement of the items (see Figure 5). Third, the concepts included in the map are cross-linked to reflect the meaningful relationship between the concepts or propositions.

概念图有几个共同的特点。其一是概念图中用字词或句子所代表的概念或命题是相互联系的,反映一个主题。其二是概念图表现的概念之间的关系通常有三种。一种是表示概念之间的隶属或平行关系。这种表示隶属关系的概念图把最有包含性的概念放在最上面,隶属的概念放在较下的位置,体现出隶属关系,或者是相反以自下而上形式排列。平行关系的概念图则勾画出概念之间的并列、交叉重合、或互不包含的关系(请参考图2)。第二种是按事件或情节的发展的时序构图(请参考图3)。第三种是按概念在空间中的关系构图,概念的排列则按事物在空间中的位置或空间运动的发展轨迹(请参考图4)。其三是图中的概念是用线条或其他标志连接起来以反映概念之间的有意义的联系。

Figure 2　Type 1. Hierarchical/Parallel map: Classification for fruit
　　图2　种类1、隶属/平行概念图:水果的分类

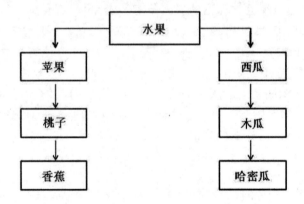

Note: The classification of target words 苹果、西瓜、木瓜、桃子、香蕉、哈密瓜、水果 in Figure 2. Type 1 map is based on our knowledge of 水果 is a general concept and the other items are subordinate concepts. 苹果、桃子、香蕉 grow on trees and 哈密瓜、西瓜、木瓜 grow on the ground; thus, these two groups of concepts are mutually exclusive in terms of their growing conditions, but they share the similarities as fruit.

注释:图2是对目的词"苹果、西瓜、木瓜、桃子、香蕉、哈密瓜、水果"认知加工的概念图。该图是根据个体把"水果"看成是包含性概念,而其他是隶属概念而制成。其中"苹果、桃子、香蕉"长在树上,"哈密瓜、西瓜、木瓜"长在地上,所以这两组从生长的形式上来说是互不包含,但是它们具有水果的共性。

Figure 3　Type 2. Temporal map：my day
图 3　种类 2、按时间推进概念图：我的一天

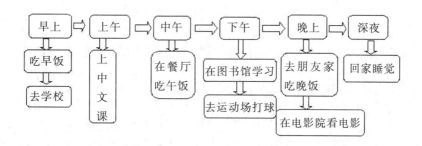

Note: Figure 3 is outlines the activities that the student completed during a particular day. The target words included in the map are:

注释：图 3 总结了学生一天中按时间推进所进行的活动，所包含的目的词是：

睡觉、回家、看电影、电影院、运动场、早上、中文课、打球、学习、深夜、晚上、图书馆、餐厅、学校、中饭、早饭、晚饭

Figure 4　Type 3. Spatial map: my school
图 4　种类 3、按空间位置排列概念图：我的学校

Note: The target words 图书馆、电脑中心、学生活动中心、教学楼、教室、运动场、医院、餐馆 in Figure 4, Type 3 maps are arranged according to their spatial relationships.

注释：图 4 中的目的词"电脑中心、学生活动中心、教学楼、教室、运动场、医院、餐馆"是根据它们在空间中的位置关系排列。

Based on this concept mapping theory and its application in vocabulary instruction, the instructor can use internet-based concept map tools such as Web 2.0 tools to have students design different types of concept maps to make meaningful connections between words. Teaching Example 18 illustrates how to use the Web 2.0 concept map tools in vocabulary instruction. However, if this technology is not available, the instructor can have students work out the map by hand. This may save time and also provide opportunity for handwriting words. Incorporating handwriting mode into instruction can enhance word memorization.

根据上述描述的把这一概念图理论运用到字词教学中,教师可以运用网路概念图工具,比如 Web 2.0 工具让学生在电脑上设计各种概念图,促进有意义字词学习。教学示例 18 展示了如何在字词教学中用 Web 2.0 设计概念图。如果学校没有相应的技术设施,教学中可以让学生手绘概念图。这不但节省时间,同时给了学生手写汉字的机会。把手写汉字结合在字词教学中能增强对字词的记忆。

Teaching example 18.　Design a semantic map about family members: Establishing meaningful relations between words.

教学示例18　设计关于家庭成员的概念图——建立词语间意义关系

Words to be learned　要学的生词：

散步、可怕、忘不了、确实、年代、曾经、除非、否则、商量、做生意、打听

(from the *Integrated Chinese Level 2, lesson 9 Travel* by Yuehua Liu, Tao-chung Yao *et al.* Cheng & Tsui Company)

Instructional tools and materials: 教具和资料

PowerPoint, Cacoo online concept mapping tool 投影片, Cacoo 概念图绘图网站: http://cacoo.com/

The objective of this activity 活动目的:

To review the target words just introduced and to discover meaningful relationships of these words in order to make a connection between the target words and their existing knowledge structure. 复习所学词汇,帮助学生发现词与词之间的意义联系,从而将生词和已有知识联系起来。

Steps for the activities 活动步骤:

Step 1. Present the 11 listed words and ask students to review these words quickly by using electronic flashcards. Step 2. Provide the topic: Introduce my family members to students and ask them to work in pairs and build a concept map around the center phrase that uses the 11 words. Step 3. After students have completed their designing, a few groups are invited to share their design with the whole class. By assessing each other's work, students are also reinforcing their vocabulary and their semantic relationships in their memory.

步骤1：老师展示以上所列的11个生词，要求学生用抽电子卡认字方法来快速复习这些词汇。步骤2：老师给出一个话题"介绍我的家人"。学生们分小组，用这11个词围绕该中心话题建立一个概念图。步骤3：学生完成设计后，以小组形式向全班展示他们的成果。评估成果这一过程也可以进一步巩固学生对于词汇本身和词语之间语义关系的记忆。

The reason to choose the Cacoo online concept mapping tool for this activity is that it has designed shapes and columns that help students easily analyze relationships. The other reason is that Cacoo supports Chinese input.

之所以采用Cacoo概念图绘图工具，是因为该网站提供现成的图形和符号，方便学生构建图形之间的关系。而且，Cacoo还可以输入中文。

Figure 5 is an example of semantic map completed by a student. The central lines and columns illustrate the similarity that father and mother share in the family by using 出生 (chūshēng: born), 年代 (niándài: a decade of a century), 曾经 (céngjīng: once) 做生意 (zuòshēngyì: do business) and 打听 (dǎtīng: inquire about).

图5是学生完成的一个概念图。图中间用线条和方框标注了家中父母的共同点，用到了"出生""年代""曾经""做生意"和"打听"这些词。

Figure 5　Concept map: Introducing my family members
图5　概念图：介绍我的家人

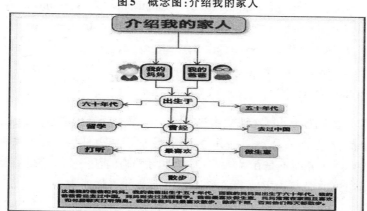

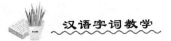

(Teaching example 18 is contributed by Xiaoyuan Zhao, Lecturer of Chinese, University of Iowa, USA)

6.3.3 Contextual approach
语境化途径

The contextual approach refers to applying or using learned words in simulated or real life communicative situations to solve a problem or fulfill a communicative task. This approach bridges the gap of classroom learning with real life communication. By practicing word use in simulated or real-life situations, students will be able to pay attention to both the linguistic form and meaning of the words. It will also help students to notice the pragmatic aspects of word usage in a complex linguistic situation.

语境化途径是指把已学的字词在模拟真实语境或真实语境中运用,解决问题或完成交际任务。这一途径能使课堂学习与实际生活结合起来。通过对字词在语境中运用,不仅能使学生专注于字词的形式和内容,还能注意到在复杂的语境中字词的语用方面的知识。

- **Simulated real-life activities**
  模拟真实语境活动

Simulated real-life activities can be completed in the classroom setting. The key points for designing this type of activity is that 1) the content of activities should originate from students' real-life situations so that students will not feel they are doing exercises; rather, they will feel that they are engaged in the activities to solve a problem or complete a task that they are facing in their real-life situations. 2) students have background knowledge for the events to be used in the activity, so that students will not be distracted or use extra time to familiarize themselves with the event itself; instead, they can focus on practicing words during the task completion. Teaching examples 19-21 illustrate the use of these types of activities in the classroom.

模拟的真实语境活动可以在课堂中进行。设计这类活动的要点是:1)活动的内容应该源于学生生活,使学生有一种亲临其境之感,让他们觉得他们是在解决他们面对的实际问题或完成实际任务而不是在做练习;2)学生对面临的任务有一定的背景知识,这样,学生不需要用额外的时间先去熟悉了解任务中涉及的事件或为了去熟悉某个事件而分心,相反,他们可以把全部注意力投入到怎样去完成任务上。教学示例19-21给出如何用模拟真实语境活动进行字词学习。

Teaching example 19. Simulated real-life activity: IQ test
教学示例 19 模拟真实语境活动：智力竞赛

IQ (Intelligence Quotient) contest can often be seen on TV channels in the United States. From elementary schools to colleges, students who are interested or qualified can join IQ groups as extra class activity. Therefore, students are familiar with this type of activity. The purpose of this activity is to help students review and practice the introduced target words in a linguistic context.

智力竞赛在美国的电视节目上很常见。从小学到大学,感兴趣或者资质符合的学生都可以参加智力竞赛小组这样的课外活动。因此,学生对于此类型的活动比较熟悉。该教学活动的目的是帮助学生在语境中复习和练习生词。

Target words 要学的生词：

图书馆、瓶、杯、罐、工作、家、打工、学校、喝、好吃、好玩、好看、可口可乐、百事可乐、雪碧、汽水、矿泉水、水、咖啡、饮料、茶、啤酒

Task sheet 任务单：

智力竞赛 Intelligence Quotient Contest

- What are the three most popular drinks in the U.S.哪三种饮料在美国最流行?
- What are the three places that you spend most of your time every week? 哪三个地方你经常去?
- What are the two most common packing formats for drinks? 哪两种饮料的包装形式最常见?
- How many drink names are you able to speak and write in Chinese? 你能用中文说和写哪些饮料?

Procedures 活动步骤：

Step 1. Students are grouped in pairs. Each pair is required to write out the answers to the questions listed in the task sheet. They then practice orally by asking questions to each other.

Step 2. Students are asked to perform a simulated intelligence test, either orally or written (to write out the answer in the white board) in the class without looking at the answers.

步骤1：学生两人一组。每组要回答任务单上的问题，并互相演练口头问答。

步骤2：学生表演模拟的智力竞赛。学生不看事先给出的答案，用口头或者书面形式（在白板上写出）回答任务单上的问题。

The class is divided into two groups. The testing rules are worked out based on mutual agreement between two groups, such as the time to be used to answer questions, and the score for each correctly answered question. During the contest, for the first round, group A sends a person to act as an interrogator and group B sends a person to answer as the interrogatee. The interrogator can ask any question listed on the sheet. The interrogator must answer questions quickly and accurately. For the second round, group A and group B exchange roles. The activity continues until each person in the group has the opportunity to serve either as an interrogator or an interrogate. Finally, scores are added up to decide the winner.

全班分为两组。具体规则如回答问题的时间或每题分值等都由两组协商决定。第一轮中，A组派出的代表作为提问方，B组的代表为答题方。提问方可以问任务单上的任何问题，答题方则必须快速而准确地做出回答。第二轮比赛中，A组和B组交换角色。活动一直进行到每个成员都已经扮演了提问和答题两方的角色后才结束。最后，计算分数，决出胜者。

(Teaching example 19 is contributed by Helen H. Shen)

Teaching example 20: Simulated real-life activity: Open house
教学示例20 模拟真实语境活动：样板房开放日

Opening house events are held by real estate companies to sell houses and apartments in the U.S. An open house activity is usually arranged during weekends. Students are familiar with this type of events. The purpose of this activity is to review the new words that have just been introduced.

美国的房地产公司常常举办样板房开放日活动来销售住宅。这类活动一般安排在周末。学生对此比较熟悉。该教学活动的目的是复习刚刚学过的生词。

Procedures　活动步骤：

Step 1. The teacher presents the task to the class: "You are an agent of a real estate company. Your goal is to sell apartments. Your job is to provide an honest introduction of one of the apartments listed below to your customers. In your description, please use your knowledge of the apartment to provide complete information. Your description should be based on the picture provided and must include the words listed on the card on the right."

步骤1：老师向全班提出任务："你们是房地产经纪人，要销售下面列出的三套公寓。在样板房开放日活动中，你需要带着客户边看房边介绍关于其中一套公寓的真实情况。描述时，请就你对该公寓的了解，提供尽量完整的信息。你的描述要基于以下图片，并包含右边提供的生词。"

一号公寓：

楼梯
走廊
地毯
租金/房租
稍微　有点贵

二号公寓：

隔壁
体育场
篮球
比赛
激动
大喊大叫

三号公寓：

| 一室 |
| 一厅 |
| 包水电 |
| 安静 |
| 受 影响 |
| 厨房 |

Step 2. Each student chooses one of the three vocabulary lists to work out a written description of the house based on the photo.

Step 3. Each student finds a partner and takes turns acting as agent and customer for the open house activity.

Step 4. The teacher asks each pair to perform in front of the whole class. Students and the teacher provide comments on the language and word use after each pair's performance.

步骤2：每个学生选择三张生词表中的一张，根据图片写出公寓的书面介绍。

步骤3：每个学生找一个搭档，轮流扮演房屋经纪人和客户介绍和参观公寓。

步骤4：每一组在全班面前表演经纪人和购房者，其他学生就他们的用词和语言表达给出点评。

(Teaching example 20 is contributed by Zhao Xiaoyuan, Lecturer of Chinese, The University of Iowa)

Teaching example 21.　Design a Simulated Online Store
教学示例21　设计虚拟网店

Target words 需学的生词：

衣服、T恤衫、毛衣、牛仔裤、样子、名牌、洗衣粉、牙膏、香皂、卫生纸、杯子、浴巾、化妆品、减价、打折、纯棉、质量、物美价廉、好看、现金、信用卡

第六章　汉语二语字词教学模式

Instructional tools and materials 教具及材料：

Online diagram tool, the task sheet 网上绘图工具，任务单

The objective of this activity is to help students review and practice target vocabulary by describing clothing items, daily necessity items, and money in Chinese. This activity will help to establish vocabulary networks and to use the target vocabulary in simulated real-life situation. Students work individually and design a simulated online store using online graphing tools. They can also use an online dictionary to look for new words to use in their design. Figure 7 is a completed sample by a student. This student designed a clothing store and described each of her items using learned vocabulary and marked a price for each item. After completion of the design, we assess the students' learning outcome by letting them invite each other to visit their stores and provide feedback. The teacher also visits the store and provides feedback.

　　该活动的目的是帮助学生通过描述衣物、日用品和货币来复习相关字词，在头脑中建立字词网络，并在实际生活中使用这些字词。具体说来，该活动是让学生独立地使用网上绘图工具来设计一家网店。他们也可以用网上词典来查阅需要使用的生词。图6是学生的成果展示。该学生设计了一家卖衣服的网店，用其所学词汇描述了所售商品，并标出价格。完成该设计后，学生们互相访问彼此的网店页面，给出反馈意见。老师也访问学生的网店页面并给出反馈。

Figure 6　On-line store
图 6　网上商店

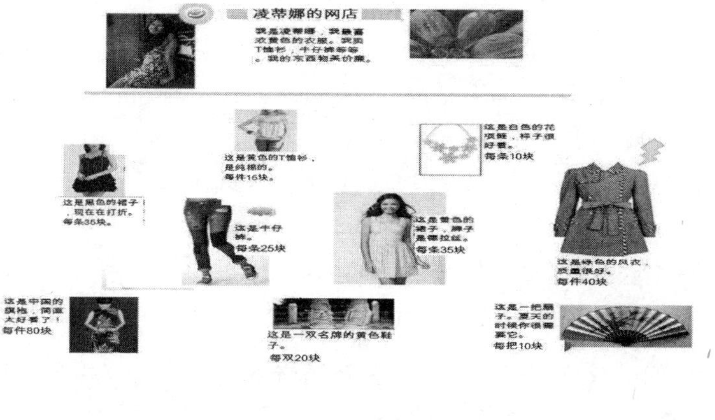

(Teaching example 21 is contributed by Xiaoyuan Zhao, Lecturer of Chinese, The University of Iowa, U.S.A.)

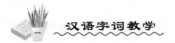

- Real-life activities 真实语境活动

Real-life activities usually are extended beyond the classroom. These types of activities allow students to focus on meaningful communication, which is very helpful for expanding the depth of vocabulary knowledge. The real-life activities can be of two types. One type is theme-based social activities, the other type is reading /writing-based vocabulary activities. The theme-based social activities have three characteristics: The activity has a theme so that students can use the words related to this theme. The activity has a goal and students are required to reach the goal by engaging the activities. The activities are intended to provide students with opportunities to practice learned target words. Therefore, this type of activity is a guided activity, which is different from natural activities happening in students' daily lives. Teaching examples 22— 26 are examples of theme-based social activities.

真实语境活动大部分是在教室外进行的。这类活动能让学生的注意力集中到有意义的交际活动中去,这对拓宽字词知识的深度很有帮助。真实语境活动一般有两类:一类是主题型社交活动,另一类是读写型的字词活动。主题型的社会活动有三个特点:活动有一个主题,学生能根据主题来练习相关字词;活动有一个目标,学生可以有目的地展开活动去达到目标;活动提供给学生练习目的字词的机会。因此这种活动是有指导的活动,它不同于学生真实生活中自然发生的活动。关于如何在教学中组织这一类活动,具体请参看教学示例22—26。

Teaching example 22.　Theme–based social activity: Conversational Corner
教学示例22　主题型社交活动:汉语会话角

The instructor can hold weekly gathering for CFL learners with native Chinese to practice conversation. In order to help students get maximum benefits from this activity, the instructor needs to develop topics and questions based on students' interests and their vocabulary knowledge as guideline for the activity. The instructor also should give a training session to the native Chinese speakers regarding how to communicate with students with limited Chinese vocabulary knowledge, so that the CFL learners can use and practice their target words learned from the lessons during the activity.

老师每周组织一次汉语学习者与汉语母语者的会话活动。为了更好地发挥该活动的效用,老师可根据学生的兴趣和已学的字词知识设定好会话主题和问题提纲作为活动指南。老师事先可就如何与汉语字词水平有限的学生进行交流,对汉语母语者进行有针对性的培训,以帮助汉语学习者在活动中有效操练学过的生词。

Teaching example 23.   Theme-based social activity: Language partner
教学示例 23   主题型社交练习：语言伙伴

The purpose of the language partner activity is to provide opportunity for CFL learners to be paired with native Chinese speakers (they could be students who are studying at the same institute or at other institutes) to practice Chinese in a natural environment on a regular basis. For practicing vocabulary purposes, the instructor can design vocabulary learning tasks beforehand and ask students to complete the tasks during their meetings with the language partners. The vocabulary learning tasks could be to find out what words are used for greeting a person or to express gratitude; or how a particular word such as 规定 can be used in different contexts.

　　语言伙伴活动的目的是通过让汉语学习者与汉语母语者（如来自中国的留学生）结成语言伙伴给汉语学习者提供一个交流平台，使他们能在较为自然的环境中定期练习中文。为了更好地操练词汇，老师要预先设计好字词学习的任务单。学生和汉语母语者会面时需要完成规定的任务。任务可以是与主题有关的例如找出表达问候或感激的常见用语，或是关于某个词如"规定"在不同语境中的使用规则等。

Teaching example 24.   Theme-based social activity: Group on-line chatting
教学示例 24   主题型社交练习：网上会话

In this activity, CFL learners are paired with Chinese students in China through video-conference activity. The instructor guided on-line chatting is an effective way to practice vocabulary. The chatting can be arranged in a computer lab. The instructor should give students a task on what vocabulary should be practiced during each chat. The instructor could also inform the native speakers about the purpose and theme prior to the activity, so that the Chinese partners can do some preparation prior to the chat. At the initial stage, the instructor should supervise the chatting and provide on-site help whenever a student has difficulty in finding the right words to complete the task (see the sample chatting task sheet below).

　　在这一活动中，汉语学习者和身在中国的学生搭配成组，视频会话。在老师指导下的网上会话是操练词汇的有效方式。网聊可以安排在机房。对于汉语学习者，老师给出会话所需使用的字词、句式（参见下面会话任务单）。对于身在中国的学生，老师则提前告知会话意图和主题，以便其有所准备。在初始阶段，老师要在机房随时指导学生，并在学生遇到表达困难时及时提供帮助。

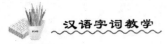

汉语字词教学

会话任务单

> **Conversation topic: Sports 会话主题：体育**
>
> 1. Ask your Chinese partner whether they like following sports by using 你喜欢……吗？请用"你喜欢……吗？"句式问你的中文伙伴是否喜欢下列体育活动：
>   打篮球、踢足球、打橄榄球、跑步、爬山、游泳、打乒乓、拳击、滑冰
>
> 2. Tell your partner about the popular sports in your country and also ask your partner to tell you the popular sports in his/her country. 请告诉你的伙伴你自己国家流行的体育活动，也请你的伙伴告诉你他/她的国家流行的体育活动。
>
> 3. Tell your partner about your favorite sports and also ask your partner about his/her' favorite sports. 告诉你的伙伴你最喜欢哪些体育活动，也请你的伙伴告诉她/他最喜欢的体育活动。
>
> Please write out the new sporting words that you have learned from your partner during the chat. 请写出从你伙伴那儿学来的新的体育活动的词。

Teaching example 25. Theme-based social activity: Vocabulary Weblog
教学示例 25　主题型社交练习：词汇博客

Students can create a weblog for vocabulary learning purposes. In the weblog, students can post a vocabulary question and ask other students to answer the questions. The questions could be a character/word riddle or puzzle, or could ask for an explanation of a certain word and its usage; or could ask to describe an object or event using specific words. Communication by visiting each other's weblog will greatly stimulate students' interests in learning and practicing vocabulary.

　　学生自建一个用于词汇学习的博客。在博客上，学生提出一些和词汇有关的问题，其他人予以回答。例如，字谜、词谜，某个词的释义和用法，或是用几个限定字词来描述某样事物或某件事。通过访问他人博客所进行的交流活动能大大激发学生对于学习和操练字词的兴趣。

Teaching example 26. Theme-based social activity: News report
教学示例 26　主题型社交活动：新闻报道

This type of activity is designed based on individual lesson content. For example, if the lesson is about earthquakes, the instructor could ask students to collect news from the internet about earthquakes to read and identify the words about earthquakes that they have learned and to identify a few words that they have not learned to find out the meaning and pronunciation for these new words. Students could also visit their friends who have first-hand experience about earthquakes. After this, students are required to report to the class about the news they have read and the old and new words they have identified in the news.

  这类活动的设计以每课的课文内容为基础。例如,如果课文内容和地震有关,学生便在网上收集有关地震的新闻来阅读。他们标出新闻中已学过的与地震相关的字词,并对新闻中提供的却尚未学过的生词注音释义,还可以从经历过地震的朋友那里获取第一手的资料。在这之后,学生向全班介绍他读过的新闻以及所标注的那些新词。

(Teaching examples 22—26 are contributed by Helen H. Shen).

- Reading/writing-based vocabulary learning activities
  读写型字词学习活动

Vocabulary learning can take place in two forms - intentional learning and incidental learning. Intentional learning occurs when learners are clearly aware of their vocabulary learning goals during the learning process. Incidental vocabulary learning refers to vocabulary learning that is a by-product of a language activity. The learners acquire vocabulary knowledge from an activity that is not a pre-planned goal. (Hulstijn 2003) Reading/writing-based vocabulary learning activities are designed to having learners acquire vocabulary incidentally through reading and writing activities. Pleasure reading is an excellent approach to gain vocabulary. The instructor can recommend that students read graded books and articles, which allow students to review previously learned vocabulary through repeated exposure during reading or writing, and to learn new vocabulary through guessing from the reading contexts. The instructor could also ask students to report their reading content by writing a summary and reporting it to the class.

In addition to pleasure reading, instructors can create themes-based reading/writing activities to help students to expand their vocabulary. In designing these types of activities, the instructor should carefully control the difficulty-level of the activities. The activities should be based on class lessons and students' language proficiency level, so that the activities will be challenging and yet within the reach of the students. Please see teaching examples 27—29 for designing this type of activities.

字词学习的发生可以有两种形式—有意识的学习和无意识的学习。有意识的学习是指学生在学习过程中意识到他们是在学习字词;无意识的学习是指字词的习得是某种活动的副产品,学生在这一活动中学到了字词,但这不是他们事先计划的一部分(Hulstijn 2003)。读写型活动设计的宗旨是让学生在阅读和写作活动中无意识地学习字词。娱乐性阅读是一种很好的习得字词的途径。教师可以让学生阅读经过教师挑选的分级的课外书或文章,让学生通过阅读来多次重复接触以前学过的字词或通过上下文猜测新字词的意思。教师还可以让学生在读完后写文章的内容摘要,用书面或口头的形式向其他学生报告自己阅读的内容和感受。除了娱乐性阅读外,教师可以设计一些主题型读写活动来帮助学生扩大他们的词汇知识。在设计这一类活动时,教师应该严格控制活动的难度。活动必须适合学生的现有汉语水平,使活动有挑战性,但学生经过努力是可以完成的。关于如何设计这类活动,请参看教学示例27—29。

Teaching example 27. Reading/writing-based vocabulary learning activity: Compare menus

教学示例27 读写型字词活动:比比招牌菜

The instructor asks students to conduct an investigation about the dishes provided by a number of Chinese restaurants in the city and to find out the featured dishes from each restaurant for comparison, and then to report the findings to the class. During this activity, students have opportunity to review dish words learned in the class and also to learn new dish words from the menus.

教师要求学生走访附近的几家中国餐馆,找出他们的招牌菜加以比较,然后向全班报告。这一活动促使学生复习已学过的有关菜肴的词汇,并从各式菜单中学习更多的菜名。

Teaching example 28. Reading/writing-based vocabulary learning activity: Class newspaper

教学示例28 读写型字词活动:班报

The instructor can motivate students to run a regular class Chinese newspaper (either on-line or off line). The topic for each issue should related to the lesson content so that students can use the learned words in their writing. Students should elect an editor and an editorial board to be in charge of the newspaper. Each student in the class should contribute stories or news to the newspaper using the target words learned.

教师鼓励学生筹办定期出版的中文班报(在线或线下的形式皆可)。每一期的主题应该与学过的课文有关,这样学生可以通过写作练习刚学过的字词。学生们自行选出一名编辑和一个编委会来管理班报。每名学生都要为班报编故事或者新闻。

Teaching example 29. Reading/writing–based vocabulary learning activity: Writing Diaries about the Chinese class

教学示例 29 读写型字词活动:中文课日志

The instructor can ask student to write a diary once a week to record the things that have happened in the Chinese class and to share these with other students in the class. Since the diaries are about the Chinese classes, the students can use the words learned from the Chinese class in their diary writings. The instructor may encourage students to share their diaries with their classmates or friends.

教师要求学生每周写一篇有关中文课的日志,并在课上与其他同学交流。因为日志的内容与中文课有关,所以在写作过程中,学生可以用到在课上学过的字词。教师要鼓励学生与其他同学或是朋友分享他们的日志。

(Teaching examples 27-29 are contributed by Helen H. Shen).

It should be pointed out that the major focus of the reading/writing based vocabulary activities is incidental learning of vocabulary and the appropriate use of learned words, rather than on the quality of reading and writing. Therefore, the activity design should make sure that students will be given plenty of opportunities to practice the learned words and also to learn new words. The evaluation should give enough weight to the accuracy of word use.

应该指出的是,读写型字词学习活动的重点是促进无意识字词学习,让学生恰当地运用学到的字词知识,而不是阅读和写作的数量。因此,活动的设计应考虑活动本身是否提供了足够的机会让学生练习所学的字词及学习新字词。在评估活动的时候应该对字词使用的准确度给予足够的分值。

In this chapter, we discussed the three dimensions of the CFL vocabulary instruction framework: cognitive process of meaningful learning, integration of four language skills for building linguistic proficiency, and adopting the three-tiered instructional approach for pedagogical soundness. Based on the above discussion, the complex relationship among the three dimensions for this framework is outlined in Figure 8. In pursuit of effective vocabulary instruction, we must know that high quality learning cannot be realized without interaction of these three dimensions.

在这一章中,我们讨论了汉语二语字词教学模式的三个维度:有意义字词学习的认知过程,为提高语言水平而促进四种语言技能的融合以及为促进教学有效性而采用三层次教学途径。在上述讨论的基础上,我们把这三个维度的错综复杂的关系用图7勾勒出来。在追求有效字词教学手段过程中,我们必须牢记,高质量的字词学习只有在三个维度的理想结合的过程中才能实现。

Figure 7   A Framework for CFL vocabulary instruction
图7   汉语二语字词教学模式

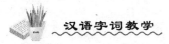

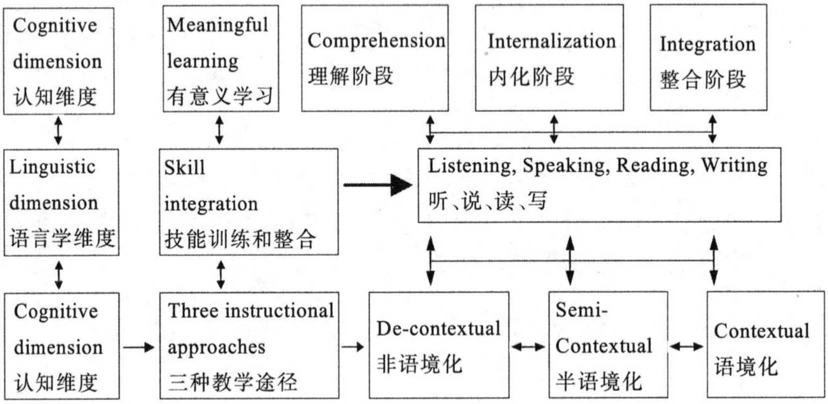

The realization of meaningful learning and skill acquisition initiates from effective implementation of appropriate instructional approaches. The instructional approach proceeds from the first tier of decontextual activities to the second tier of semi-contextual activities and to the final tier of contextual activities to support each stage of meaningful learning from comprehension to internalization to integration. At each stage of meaningful learning, the instruction must balance the four language skills in vocabulary acquisition. The training of four skills should be manifested in the teaching activities in each tier of instructional approach. That is, at each meaningful learning stage, instruction should consider integrating listening, speaking, reading, and writing skills in order to facilitate the transformation of vocabulary knowledge into skills. However, the acquisition of vocabulary knowledge from unknown to known and the development of four language skills from controlled to automaticity is gradual. Due to complexity of cognition and individual differences, the progression is not linear. We should anticipate regression and focalization at any stage. In learning reality, vocabulary acquisition is not as simple as finding that today student learns 60 words and tomorrow they learn another 60 words. Rather, we observe that on the second day, students only remember half of words introduced the day before. We should expect that some words that have reached the internalization stage may have bounced back to comprehension stage. Therefore, instruction should not be rigid and fixed; rather, it should be flexible and adjustable based on learning reality. The framework for CFL vocabulary instruction proposed in this chapter outlines the dynamic of the vocabulary learning reality. Although it is still a sketch and many details need to be ironed out and enriched through further empirical studies, we wish this framework to serve as a guideline for the CFL vocabulary instruction.

有意义学习和技能获得的实现始于有效地实施恰当的教学手段。字词教学中教学途径有序地从第一层次的非语境化活动推进到第二层次的半语境化活动,最后到第三层次的语境化活动,以支持有意义学习从理解阶段上升到内化阶段最后到整合阶段。在每一个有意义学习阶段,教师必须保持字词的听说读写四种技能训练的平衡。这四种技能的训练体现在每一层次的教学活动中。也就是说,在有意义学习的每一个阶段,教学必须考虑如何融合听说读写四方面活动,使词汇知识转换为技能技巧。当然,词汇知识从无到有,听说读写技能从有意识控制的运用发展到自动化运用是一个渐进的过程。由于认知过程的复杂性和个体性,这种发展不是直线的。我们应该估计到在任何一个阶段知识和技能的习得会出现回归或高原现象。在学习的现实中,词汇习得不是像今天学生学60个字词,明天再学60个那么简单。相反,我们可能发现第二天,学生只记得第一天学的一半字词甚至更少。我们应该预计到有些已经达到内化阶段的字词又会回归到理解阶段。因此教学手段不应该是固定的、僵化的,而应该是灵活的根据学习现状而不断调整的。我们在本章中提出的汉语二语字词教学模式勾画出了词汇习得的这种动态现状。虽然这一模式仍然是粗线条的,许多细节有待于进一步的实证研究来充实,我们希望这一模式对汉语二语字词教学具有指导意义。

At the end of this chapter, we would like to share a traditional Chinese saying with our readers: "There are ways of teaching, but there is no fixed way of teaching." Teaching is very dynamic; we need theories and methodologies to guide our teaching practice, but we also need continuous testing, verification, and development of theories and methods that best describe and fit the ever-changing teaching current.

在这一章末,我们希望与读者分享一个传统的说法:"教学有法但教无定法。"教学是非常动态性的,我们需要教学理论和教学法来指导我们的教学实践,但是我们也需要不断地检验、证实并发展教学理论和创造教学法使之适用于不断变化的教学潮流。

References 参考文献

张田若、陈良璜、李卫民（2003）《中国当代汉字认读与书写》(第2版)，四川教育出版社。

Anderson, J. R. (1982) Acquisition of cognitive skill. *Psychological Review,* 89, 369-406.

Anderson, J. R. (2005) *Cognitive psychology and its application (sixth edition).* New York: Worth Publishers.

Ausubel, D. P. (1962) A subsumption theory of meaningful verbal learning and retention. *The Journal of General Psychology,* 66, 213-224.

Ausubel. D. P. (1963) *The psychology of meaningful verbal learning.* New York: Brune & Stratton.

Ausubel. D. P. (1977) The facilitation of meaningful verbal learning in the classroom. *Educational Psychologist,* 12, (2), 162-178.

Hulstijn, J. H. (2003) Intentional and incidental second language vocabulary learning: a reappraisal of elaboration, rehearsal and authomaticity. In P. Robinson (Ed.), *Cognition and Second Language Instruction,* pp. 258-286. Cambridge, U.K.: Cambridge University Press.

Meyer, L. M. (2000) Barriers to meaningful instruction for English learners. *Theory into Practice, 39,* 228-236.

Novak, J. D., & Cañas, A. J. (2008) The theory underlying concept maps and how to construct and Use Them, *Technical Report IHMC CmapTools* 2006-01 Rev 01-2008, Florida, Institute for Human and Machine Cognition. http://cmap.ihmc.us/publications/ researchpapers/ theorycmaps/theoryunderlyingconceptmaps.htm

Novak, J. D., & Gowin, D. B. (1984) *Learning how to learn.* New York: Cambridge University Press.

Novak, J. D. (1991) Clarify with concept maps: A tool for students and teachers alike. *The Science Teacher,* 58, 45-49.

Oxford, R. & Crookall, D. (1990) Vocabulary learning: A critical analysis of techniques, *TESL Canada Journal,* 7, 9-30.

Ryle, G. (1949) *The concept of mind.* New York: Barnes & Noble, Inc.

Shuell, T. J. (1990) Phases of meaningful learning. *Review of Educational Research, 60,* (4), 531-547.

Stahl, S. A. (1983) Differential word knowledge and reading comprehension. *Journal of Reading Behavior,* 15, 33-50.

Stahl, S.A. (1985) To teach word well: A framework for vocabulary instruction. *Reading World,* 24, 16-27.

Thelen, J. N. (1986) Vocabulary instruction and meaningful learning. *Journal of Reading,* 603-609.

Chapter 7　第七章

Vocabulary instruction methods demonstration: Beginning level

汉语字词教学方法举例：初级

在这一章中，我将向大家介绍十种教学方法（这十种教学方法配有录像演示，本书所附的录像是演示版，另有完整的教学录像出售）。为了能让大家更加清楚地了解这十种方法，我将它们用于一篇课文的汉语字词教学中。这些方法有的是用于介绍生词，有的用于练习和复习生词，有的是对生词的运用。在平时的教学中，教师可以根据需要选取方法，一篇课文的生词的教学，使用多少种方法要看学生的学习程度以及教学时间而定，不能死板规定。在介绍方法之前，我先谈谈低年级字词教学的特点。

教学特点

一年级学生的汉字的积累量很少。在最初级阶段，汉字对他们来说可能就是各种线条的无意义的组合，所以系统地分析汉字就成为一年级汉字教学的重点。其目的是使学生对汉字的特点有一个整体的认识，同时创造出较有效的记忆汉字的方法，从而为他们今后的学习打下坚实的基础。在此教学思想指导下，一年级的汉字教学以识字作为主要教学目标。识字过程体现在对汉字音形义的认知，即对字形的识别及对读音和意义的认知。在本次教学过程中，教师根据学习者学习语言的记忆心理过程和特点，通过大量的图片和活动来营造生动有趣的学习环境，调动人体各个感官在汉字认知中的积极作用，激发学生的想象力和创造力，提高对汉字的认知和记忆能力。一年级的教学设计要考虑以下几个方面的因素。

1. 非语境化、半语境化教学活动和语境化教学活动的比例

教学方法侧重于运用非语境化和半语境化活动。比如说较多地运用字卡、图片以及动作、面部的表情和实物来引发学生的想象力和提高对汉字的感知度。由于学生正处于汉字学习的初级阶段，语境化教学的比例相对比较小，但是教师也通过让学生在句子中识字和在具体生活场景中运用字词的方法，提高学生的记忆和运用字词的能力。比如说，组织学生用学会的字词对茶馆和咖啡馆两个生活场景进行简单的描述。在运用语境化教学时教师需对活动的难易程度和方式进行仔细的考虑，并且要选择与学生生活紧密相关的事件或者学生熟悉的场景。比如说，要求学生对场景做成段的描述或对话就不太

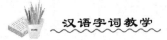

适合。学生会因为活动太难而无法完成对学习产生畏难情绪,或者可能造成字词的不恰当运用,造成事倍功半。

2. 学生活动的比例

众所周知,调动学生学习的积极性是达到学习目标的一个关键因素。汉字学习对于外国学生来说是一个很大的挑战。所以如何激发学生的学习兴趣和动力是教师教学设计的中心问题。以此作为教学指南,一年级的汉字教学以活动为中心来组织教学,让学生学得快乐,在快乐中得到知识。活动的特点可以体现在以下几个方面。首先,三个教学环节(学习生词、巩固生词、运用生词)都以活动为中心。活动设计要注意环环相扣,即学习、复习、运用。其次,在学习新词阶段,活动以建立知识的图式结构,为汉字建立意义编码为目标,使学生能够在短时间内提高对汉字的记忆能力。比如说,将春天阳光下茁壮生长的禾苗散发出的清香与生词"香"相联系。这样,学生不仅记住了字形,而且记住了字义。这个阶段的活动设计要注意编码的有意义性和控制图式结构和编码的复杂程度。简单地重复读字词不仅枯燥无味,而且达不到学习目标。而过于复杂的编码会增加学生的记忆负荷,也是不可取的。第三,在复习和运用生词阶段,活动要以对汉字的认知达到自动提取为目标。通过非语境化、半语境化和语境化的复习和操练达到教学目标。在这个阶段,活动设计要注重丰富目标词的编码,即活动能够提供不同于学习阶段时的编码,以引起学生的兴趣,进一步加强对汉字的记忆能力。比如复习"香"这个词,教师可以让学生闻其他物品的味道,并说出词组、句子,以加深对这个词的理解。

3. 教师直接指导的比例

初级阶段,学生还没有掌握一定量的部首,同时还没有形成对汉字的结构的分析能力。所以教师要比较详细地介绍分析单个的生词。目的是使学生对所学的生词的结构特点及用法有较深入的了解。同时逐步形成分析字词的能力,为今后的学习打下基础。教师的直接指导体现在教授汉字的读音和部首、分析字源和结构、帮助学生记忆抽象字词,和讲解字词的用法。

4. 汉字教学和课文内容的结合

汉字教学应当紧紧结合课文内容。我要介绍的教学方法中的字词是选自课文"入乡随俗"。生词学习应该紧紧围绕课文主题。在讲解汉字的时候,教师带入中国的茶馆的环境和特点,让学生用学会的字词简单描述中国的茶馆,比如说,用"筷子、茶壶、点心、热闹、舞台"描述茶馆的环境和特点,并让学生将茶馆和咖啡馆的环境作一个比较。同时,也可以让学生简单说说本国的或者是中国的相关的风俗,以期达到学以致用的目的。

教学方法

1. 教学内容
   课　文：入乡随俗（出处：《新实用汉语课本》第三册，第二十七课）
   新字词：筷子、搬、稍、壶、刀、叉、点心、切、香、甜、茶馆、热闹、舞台、咖啡馆、安静、干净、风俗、看法、正常、了解、发现、场所、比如、食物

2. 教学目标
   (1) 掌握部首的意义，及其在字中表音或表意的作用。
       重点部首：刀、禾、舌、手、竹
   (2) 掌握字词的字音、字形、字义，并能够认读、造句。

3. 教学步骤
   　　教师首先根据生词的特点将生词分类。词性、词义、词形等都是分类的标准。比如说，相同部首的字词、象形字、近义字词、反义字词、语义联系等等。这个步骤的目的是帮助教师根据不同的字词类别选择不同的教学方法，同时也帮助学生对生词进行记忆分类。其次，每部分的生词教学按照介绍生词、巩固生词和应用生词的步骤进行。介绍生词是以教师为主导的教学，在此环节中，我们要以认知负荷理论和认知加工深度理论作为指导：在一节课当中，教师应该根据字词的难度控制新字词的输入量，帮助学生建立知识的图式结构。但是要注意新知识的图式化的复杂程度。在一年级的汉字教学中，着重于一词一义，从简单图式到复杂图式是我们要把握的重点。复习和运用生词的目的是强化学生对生词音形义的认知，并熟练地在语境中运用生词，即达到对新知识的运用的自动化。在教学中，教师运用非语境化、半语境化和语境化的教学活动来帮助学生达到学习目的。

4. 教学评估与反馈
   　　对学习成果的评价主要在应用生词环节中进行。在学习和复习生词结束后，教师用字卡或练习纸测试每个学生对汉字的音、形、义的掌握程度。或者运用学到的汉字知识来解决问题，完成任务。比如说，根据学到的字源知识写出汉字；将声旁和义旁组合成一个学过的生词；用学过的生词根据语境造句等等。下面，我具体介绍各种方法在本课教学中的运用。

方法一：部首认字

1. 内容：介绍生词"筷子、搬、稍"。
2. 设计：教学方法属非语境化途径。运用PPT展示目的词和相关的图片。目标字词的部首要用红色标出，并结合图片使之形象化。

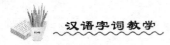

3. 步骤:
   1) 使用PPT展示目标字词,将部首单独陈列,并结合图片加深学生对该部首的认知。

(备注: a. ㇏ 出自《常用汉字图解》北京大学出版社,1997,作者:谢光辉
　　　 b. 以上图片出自 www.google.com)

   2) 教师逐个讲解部首的意义,并要求学生总结出该部首对于词义的作用。
   3) 通过齐读和个别诵读使学生掌握目标字词的正确读音。
   4) 用字卡要求学生个别认读,进一步巩固学生对目标字词的字形和读音的熟悉。
4. 反思:该方法是通过强调部首在目标字词中的意义来加强学生对汉字的识别和记忆能力。根据认知加工深度理论,利用合体字的部件的独特性对汉字的缀字法进行分析来揭示汉字形和义的联系是比较有效的意义编码。教师在使用这种方法时要强调部首的独特性,并用故事或图片的方式加深学生对其意义的记忆和认知。同时教师要注意要求学生说出此部件对汉字的意义的作用,以此来加强学生分析汉字的能力。

方法二:部件拼合

1. 内容:复习生词"筷子、搬、稍"。
2. 设计:教学方法属非语境化途径。教学用具是字卡。字卡上分别写上合体汉字的部件,即声旁和义旁。
3. 步骤:
   1) 教师把目标汉字的部首卡和声旁卡排成一排,两个学生上前准备拼字。
   2) 教师读词,学生快速找到部首卡和声旁卡,拼成目标汉字。这个活动可以培养学生快速准确地辨别汉字部件的能力。
4. 反思:该方法是复习巩固学过的部件,以加深学生对汉字部件的记忆和认知。此活动还可以有变化的形式,比如说学生手持卡片,教师读词,持有部首卡和声旁卡的学生走上前,拼出目标汉字。

方法三：看图说字

1. 内容：复习生词"筷子、搬、稍"。
2. 设计：教学方法属半语境化教学途径。教学用具是字卡和PPT。
3. 步骤：

   1) 教师用PPT展示下列和目标汉字相关联的图片

a

b

c

（备注：以上图片出自www.google.com）

   2) 教师根据图片问问题，要求学生说出含有目标字词的句子。

      图a: 他们在用什么工具吃饭？

      图b: 他们在做什么？

      图c: 这个盘子比那个盘子稍大还是稍小？

   3) 教师出示目标汉字字卡，根据图片说出含有目标汉字的句子，然后要求学生复述句子。

      图a: 他们在用筷子吃饭。

      图b: 他们在搬沙发。

      图c: 这个盘子比那个盘子稍小。

4. 反思：该方法是根据认知理论中的双重编码理论，将具有直观性的图片与汉字词相联系,将字词的音形与意象挂钩,形成"意象编码,即在学生的头脑中形成一幅与某一字词相对应的图像",帮助学生建立已知音义和未知的形之间的联系,同时将孤立的字词和语境相结合使之成为有意义的概念。教师在使用这种方法时要注意四点,一是意象和字词要有紧密的关联性,即学生可以通过具象联想起字词的音和形;二是要注意对一个字或词不要运用过多的具象,以免增加记忆负担;三是要运用具有生活真实性的具象,使学生的学习内容与真实的生活联系起来;四是如果选择图片,图片要清晰明了。

方法四：追溯字源

1. 内容：学习生词"壶、刀、叉"。
2. 设计：教学方法是非语境化教学。教学用具是字卡、实物和PPT。
3. 步骤：

   1) 教师用PPT展示目标汉字。

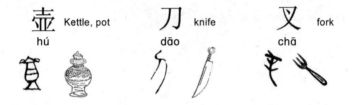

（备注：以上图片出自《常用汉字图解》北京大学出版社,1997,作者：谢光辉）

   2) 通过齐读和个别诵读使学生掌握目标字词的正确读音。
   3) 教师用PPT展示字源和相关图片,并对字源进行讲解。
   4) 教师用字卡对所学的字词进行复习,让学生个别认读。
   5) 教师展示具体物品：刀、叉、筷子。学生说出相关的字词。

4. 反思：该方法是基于认知深度加工理论,通过对汉字字源的解释来对汉字进行意义编码,揭示汉字义和形之间的联系,加深学生对汉字的理解。使用该方法时教师要注意对字源讲解的深度和广度的把握,以免造成记忆负担。汉字的字源图片要清晰,使学生能够清楚地认识到古体字和今体字之间的联系。该方法也有变化形式。比如说,让学生为汉字配图。或者通过汉字的古体形态来猜测意义。目的是调动学生的创造性,提高对汉字的记忆能力。

方法五：看图写字

1. 内容：复习生词"壶、叉"。

2. 设计:教学方法是非语境化教学。教学用具是PPT。

3. 步骤:

　　1) 教师用PPT展示汉字字源,要求学生根据字源写出汉字。

　　2) 学生用三十秒钟准备。

　　3) 两个学生上台将目标汉字写在黑板上。

　　4) 教师进行评价。

　　5) 如果学生写得不正确,教师要示范正确的写法,并要求所有学生在纸上写出目标汉字。

4. 反思:该方法的目的是加深学生对汉字的形体特点的理解和认知,提高对汉字的记忆能力。比如说,学生看到"壶"字,脑子中能够闪现壶的形体特点,即能反映出这个字的意思。同时也培养学生正确书写汉字的能力。

方法六:感知汉字

1. 内容:学习生词"点心、切、香、舔"。

2. 设计:教学方法是半语境化教学。教学用具是PPT、白板、实物。

3. 步骤:

　　1) 使用PPT展示目标字词。

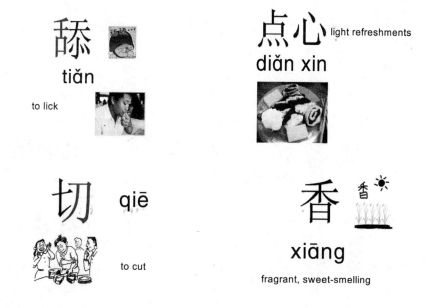

(备注:以上图片出自《常用汉字图解》北京大学出版社,1997,作者:谢光辉;

《新实用汉语课本》北京语言文化大学出版社2005,作者:刘珣等;以及 www.google.com)

2) 通过齐读和个别诵读使学生掌握目标字词的正确读音。

3) 讲解目标字词的部首,加深学生对其部件的理解。

4) 运用图片和想象使学生对目标字词有更感性的认知。

5) 教师运用动作和实物,引导学生说出目标字词。巩固、强化学生对目标字词特点的理解。

6) 一个学生进行表演,做出动作,下面的学生根据动作说出相关的字词。

4. 反思:该方法是基于认知理论中的多重感觉通道理论。通过动作、想象和实物来调动各种感官在学习中的积极作用,以加深学生对目标字词的理解和认知。教师在使用这种方法时,首先要注意的一点是选择适合的学习内容,即确定哪些字词可以通过人体的感官或动作来学习以达到比较好的记忆效果。比如说,动词、形容词和与人体的感官相联系的词等就比较合适。其次,表演不仅仅是为了让学生高兴,活跃课堂气氛而设,更重要的是要让学生通过各种感官的感知,将字词的形体特点和意义相联系,使之成为一种具象编码储存在记忆当中。即通过学生的亲身经历来加强对汉字的记忆和理解。

方法七:就景说词

1. 内容:学习生词"茶馆、热闹、舞台、咖啡馆、安静、干净"。
2. 设计:教学方法是语境化教学。教学用具是PPT、字卡。
3. 步骤:

1) 教师用PPT展示目标字词。

茶馆

热闹 Bustling with noise and excitement
rè nào
闹 门 市

舞台 stage
wǔ tái

咖啡馆

干净 clean
gānjìng

安静 quiet
ān jìng
安

(备注:以上图片出自《常用汉字图解》北京大学出版社,1997,作者:谢光辉;《新实用汉语课本》北京语言文化大学出版社2005,作者:刘珣等;以及 www.google.com)

2) 教师根据字词设置语境"茶馆和咖啡馆"。在语境中讲解新词,结合部首和字源知识,并且复习学过的部首知识。

3) 运用字卡复习生词。首先齐读,然后要求个别学生认读,以检查学生的掌握程度。

4) 学生讨论,提出问题。

5) 学生根据语境,即茶馆和咖啡馆,运用目标字词造句。

4. 反思: 运用该方法的目的是培养学生能够根据语境正确地运用目标字词的能力。使用该方法时,教师应注意语境设置要与学生的日常生活紧密相关,而且是学生经历过或者较熟悉的。

方法八: 对比认字

1. 内容: 复习生词"静、净"。
2. 设计: 教学方法是非语境化教学。教学用具是PPT。
3. 步骤:

1) 使用PPT展示目标字词。

Compare

静 净

Discuss the similarities and differences between two characters

(备注:以上图片出自www.google.com)

2) 学生互相讨论这两个同音近形字在形体上的相似点和不同点。

3) 学生对讨论结果进行发言。

4) 教师总结。

5) 教师说出由两个汉字组成的词,要求学生进行分辨。

4. 反思: 该方法是基于认知理论中的竞争理论。通过对比帮助学生了解形近字的不同点和相同点,以便在头脑中建立明确的图式结构,做到对目标词的准确提取。运用该方法时,教师要注意培养学生自己去揭示相似概念的相同点和不同点的能力,并能够在语境中准确地提取目标词语。

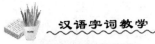

方法九：据图解字

1. 内容：学习生词"风俗、看法、正常、了解"。
2. 设计：教学方法是语境化教学。教学用具是PPT。
3. 步骤：

   1) 使用PPT展示目标字词。

（备注：以上图片出自《常用汉字图解》北京大学出版社，1997，作者：谢光辉；以及http://tell.fll.purdue.edu/JapanProj//FLClipart/, "What's in a Chinese Character" Publisher: New World Press (November 1, 2002) by Tan Huay Peng）

   2) 教师运用图片讲解字词的记忆方法，帮助学生记忆抽象的字词。

   3) 教师用字卡进行复习。

   4) 学生两人一组进行讨论，运用这些词提问和回答。

   5) 学生分组演示他们的讨论结果。

4. 反思：该方法基于为汉字提供双编码理论来教授汉字。教师根据汉字的形体特点或者部件特征将其形象化，适用于教授抽象的字词。这种形象化可以通过运用图片、故事来达到。也可以出自教师自己的创造力，或者可以发挥学生的创造力，使抽象的汉字变得生动有趣，容易记忆。运用该方法时教师要注意让学生建立形象和汉字之间的紧密联系，并具有趣味性。

方法十：读句填词

1. 内容：复习生词"茶馆、舞台、点心、壶、筷子、叉、风俗、正常、安静、热闹、了解、看法"。
2. 设计：教学方法是语境化教学。教学用具是PPT、任务单。
3. 步骤：

   1) 学生两人一组。
   2) 教师给每一个人发一张任务单(如下)，每张任务单上有一个句子，每组的句子是一样的。学生互读句子，填空。

   任务单：
   a. 今天我去(1茶馆)喝茶，那里有一个(2　　)。
   　今天我去(1　　)喝茶，那里有一个(2舞台)。

   b. 我吃了一盘(1点心)，喝了一(2)茶，太香了。
   　我吃了一盘(1　　)，喝了一(2壶)茶，太香了。

   c. 吃中餐的时候，我用(1筷子)，吃西餐的时候，我用刀子和(2　　)。
   　吃中餐的时候，我用(1　　)，吃西餐的时候，我用刀子和(2叉子)。

   d. 不同国家的人有不同的(1风俗)，对我们来说，这(2　　)。
   　不同国家的人有不同的(1　　)，对我们来说，这很(2正常)。

   3) 教师用PPT展示每个句子，学生齐读。

4. 反思：该方法是以阅读为基础的字词运用练习。主要培养学生在句子中识字的能力，同时也锻炼了正确书写汉字的能力。教师在运用该方法时要注意句子的难度和长度，以免学生产生畏难情绪。

Chapter 8　第八章

Vocabulary instruction methods demonstration: Intermediate level

汉语字词教学方法举例：中级

在这一章中，我将重点介绍十种中级汉语字词教学方法。具体的方法演示请观摩配套出售的教学录像，本书所附为演示版。在介绍方法之前，我先向大家介绍一下中级汉语汉字词教学的特点。

教学特点

中级的学生已经累积了基础的汉字部首与词汇知识。在这个阶段，我们的汉语字词教学方法设计包括三个特点：一是加强新旧汉字知识之间的联系，通过习得的部首、词汇以及相关背景知识来激活对新词的认知，进而建立或扩充相关字词的图式结构。二是鼓励学生对新的汉字词进行自发性的认知加工、强化学生对字词音、形、义的编码能力及增加词汇的网络知识。三是适当运用小组合作学习(Collaborative learning)，进一步激发学生学习热情，多创造每个学生在课堂上用中文交流的机会，使课堂充满多向的互动，在互动中练习字词。

针对这个阶段学生的汉语水平，课堂活动的安排采取非语境化、半语境化、语境化教学三项并用的模式。我在这章中要介绍的10个课堂活动当中有4个非语境化教学活动、4个半语境化教学活动以及2个语境化教学活动。课堂活动的三大步骤从非语境化教学过渡到半语境化教学到最后的语境化教学活动。在语境化教学活动中同时评估学生的整体学习成果。中级学生词汇量有限，但是他们对于汉字知识、汉语语法已有概念性的认知，在此基础上我们要让中级学生开始有目的地接触和积累同义词、近义词或反义词。在这个阶段，自发性的认知加工能力能有效地帮助学习者建立复杂图式。因此在学习、巩固生词的步骤中，教学方法的顺序是由教师直接或间接指导开始，由收到放，逐步培养学生主动建构信息，自己建立字词图式结构的能力，再进一步地将字词学习与使用的语境有效地结合起来，完成交际任务。整体看来，教师指导与学生主导的教学活动比例各占五成。

教学方法

下面我向大家介绍十种汉字教学方法在一堂字词课上的应用。我将先向大家介绍本课字词教学的内容、教学目标、教学步骤的总体设计及教学评估与反馈,然后,逐一介绍方法。

1. <u>教学内容</u>

这堂课采用的教材是《跟我说汉语》教材中的第十六课《一份简历》(北京:人民教育出版社 2006)。课文内容是一份中文简历以及三段对话。第一段对话是主人翁小雨和她的朋友安妮在电话上谈及找工作的原因。第二段是实际面试的经过。第三段对话是面试成功后朋友之间的谈话。词汇表上一共有42个生词,从中挑选出下面32个目标词进行重点学习:

简历、姓名、学历、高中、性别、身高、邮政编码、电子邮件、电话、手机、背景、熟练、输入、进行、日常谈话、经历、旅行社、寒假、讲解员、个人、自信、诚恳、责任心、善于、健谈、适合、面谈、面试、学费、交谈、做生意、工资

为了营造一个利于目标词汇习得的环境,课堂活动以"找工作"这一主题为主轴进行展开,例如 写简历、面试、描述个人特点等。最后完成与主题高度相关的学习任务。在教师的引导下将汉字教学和课文内容紧密结合,这个过程旨在促进学生自然和有意义的字词学习和应用。

2. <u>教学目标</u>

本课的生词多与描述个人性格与学习经历有关,有些字词意义相近但有其不同点。教学的侧重点主要有两个方面。一是学生要能区分相似字词概念之间的不同点并与相关概念、知识联系起来,在头脑中建立起词库。二是,学生要能运用所学的生词,以口头或书面的方式介绍自己。反映在实际的交际活动上就是要能看懂并正确填写中文简历表格,并且能在模拟的面试过程中展现出用中文进行应对的能力。

课堂活动的安排是以这两个侧重点为准则,循序渐进地落实在三个教学步骤上。第一阶段以字词的音、形、义加工为主,培养学生的认字能力;第二阶段是巩固生词并了解它们的使用范围,在此基础上了解生词与其他知识的联系,提高学生对目标字词的快速反应能力。活动的设计结合了听、说、读、写的技能训练。第三阶段是完成模拟实境的教学任务,着重词汇输出能力。

3. 教学步骤与方法

本课的汉字教学由三个步骤、十个方法组成。三个步骤依序为"介绍生词"、"巩固生词"和"应用生词"。每个步骤包括两到四个方法,教学步骤与方法名称如下表所示:

步骤一 介绍生词	1 按意补字
	2 画说汉字
	3 解说汉字
	4 温故知新
步骤二 巩固生词	5 故事串词
	6 排除异己
	7 汉字网络
	8 掀掀乐*
步骤三 运用生词	9 毛遂自荐
	10 精挑细选

*该名称由学生创造,意思是掀卡片很有乐趣。

介绍生词的4个方法设计以认知加工深度理论为基础,重点在于培养学生对生词音、形、义的编码与加工能力。方法1和2为老师直接指导或引导下的编码与意义加工,这两个方法是为了方法3"解说汉字"作铺垫,让学生在解说汉字时能应用在前几个活动中所习得的技巧和知识,进行自发性的认知加工。在介绍新词时,我们尽量使新字词与部首、字源或相关字词知识相联系以减低认知负荷,帮助学生更好地记忆生词。为了使这四种教学方法取得最好的教学效果,我们在下表中列出哪些方法适合教哪些新字词。

		教学方法	目标字词选择建议
介绍生词	1	按意补字	可用于教学部件与字义高度相关的生词。
	2	画说汉字	可用于学习那些能借助古文字形、图片来帮助记忆,或是需要教师经过解说才容易理解的字词。
	3	解说汉字 (用英文解说生词)	可用于教学: 1.音、形、义与学生学过的部件中度或低度相关的字。可以让学生思考、联想,通过自己分析解说来帮助学习。 2.音、形、义与部件完全无关的字,让学生发挥创意。
	4	温故知新 (用中文介绍生词)	适用于能用中级汉语解释清楚的生词。

在巩固生词的阶段,我们更加注意让生词与学生的原有知识、个体经验、相关语境发生联系。并且应用竞争理论让学生进行对比和比较,复习巩固学到的新字词。更重要的是鼓励学生自己进行分类,使学习生词更具系统性,更加个体化,避免生词以孤立、零散的形式储存在大脑中。

步骤三设计了两个与求职相关的活动,这是大部分的学生都感兴趣的交际任务,借此激发学生的学习动机。通过面试任务的驱动,激发学生用中文应对求职的需要,进而寻找表达个人意愿或情况的字词,然后评估所选字词是否适合这个特定的语境。由于学生是以小组合作的方式来完成任务,成功率比较大,因此学生一般都敢于参与最后的表演任务。

4. 教学评估与反馈

在汉语字词教学中,增加学习者的汉字知识与发展他们对汉字的兴趣同等重要。课堂教学评估的目的除了测试教学成果之外,最终目标是要培养学生对字词进行深度加工的能力,让学生热爱字词学习。所以评估过程也应该体现这些因素。这堂字词课的教学评估形式可概括分为三种:核对答案、分享信息、角色表演。

"核对答案"一般是使用在有固定答案的学习活动当中,用以评估学生对教学内容的理解状况。传统教学的方式是学生做完练习之后由老师核对答案,或者由个别学生提供答案,教师再给予适当的反馈。为了让学生能进一步的展现学习过程,鼓励学生思考。核对答案时,发言的同学必须解说自己的思考过程。比如在"按意补字"的活动中,发言者提出他自己对"龄"这个字的部件为什么是"齿"的看法。其他的学生可能有不同的阐释方法。虽然答案是固定的,但通往答案的途径却可以是多样的。

"分享信息"是让学生展示自己或小组的分析、学习成果。所有的学生都可以从同学的学习成果中吸取对自己有用的成分。教师可以进一步提供引导性的反馈帮助学生运用习得的部件知识来记忆新字词。这个评估方式主要适用于没有固定答案的字的教学活动中。以"解说汉字"这一方法为例,每个学生依据自己的经验、理解和创意叙说记忆字词的方法。对于某些古文字形、部件音义与现行汉字相去甚远的字词来说,这种分享过程就是最好的学习。"分享信息"评价活动,教师评价的不仅是学生对目标字词的理解,它也包括对学生自发性的汉字词学习策略的评价。这也是中年级汉字课堂教学要掌握的重点。

"角色表演"主要用于评估任务型的教学活动,要求学生以分角色表演的形式在语境中呈现所学的字词,完成交际任务。在准备这一活动的过程中,遇到无法解决的问题,可以求助老师或其他同学。学生在"角色表演"活动中不仅仅参与角色表演,也参与评估,评估自己和其他同学的语言表达用词能力,所以他们不只是被评估的对象,他们也是评估者。我下面要介绍的方法10"精挑细选",具体地展示了这一方法的运用。在这一方法中,让学生扮演工作面试中的两个角色:考官和应试者。教师在评价时要特别注意给予反馈的时机与方式,由于表演活动是在全班的同学注目下进行的,过度的纠正型反馈容易打击学生的积极性与自信心,造成学生对活动的排斥心理,因此评论必须切中要点、重质不重量,切忌频繁地打断学生表演加以评论。需要指出的是,教学目标和搭配的课堂活动设计在很大程度上决定着学生的学习成效。如果多数学生都在表演时出现大量错误,无法顺利完成任务,这代表教学目标与学习活动出现落差,需要改进。所以学生的错误是提供给教师的有用的反馈信息,它可以为教师改进教学活动设计提供重要的参考。

下面,我将对上述提及的每种方法给予具体的说明,并在"反思"的部分列出备课或教学时应注意的事项及各教学活动的衍生变化。

方法一: 按意补字

1. 方法界定:

"按意补字"是用来介绍生词,以教为主的活动,适用于非语境化的教学环境下进行。这套方法属于教师引导下的认知加工范畴,可引导学生通过自己的独立思考找出部件音义与目标字词之间的联系。

2. 内容:

诚恳、工资、团队、邮政编码、健谈、年龄

3. 设计:

在学习单上列出目的词、拼音及英文注释,根据生词的音或义,挖空其中关联性高的部件,然后让学生通过讨论、推理、猜测填补遗失的部件。教学用具包括部首卡、学习单、投影机(或实物投影仪)、黑板。

4. 步骤:

(1) 先复习重要偏旁部首,部首卡举例如下:

(2) 分发学习单，学生两人一组进行讨论，根据目标生词的发音或意义寻找相应的部件。

"按意补字"学习单

Instructions: For each new vocabulary word, please fill in the box with the missing components based on its pinyin or English meaning.

1 　chéng kěn 诚 ?　(adj.) sincere

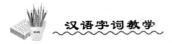

2	gōng zī 工 次?	(n.) salary
3	tuán duì 团 阝?	(n.) group
4	yóu zhèng biān mǎ 邮 政 编 石?	(n.) postcode
5	jiàn tán 健 炎?	(adj.) very conversational

(3) 学生以组为单位,上台用投影片、投影机(或实物投影仪)讲解他们的推测逻辑和讨论结果。

5. 反思:

(1) 教师在设计教学活动时,要特别注意目的词的挑选。每个部件应只适用于一个生词,学生必须找出最佳搭配来补字。要避免学生根据音、义任意搭配,以致于造成过度类推、解释合理却不成字的情况。

(2) 对于难度高的生词,应鼓励各组学生分享他们的加工方式。

方法二:画说汉字

1. 方法界定:

"画说汉字"是用来介绍生词,以教为主的活动,适用于非语境化的教学环境。这套方法属于教师直接指导下的认知加工范畴,通过生动、细致的具象编码来增强记忆效果。

2. 内容:

身高、背景、寒假、适合、面谈、交谈。

3. 设计:

老师通过字源、字形或偏旁部首知识的解说为新字词提供多重编码方式,使之形成多种提醒线索。使学生对汉字的解构、特点有较深入的认识。主要的教学用具是投影仪。

4. 步骤：

   (1) 老师通过使用投影仪展示目的词的字源和古文字形来帮助学生学习汉字。作为实例，投影片及图片引用出处列举如下：

图片、课文出处：《跟我说汉语》（第16课）

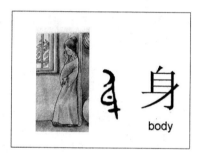

图片出处：Picture Chinese (Long River Press)
古文字图片出处：《常用汉字图解》（北京大学出版社）

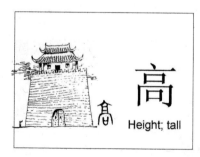

图片、古文字出处：《常用汉字图解》（北京大学出版社）

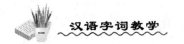

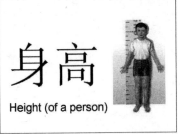

图片出处：网络图片
(Google image search key word: height)
healthguide.howstuffworks.com

图片出处：看图学汉字 *Picture Characters: Learning Characters Through Pictographs* (Published by China Books)

图片、古文字图形出处：《常用汉字图解》（北京大学出版社）

第八章　汉语字词教学方法举例：中级

图片出处：网络图片
(Google image search key word: snow) www.freefoto.com

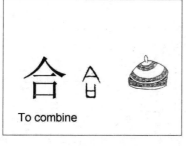

图片、古文字出处：《常用汉字图解》(北京大学出版社)

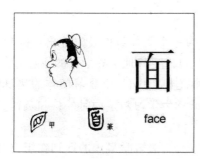

图片、古文字出处：《常用汉字图解》(北京大学出版社)

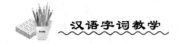

面谈

To speak to sb. face to face

交 cross

图片、古文字出处:《汉字演变五百例》(北京语言学院出版社)

交谈

To talk to each other

5. 反思:

(1) 老师为每个目的词设计投影片时,要为每个图片组件设定好出现的顺序。实际教学时,按照介绍顺序演示辅助图片可以更好地引导学生的注意力。

(2) 如果学生不熟悉目的词中的重要部件,建议增加一个复习部首的热身活动来激活学生头脑中相关的部件知识,降低学生学习新字词时的认知负荷,从而使学习过程更为顺利。

(3) 这个活动适合初、中级的汉字词教学。与初级教学最大的区别在于,中级教学应更注重学生对部件自动化辨识能力的培养,因此投影片上不再以颜色标出重要部件,也不直接告知学生部首的意义。中级汉语的学生应该能够自己辨识已习得的部首,老师主要起促进学生自己为字词建立提醒线索的作用,而不是单向地解说、传授。

(4) 虽然我们强调学生的参与,但整体来讲,这仍然是一个以教师为主导的教学活动,由于信息量大,目的词控制在10个左右比较合适。

方法三:解说汉字

1. 方法界定:

"解说汉字"是用来介绍生词,以教为主的活动,适用于非语境化的教学环境。这套方法属于学生主导的认知加工范畴,教学目的是要促进学生主动积极地选择适合自己的方式编码,给字词编码带来独特性。

2. 内容:

简历、经历、面试、个人、面谈、手机、住址、电话、健谈、自信、诚恳、责任心、善于、熟练、输入、培训、做生意、进行

3. 设计:

将目标词汇按四大主题分类,让学生先分组讨论,再上台报告介绍生词。教学用具包括幻灯片和幻灯机(或实物投影仪)。下面是每个主题的内容。

(面试)　　简历、经历、面试、个人、面谈
(联系方式)　手机、住址、电话
(个人特点)　健谈、自信、诚恳、责任心、善于
(工作能力)　熟练、输入、培训、做生意、进行

4. 步骤:

(1) 学生三人一组,教师以幻灯片形式传给每组一个主题。幻灯片范例如下:

```
主题:面试                    主题:联系
----------------             ----------------
简历                         手机
经历                         住址
面试                         电话
个人
面谈
```

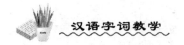

主题:个人特点	主题:能力
健谈 自信 诚恳 责任心 善于	熟练 输入 培训 做生意 进行

5. 反思:

(1) 因为这是三到四个人为一组的活动,集体创意度高,教师可以考虑将少许较高难度的字,尤其是那些字义与部件关联度低,古文字形也无法帮助理解记忆的字词,分配给提早完成任务的小组进行讨论。学生们的创意往往超乎我们的预期,这会让课堂活动增加一些趣味。

(2) 这是一个以学生为中心的教学活动。学生自己想办法运用字形或部首知识分析目的词的音和义的过程也是自学字词的过程。学生在分组讨论时,教师应特别注意各组学生的讨论状况,并提供必要的协助。

(3) 派生活动:

　　a. 鼓励学生在能力所及的范围内用中文进行解释。此外,如果目标生词适合运用多重感觉通道理论来增强学习效果,教师还可以鼓励学生通过表演、画图的方式请其他组的同学猜他们报告的是这一课里的哪个生词。

　　b. 学生自己找同类的生词。老师发给每组同学一张只有主题的空白幻灯片,让学生自己从生词表上寻找与主题相关的字词并做进一步的解说。这样做的优点是可以让学生自己给字词归类,自己选择要讲解的生词;缺点是寻找的过程会占去较多的课堂时间。

方法四:温故知新

1. 方法界定:

　　"温故知新"是用来介绍生词,以教为主的活动。这是一个属于半语境化教学活动,通过旧词来学习新词,强调新旧词汇相联系的图式化学习。

2. 设计:

　　用目标词汇和与其相对应的中文解释做成两组卡片,让学生做双向的配对,通过旧词或本课刚习得的新词来学习新的概念,再从新概念的角度回想其与旧概念之间的联系。教学用具包括白板(或黑板)和两组字卡(即生词卡和中文解释卡)。

4. 步骤：

(1) 老师先领读生词卡，并把生词卡放(或贴)在白板上。生词卡示例如下：

讲解员	自信	工资
性别	手机	日常
谈话	住址	电子邮件
学历	健谈	

(2) 学生两人一组随机抽取一张中文解释卡，两人进行讨论后，从白板上的生字卡中找出相对应的生词，然后上台将中文解释卡放在目的词的旁边。中文解释卡示例如下：

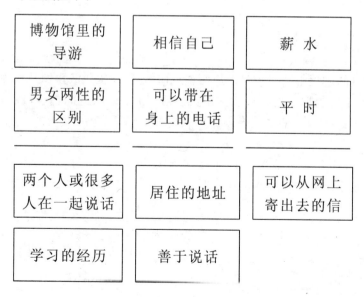

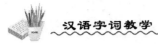

(3) 各组完成配对后,老师迅速过一遍所有的卡片核对答案。

(4) 接下来,老师拿掉白板上的生词卡,只留下中文解释卡,让学生看着白板上的中文解释卡与同一组的同学讨论,逐一回想与中文解释卡相对应的目的词。

5. 反思:

(1) 目的词得事先经过挑选,中文解释需符合中级汉语词汇水平,最好能用上学生刚学过的词来解释这个活动里的目的词。举例来说,学生在前面的活动中学习了"经历"这个生词,在当前这个活动里教师就可以运用"经历"来 对"学历"加以解释,突显新旧字词之间的意义联系,尽可能地在课堂上复习与运用新知识。

(2) 派生活动:

  a. 可再加上活动步骤5,让每组学生用目的词造句、编短对话或小故事。

  b. 提高活动难度,让学生分组讨论,自己用中文解释目标生词。

方法五:故事串词

1. 方法界定:

  "故事串词"是用来巩固生词,以复习为主的活动。这是一个属于半语境化教学活动,教师让学生在故事中复习生词,引导学生注意生词的正确使用方式,并且运用一系列的图片来激活相关信息的提取,从而提供一种有利于记忆的编码形式。

2. 复习内容:

  适合、简历、自信、交谈、熟练、输入、面试。

3. 设计:

  在讲故事的过程中利用生字卡加强重点词的复习,提供故事图片作为一种提醒线索,帮助学生提取目的词。教学用具包括字卡、故事图片、白板(或黑板)、胶带。

4. 步骤:

(1) 老师用图片引出故事段落,用目的词造句说故事,以句为单位让学生跟着复述,然后把字卡放在相应的图片之下。故事图片与相对应的字卡示例如下:

图一　图二　图三　图四　图五

适合　简历　自信　熟练　面试

交谈　输入

(2) 将学生分组（两人一组），让他们看着白板上的图片和字卡练习刚刚学到的句子。

(3) 老师挑选小组（或小组自愿）复述之前学到的句子，重现故事内容。

5. 反思：

(1) 如果课文内容是与节庆或文化相关的主题，这个活动将能发挥更好的教学效果。比如在端午节的主题之下，老师可以利用屈原投江的故事来设计这个活动，用串连目的词的方式说明龙舟和粽子的由来。如此一来，学生不但复习了目的词，还获得了节庆典故知识。生动的历史或民间故事不仅能激发学生的学习兴趣，还能将文化知识融入汉语字词的教学当中去，帮助学习者更有效地建立复杂图式。

(2) 活动里的图片应尽量选择真实生活的写照，现在网络上的多种搜索引擎可以帮助老师们寻找任何主题的图片。真实的照片能够更好地展示真实的社会和文化，亦能在更大程度上帮助学生理解语境和语言赖以产生的文化背景，从而加强目的词的编码与记忆。

(3) 派生活动：

　　a. 针对水平较高的学生，老师可以先说故事，再让各组同学用自己的话复述故事，针对相同的内容可提供不同的表达方式。

　　b. 另一个提高难度的方法是教师只展示图片，学生分组讨论，然后看着图片自己编故事，教师应鼓励学生尽可能地用上本课刚学习的生词。这类派生活动能让各组学生从不同的角度进行表达，各组相互补充，对同一图片可用不同的语言结构或情节来进行描述。

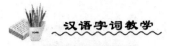

方法六：排除异己

1. 方法界定：

"排除异己"是用来巩固生词，以复习为主的活动。这是一个属于半语境化教学阶段的活动，该教学活动是让学生运用对比和比较的手段思考相似概念之间的差异，再按照词性、事物属性或事物的关系进行归类。

2. 复习内容：

诚恳、自信、面试、面谈、交谈、工资、学费、电话、手机、电子邮件、大学、高中、学历、讲解员

3. 设计：

将目的词和与之相关的其他词汇搭配成组。这里所谓的其他词汇包括了本课的新词和学生以前学过的旧词。让学生讨论各组字词的相似点和不同点。教学用具是词汇卡。

4. 步骤：

(1) 将学生分组，每组抽取一张词汇卡。词汇卡示例如下：

(2)

面试、面谈、交谈
工资、寒假、学费
电话、手机、电子邮件
大学、博物馆、高中
诚恳、自信、学历
导游、讲解员、歌星

(3) 每张词汇卡上都有三个词，学生首先需要讨论这些词之间的联系、差异，然后从中挑出一个与其他两个不同类的词语。

(4) 学生轮流上台报告他们讨论的结果。

5. 反思：

(1) 这个活动主要是应用竞争理论在教学上的启示，帮助学生日后能成功地提取目的词，避免与目的概念有某种联系的其他词相混淆。课堂时间充裕的话，建议先让学生讨论三个词的相同点，对相同点的了解有利于字词的分类和图式结构的建立，然后再进一步讨论三个词的不同点，使学生对每一个目的词所代表的概念有更精确的理解和区分。

(2) 除了按照性质、事物属性来对字词进行分类之外，还可以按词性、部首或关系来分类。至于选用哪种分类进行方式，要根据目的词的特性与课文主题来决定。

(3) 活动派生类型：

    a. 老师可以指定挑选同义词还是反义词以缩短学生讨论过程，简化活动设计。

    b. 让各组学生自己从生词表中挑出三个生词，他们要能说明这些词的共同点以及个别的细微差异。教师在课堂上采用这个派生类型时，要特别注意各组选择的词语，避免小组之间有太多重复的情况发生。

方法七：汉字网络

1. 方法界定：

"汉字网络"是用来巩固生词，以复习为主的活动。这是一个属于半语境化教学活动，教学目标是建立新字词与其他已经学过的字词、个体经验或语境的联系，帮助学生在复习过程中将新字词图式化。

2. 复习内容：

与"做生意"，"个人特点"，"简历"相关的生词

3. 设计：

老师呈现三个主题，鼓励学生依据个体经验围绕主题自己对层次进行分类，分类时特别强调新字词之间的各种联系，并让学生在白板上将这些联系以网络的形式展示出来。教学用具是主题卡、白板和白板笔。

4. 步骤：

(1) 老师将如下三个主题贴（或直接写）在白板上：

| 做生意 | 个人特点 | 简历 |

(2) 学生三到四人一组,每组负责一个主题。学生自己从本课生词表中选出与指定主题有关系的词,并且讨论这些新字词间的联系。

(3) 学生小组上台用白板笔画出汉字网络,然后串词说句子解释生词与主题的联系。网络范例如下:

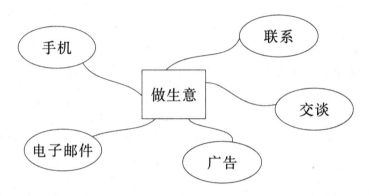

5. 反思:

(1) 这套教学方法是让学生思考如何将孤立的字词组成有联系的整体。归类的目的是使生词与其他概念建立联系,而非零散地储存在大脑中。由于学生是根据自己的经验、想法进行的分类,建立出来的图式结构对他们而言是有独特意义的。正因为如此,这个活动没有标准答案,只要他们能够合情合理地说明网络间的联系,就有助于减少非图式化的认知负荷。此外,学生自发性的组织图式还能有效地控制图式结构的复杂度,从而使学习更有效率。

(2) 派生活动:

  a. 加上步骤4:擦掉主题,让学生根据汉字网络上的提醒线索,回忆复述主题,加强表征之间的联结和转换。

  b. 再加上步骤5:保留主题,擦掉网络中的生词,让学生分组讨论、回想,根据前几个步骤中所建立的联结线索,提取相关信息,补上目的词,重建网络,从而巩固新字词的图式结构。

方法八:掀掀乐

1. 方法界定:

  "掀掀乐"是用来巩固生词,以复习为主的活动。这是一个小组竞赛活动,用于训练学生对目标字词的快速反应能力,通过竞赛的形式激发学生的集体荣誉感、提高学习积极性。

2. 复习内容:

  责任心、能力、博物馆、导游、交谈、个人、日常、简历、自信、寒假、面谈、工资

3. 设计:

　　让学生分组竞赛,掀卡片抢答,用目的词造句。教学用具是1张纸板,贴上12张生字卡,将所有的生字卡对折遮盖目的词。

4. 步骤:

(1) 老师将全班学生分成两组,两组轮流派人上台掀开纸板上的对折卡。卡片范例如下所示:

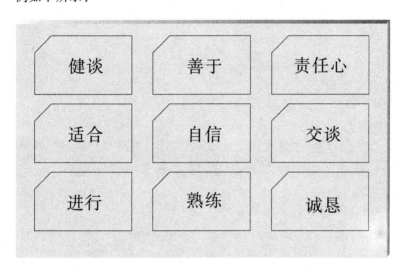

(2) 掀开卡片的学生如能说出目的词的英文意思,得一分;同组队员若能用目的词造一个句子,再得一分。反之,同组的组员若不能顺利得分,就得把机会让给另一组,让其他人抢答。

(3) 积分高的小组获胜。

5. 反思:

(1) 在汉语字词教学中适当运用竞赛活动能够活跃课堂气氛,使教学手段更多样化,让枯燥的字词复习转变为学生乐于接受的游戏活动,可以激励学生的学习热情,与此同时,还可以在有限的复习时间内大幅度地增加提取信息的频度。老师在竞赛过程中应当鼓励同组成员互相帮助提醒,提高所有学生的参与度。

(2) 派生活动:

　　a. 让掀卡片的学生用动作、画图或用同义词解释等方法让其他组员猜目的词。这类派生活动应用了多重感觉通道理论,让学生进行表演性的教学活动,为目的词提供多重编码方式。需要指出的是,教师在应用这种派生活动时必须考虑哪些字词的编码适用于表演性活动,如此才能在不浪费课堂时间的前提下,为学生带来最佳记忆效果。

b. 一种简化活动的方式是运用两组字卡(一组目的词,一组英文解释或中文解释),让学生进行掀卡配对,完成最多正确配对的小组获胜。"掀掀乐"是一个弹性很大的活动,老师们可以配合实际课堂教学情况调整抢答方式、掀卡片的方式以及卡片配对的选择。

c. 另一个提高参与度的派生活动是学生两人为一组,同组的一人拿目的词卡,另一人拿英文解释或中文解释卡,组内配对完成后,两人再一起为每个目的词造句。这种活动能在单位时间内大幅度地提高每个学生的参与度。缺点是教师得事先准备大量的小卡片供各组使用,建议将卡片的制作(至少目的词的部分)布置为学生课前的预习作业。

方法九: 毛遂自荐

1. 方法界定:

"毛遂自荐"是一个属于语境化的教学活动,教学目标以应用新词为主,使学生能看懂中文简历表格并且能用中文正确地填写、介绍自己。

2. 内容:

本课所有生词

3. 设计:

让学生填写一份中文简历,并根据简历内容上台介绍自己。

4. 步骤:

(1) 老师将中文简历表格发给每个学生,让他们根据个人实际经验、状况填写简历。表格范例如下所示:

简历

姓名:	年龄:
性别:	电子邮件:
邮政编码:	手机:
教育背景: ☐ 大学毕业 ☐ 高中毕业 ☐ 其他:_____	
工作经历:	
个人特点:	

(2) 填写完毕后,指定学生或让学生自愿上台介绍自己。
5. 反思:
(1) 填写个人简历是求职过程中不可或缺的准备工作之一。许多学生学习中文的最终目的就是希望他们的中文能力能在找工作时为他们带来优势。这个活动将目的词教学与相应的语境、任务结合起来,让学生吸收、理解、运用新字词,训练读、写、说的能力。
(2) 派生活动:

  a. 若要进一步加强小组阅读训练,老师可以收集所有学生填写好的简历,再将姓名部分遮盖起来,把简历发给不同组的同学,让学生读一读,猜一猜这是哪个同学的简历。

  b. 另一个活动也是利用学生完成的简历所衍生的:学生两人一组,老师给各组分发一则招聘广告和两份其他同学填好的简历,让学生讨论,根据广告内容与简历的描述决定要面试的人选。小组报告时要解释为什么这个人适合这项工作。这种形式一方面可以促进学生思考、理解和记忆,另一方面也为最后的任务活动做了一个很好的铺垫。招聘的条件与工作机会的类别也可以让学生自行决定,以提高学生的阅读理解动机,找到最好的面试人选。

方法十: 精挑细选

1. 方法界定:
  "精挑细选"是一个属于语境化的任务型教学活动,教学目标是要让学生在模拟实境的任务中运用本课所学到的生词进行面试应对。
2. 内容:
  本课所有生词
3. 设计:
  提供给学生一个模拟真实生活中的面试情境,让学生在交际活动中运用新字词。教学用具是在前一个活动中所完成的简历。
4. 步骤:
(1) 学生两人一组拿着填好的中文简历模拟面试过程。
(2) 学生运用本课学到的生词进行面谈。
(3) 分组上台演示面试经过。
5. 反思:
(1) 最后任务的演示是要把语言形式与实际意义结合起来。为了完成这个任务,学生将主动积极地产生需求并寻找恰当的字词以正确表达自己的思想,因此,完成任务的过程也是一个重要的学习环节。这个任务的目的是要增强学生的

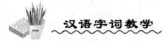

学习动机,使其在积极参与任务的过程中促进自然且有意义的语言应用。

(2) 这个活动采用合作学习的模式,利于学生创造性地运用所学到的字词知识,也利于加强学生彼此之间及与老师之间的交流,因此课堂上的语言交流量大为提升,这将促使学生在掌握知识的过程中积极主动、互助共进,克服课堂表达的羞怯感,从而提高教学效果。

在本章开始时提到,上述十种方法配有教学实况录像,由于时间限制,在录像里所展示的上述十种方法是以最简练的方式呈现,实际应用时,老师们可根据学生的掌握程度和字词的难易度,灵活掌握时间,采用不同的方法并对这些方法进行改变以适应教学实际。

Chapter 9 第九章
Vocabulary instruction methods demonstration: Advanced Level

汉语字词教学方法举例:高级

在这一章中,我将介绍重点介绍十种高年级字词教学方法。具体的方法演示请观摩配套出售的教学录像,本书所附为演示版。在介绍方法之前,我先向大家介绍一下高年级字词教学的特点。

教学特点

在高年级对外汉语教学中,汉字教学往往会成为被忽视的对象。究其原因,无外乎是认为高年级汉语学习者已经具备了相当的自学能力,因而如汉字、词汇这样的基本语言知识就不再需要教师进行专门、详细的讲解了。实则不然。熟悉高年级对外汉语教学的人都知道,这一时期学习者接触到的词汇中包含有大量的具有重要语法意义的虚词,如副词、连词、关联词等等,以及在语用学层面与不同语体、语境相适宜的实词。因此,汉字和词汇的教学在高年级阶段绝不是语言知识教学中一项孤立的内容,而是密切联系着各种语言知识及各项语言技能。可以说,汉语学习者能否在高年级阶段实现在语言的准确度、多样化和流畅度上的全面而显著的提升,字词教学依然是举足轻重的。

当然,相对于初级和中级汉语字词教学而言,为了与高年级汉语学习者的水平相适应,高年级字词教学应该体现出自己鲜明的特点。首先,在教学组织上,突出以学生为中心的理念。教师应大大减少直接讲解和指导的比例,在课堂中转变为引导者和辅助者的角色,带领学生运用他们已有的知识和能力去获取新知识,建立新旧知识之间的联系网络,推动学生的主动性学习。其次,教学活动的设计应突出合理的复杂性。减少学生表演活动和非语言的意象编码活动,更多地运用语言直观的活动,做到直观而不直接。图式化教学中,教学活动帮助学生所建构的知识图式应实现由简单向复杂的过渡。另外,在完成活动的过程中,力求融入对学生听、说、读、写各项语言技能的综合训练,使字词教学真正体现出高年级水平。第三,减少非语境化教学活动,而侧重于半语境化、语境化教学。通过具体语境,让学生感受到词汇知识是生动的、有意义的,从而能促进学习的积极性,加深他们对词汇的理解和记忆。同时,通过设计典型性语境来强化学生对目标词语的正确运用,以及对目标词语使用范围的正确理解。第四,汉字教学不能独立于课文内容之外,而应与课文紧密结合。运用课文中所提供的语料,能帮助学生了解目标词语的常用方法和语境,也有助于保持教学内容的一致性、连贯性。因此,教师应在词汇的例句和练习中优先选用课文中的句子、语段或相关资料(如录像等)。在学习汉字词汇的同时,加深学生对课文内容的印象,使汉字学习和课文学习相辅相成。

教学方法

下面我将具体列举十种高年级汉字教学方法,为了方便起见,这十种方法运用在一堂字词教学课中。在实际的教学中,老师们可以根据教学实际选择使用。

1. **教学内容**

    本课所使用的教材为《中国社会文化写实》,(Hong Gang Jin, De Bao Xu, James Hargett 2000; *China Scene: An Advanced Chinese Multimedia Course*; Cheng & Tsui Company)。选用的课文是第十一课《市场经济》。这一课以改革开放后一个自发形成的个体批发市场——白沟市场为缩影,反映了市场经济给中国带来的巨大改变以及欣欣向荣的发展态势。

    本课学习和练习的生词有:经商、日趋、红火、仍旧、赔钱、起家、照常、自产、挑战、手头、行情、利润、例外、决策、不断、大多、绝对、机遇、依据、超前、批量、了不起、指令性、客流量、可想而知、购销两旺、车水马龙、随处可见、个体经济、日用小商品、白手起家、先决条件

2. **教学目标**

    字词课的教学目标如下:

    (1) 通过主动性学习活动,使学生掌握目标词语的基本知识,包括词性、词义和基本用法等。

    (2) 帮助学生建立起新的词汇知识与已有知识、图式之间的联系系统,以旧知识来促进对新知识的理解、学习和记忆。

    (3) 运用真实的典型性语料,引导学生对目标词语和相似的已学旧词进行辨析、比较,从而强化学生对目标词语的意义和确切使用范围的正确理解。

    (4) 通过一系列模拟真实语境的活动,促使学生主动运用目标词语,加速新知识的内化过程,帮助学生实现对目标词语的正确、熟练应用。

3. **教学步骤**

    本课向大家展示了十种针对高年级汉语学习者而特别设计的字词教学方法。诚然,能够应用于高年级字词教学中的教学方法远远不止十种。在这里对这十种方法的设计和选用,主要是基于对课文内容和目标词语特点的考量。每种教学方法都不是万能的,都有其适用的词语类别和范围。因此,教师在设计教学方法时必须从目标词语本身的类别、特点出发,并结合课文形式和内容的特点,如此

设计出的教学方法和活动才有可能实现效度的最大化,才能有效地、有针对性地促进学生掌握新的字词知识。本课旨在通过十种有代表性的具体教学方法(见下表)的展示,使大家能直观地感受到高年级汉语字词教学的特点。

如表所示,本课展示的十种教学方法可以划分为三大教学环节:介绍生词,复习、巩固生词和应用生词。首先,在介绍生词环节中,所使用的教学方法有四种:引导学生发挥学习主动性的"生词侦探";兼有图片、动作等意象编码及语言直观手段,建立起新旧知识联系,并带领学生利用词素线索,对目标词进行深层次加工的"按意索词";运用语料库教学法,训练学生以典型性语料为基础,通过理解、分析、比较来明确目标词语的准确意义和使用范围的"深究细品"和"辨析比词"。接下来,复习、巩固生词环节展示了三种教学方法:通过寻找近义词的活动,联系起相似的旧词和新词,从而帮助学生更好地理解和记忆新词的"以旧换新";为连词和关联词专门设计的学生合作活动"你说我接";以及兼顾新词复习与多种语言技能(如听力)操练的"视听搜词"。最后,为应用生词环节所设计的三种教学方法分别是:运用视听手段和不同形式的语境化综合技能任务来强化学生正确使用新词的能力的"解说录像"、"采访准备"和"现场采访"。

十种教学方法列举

教学环节	教学方法
介绍生词	生词侦探
	按意索词
	深究细品
	辨析比词
复习生词	以旧换新
	你说我接
	视听搜词
运用生词	解说录像
	采访准备
	现场采访

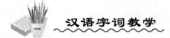

以上十种教学方法的设计除了遵循由介绍到巩固到应用的逻辑主线之外,其中所使用的教学活动也是依照从非语境化到半语境化再到语境化的逐步过渡来安排的。同时,以少量的意象编码活动和大量不同形式的语言编码活动相搭配,增加课堂教学的多样性。另外,在对学生使用目标词语的要求方面,也建构起由单句向复句和语段过渡,由相对控制式的操练向开放式的操练过渡的难度坡度。

4. <u>教学评估与反馈</u>

在字词教学中,对学生的学习效果进行即时检测,并给予及时有效的评价和反馈也是一个重要的组成部分。在本课展示的十种教学方法中,几乎每种方法都包括有评估与反馈这项内容。比如,在学习新字词的环节,"生词侦探"这个主动性学习活动中,每个学生都要介绍一个目标词语的词性、词义,并且造句,教师和其他学生就会对他介绍的知识内容和对目标词语的使用情况进行监督和评价,及时纠正出现的错误,引起注意,避免错误习惯的形成。又如,在"深究细品"和"辨析比词"等方法中,紧跟在介绍新知识之后的判断正误、改写句子、完成句子、选词填空等各种有很强针对性的练习,也是一种及时监测学生学习效果,强化对新知识、新图式正确理解、记忆和应用的有效手段。除此之外,在对新字词的复习和应用环节中,教师更会特别留意学生的语言使用情况,及时进行评估和反馈,强调新字词的正确使用,引导学生发现并纠正典型性偏误,帮助学生提高语言的准确度。

需要指出的是,在高年级汉语字词教学中,教师应有意识地将评价与反馈的机会更多地留给学生,激发学生之间的讨论,引导学生主动地进行这种元认知层面的思考和训练。这样,学生在互相监督和评价的过程中,又能再一次地加深对正确知识的印象,加速新字词知识的深加工和内化。下面是具体的方法演示。

方法一:生词侦探

1. 内容:

介绍"经商、了不起、利润、仍旧、决策、壮大、不断、指令性、超前"九个生词。

2. 设计:

作为这次生词课的第一个活动,我设计了这个非语境化的、促使学生主动学习的教学方法,来介绍一些对理解本课课文内容很关键的实词。所使用的材料和教具如下:

(1) 展示全部目标生词的PPT:

经商	了不起	利润
仍旧	决策	壮大
不断	指令性	超前

PPT1

本张PPT上展示的是本教学法中学生要学习的一组生词,共九个。之所以将它们归为一组,是因为这些生词都是与课文主要内容紧密相关的,是理解课文内容和讨论相关话题时必须掌握的重要实词。这里,用一页PPT将整组生词展示出来,旨在给学生在接下来的猜词活动中提供一个生词范围,有助于他们准确定位目标词。

(2) 活动任务单。每张任务单上给出不同的生词,并指明学生需要去了解的有关这个生词的知识点,下面是任务单示例:

生词	词性	中文意思	句子
经商			

3. 教学步骤:

(1) 使用PPT展示这个活动介绍的所有目标生词。

(2) 教师布置活动任务,提醒学生在学习目标生词过程中需要注意的知识点,介绍任务单。

(3) 下发任务单,给学生两分钟的时间自行完成对目标词语的学习,填写好任务单上所要求的内容。

(4) 请每个学生逐一报告自己分配到的生词的词性和中文意思,其他学生充当生词侦探,根据这些线索猜出目标词语。然后,由这名学生使用目标词语造句,教师引导其他学生进行评价,对不准确的使用情况通过全班讨论来加以纠正。

(5) 检查学生是否还有疑问,回收任务单。

4. 反思:

通过这个教学方法的展示,大家可以看到,在对高年级学习者进行字词教学时,即使是一个非语境化的介绍生词的活动也不应该是简单的、被动的,而应成为促进学生主动性学习的契机,培养学生对词语的基本知识和用法的自学能力。另外,任务的设计应该体现出层次感和复杂性。学生完成任务的过程是一个从学到用的过程。同时,报告、猜词和互相评价、纠错的步骤更兼顾了词语知识的学习和语言技能的训练,如口语和听力。而活动中训练学生用中文来解释目标词语,这样做能有效帮助学生建立起新词与旧词,新知识与已有的语言、知识之间的联系。因此,"生词侦探"这一教学方法很好地达到了促使学生进行主动性学习和以学生的旧有知识促进对新知识的理解、学习和记忆等教学目标。

需要注意的是,这个教学方法所强调的不是一个学生对一个目标词语的掌握,而是全班学生对全部目标词语的掌握。而这一点正是通过一些学生之间的互动环节来实现的。一人介绍,全班猜词,让教师得以了解其他学生对目标词语的熟悉程度。同样,一人造句、全班评价、纠错的互动也间接反映出其他学生对目标词语的理解和学习效果。因此,教师应该对学生互动过程中出现的一些信息保持高度敏感,以确保学生们对所有的目标生词有一致的学习成果。

此教学方法在使用中还可以有下面几种变型。一是任务单上不指定生词,而是由学生在目标生词的范围中自选一个,进行活动。那么,后报告的人就有可能因为被别人介绍了自己选的词而需要临时换词来报告。这种情况也能帮助强化学生对全部目标词语的熟悉和掌握。二是如果教学对象是低年级学习者,受其中文语言能力所限,可将用中文来解释目标生词的要求改成用学生母语或用表演的方式来进行,以降低本活动的难度,从而提高其在低年级汉字词教学中的可操作性。

方法二:按意索词

1. 内容:

介绍"手头、车水马龙、个体经济、赔钱、日用小商品"等生词。

2. 设计:

这一组生词中,有的表意非常形象,有的具有某种典型结构。因此,根据这些因素,我设计了这个非语境化的教学方法。这个方法的特点是不但使用到了图片、动作等意象编码手段帮助学生更加形象地理解目标词语,而且能运用多种手段,引导学生对目标生词进行深度加工,促进理解和记忆,加速内化过程。比如,通过对词素的精细分析来加深理解、进行比较。或者,利用词语的典型结构进行分类、联系,建立同类生词网络。在本方法中使用到的材料和教具有:

(1) 展示和介绍生词的PPTs:

图片一

PPT2

(图片来源:http://fzzg.zhulao.gov.cn/ShowArticle.asp?ArticleID=4084)

上面这张PPT的使用具体分为两步:第一步,展示本教学法介绍的整组生词,共五个。这五个生词具有一些共同的特点,或表意形象、生动,词素与整词词义联系紧密;或具有某种典型结构,可以通过词素来归类,建立生词网络。这些特点使得这些生词得以成为使用词素分析法来按意索词的合适对象。第二步,展示一张马路上交通繁忙的图片,目的是运用意象编码手段,引导学生定位第一个目标词"车水马龙",对词语意义首先获得一个形象的认识,帮助记忆。

> **车水马龙**
> —— 车像流水,马像游龙。形容车马或车辆很多,来往不绝。
>
> 猜一猜,下面哪一词的意思和"车水马龙"差不多?说出你的理由。
>
> 闭门造车　　川流不息　　马到功成

PPT3

这张PPT的上半部分,是教师引导学生通过看图片和分析词素说出对目标词"车水马龙"的理解之后,给出词语意义的标准解释。并再次提醒学生注意,各个词素的意义如何反映在词语的整体意义中,而整词的词义又是怎样通过词素之间互相结合来构成的,从而加深学生对词素分析的具体方法和作用的认识。PPT的下半部分,展示了一个为目标词找近义词的深加工活动。这个活动中所备选的三个词都直接或间接地含有目标词的词素或部分词义。活动过程中,学生需要再次运用到词素分析技巧来选出答案。这样做既深化了对目标词语的理解,建立了近义词之间的联系,也有助于学生实际掌握词素分析法。

图片二

PPT4

（教师自有图片）

图片二引入对第二个目标词的学习，同样用到了以图引词的意象编码手段。PPT的上半部再次给出整组生词，提供选词范围。下半部展示一张超市宣传单的局部，引导学生说出目标词"日用小商品"，然后再围绕目标词进行接下来的活动。

手头
　　——伸手可以拿到
例：
　　这段时间我手头很紧，上个月的工资已经快用完了，可这个月的工资十天以后才发。现在我只能这样安慰自己："忍忍吧，等拿到工资以后手头就宽裕了。"
（手头紧／手头宽裕）
　　——表示坏／好的经济状况

PPT5

上面这张PPT是配合本教学法中第三个目标词的学习的。其上内容的展示分为如下步骤：一，展示整组生词，教师以手中执笔的动作，引导学生定位目标词"手头"。二，整组生词消失，仅剩目标词，并给出其本义的标准解释。三，展示一段语料,提醒学生注意"手头"在使用中的一些特殊搭配。四,引导学生在文本中推断出"手头"的引申义及其特殊搭配的具体意义,给出标准解释。

```
手头    车水马龙    赔钱
 个体经济    日用小商品

       赔钱

      动词＋钱

   赚钱  挣钱  攒钱
      凑钱  花钱
```

PPT6

使用上面的这张PPT来学习第四个目标词。具体步骤如下:一,展示整组生词,通过找反义词的活动,引导学生定位目标词"赔钱"。二,给出目标词,提醒学生注意其结构。三,在学生说出正确答案后,给出目标词具有的典型结构。并引导学生说出更多具有这种结构的词,以结构进行归类,建立生词网络,帮助新词内化。四,展示例词。

```
手头    车水马龙    赔钱
 个体经济    日用小商品

个体经济

   私营经济    国营经济
   市场经济    计划经济
```

PPT7

上面是第五个目标词所使用的PPT,使用方法同前一张相似。先通过找近义词的手段,引导学生在整组生词中找出目标词"个体经济"。然后,带领大家总结各种经济体制,并成对给出例词。

(2) 一支用来形象示意的笔。

3. 教学步骤:

(1) 在PPT上展示本组目标生词,学生集体朗读,检查熟悉度。教师注意正音。

(2) 展示图片一,引导学生说出目标词语"车水马龙"及他们的理解,并给出标准解释。

(3) 进行一个找出近义词的活动。在给出的一组词语中,训练学生通过精细分析各个词素,辨析比较,确定"车水马龙"的近义词"川流不息",强化对目标生词的理解。

(4) 展示图片二,导入目标词语"日用小商品"。并通过提问的方式,联系到学生已知的"超市"、"药店"等相关词语,建立起生词网络。

(5) 用手中执笔这一动作,引导学生理解"手头"一词的本义。

(6) 展示一段真实语料,请学生朗读。引导学生们基于文本分析出"手头"的引申义,并了解常用搭配。

(7) 通过找反义词的手段,导入目标词语"赔钱"。

(8) 点出"动词+钱"这一典型结构,让学生说出更多有着这种结构的词,进行复习和归类,联系起原有知识和图式。

(9) 通过找近义词的手段,引导学生说出目标生词"个体经济",并带领大家总结各种经济体制,用"……经济"的结构为纲,串起同类词语的网络。

4. 反思:

高年级的学习者,因为之前的知识积累和技能训练,已经拥有了相当的词汇量和语言能力。这也就使得通过分析词素来理解新词成为可能。而词素分析的方法是一种认识、理解生词的有效手段。因此,在高年级汉字词教学中,教师应有意识地培养学生使用词素分析法的习惯,促使学生在自学能力上也达到相应的高水平。这正是我把此种教学方法命名为"按意索词"的主要原因。不难发现,无论是在意象编码活动中,还是在以典型结构分类的活动中,词素所发挥的作用都是被强调的重点。对图式化教学而言,词素往往就像是联系起新旧知识的桥梁。用旧知识来促进对新知识的学习;学习新知识的同时又复习了有共同点的旧词。如此以旧促新,以新带旧,温故与知新相辅相成。同时,生词网络联系的建立,能帮助学生整理原有知识,并将新词融入已有图式之中,从而实现更深的理解、更牢的记忆和更快的内化。

在本方法的教学展示中,还可以看到一段精彩的学生互帮互助片段。这又再一次涉及教师如何能激发学生之间的互动这一话题。我在这里使用的可以说是一种"打太极"的方法。当学生提问时,教师不要急于作答,而是在第一时间把问题抛还给全班学生,借以引发思考和讨论。事实证明,这一点是非常有效的。录像中,另外一位学生就很好地解答了自己同学的问题,之后教师再做了一些补充。这种学生间自觉地合作互动正是高年级课堂特点的一个重要体现。

方法三: 深究细品

1. 内容:

　　　介绍"红火"等生词。

2. 设计:

　　本教学法介绍的生词有一个共同的特点,那就是有自己特定的使用范围、修饰对象。因为学生已经学习过这些词语的近义词,所以学习的重点已经不再是词义了,而是需要强调其确切的使用方法和语境,与其他近义词相区别,提高学生使用目标词语的准确度。有鉴于此,在这个半语境化教学方法中,我选用了语料库法。从一组体现目标词语典型使用语境的真实语料出发,带领学生先体会后总结,归纳出关于目标词语的重要知识点和使用规则。这里的教学活动使用了以下材料和教具:

(1) 用于展示例句、介绍生词和进行练习的PPTs:

> 1、美国的旅游业一天比一天红火,9年来持续增长。
> 2、奥运期间,北京市各大商场生意红火,中外顾客购物踊跃。
> 3、今天的中国农民越来越富裕,日子越过越红火。
> 4、近年来,各类职业学校办得很红火。

PPT8

　　本张PPT展示了从语料库中选取的包含目标词语的典型例句,共四句。在这些例句所体现的"红火"一词的典型使用语境中,首先让学生来体会、分析、推断出"红火"的词义。接下来,提醒学生注意、归纳"红火"所修饰的对象范围和其特点。

> 词语用法：
>
> "红火"一般用于形容<u>生意</u>、<u>行业</u>、<u>生活</u>等兴旺、热闹。

PPT9

在逐步引导学生从语料中发现、体会目标词"红火"的意义和使用特点后,本张PPT给出了"红火"正确使用范围和方法的正式总结。

> 练习：
>
> 一、判断正误：
>
> 1.这条马路很红火。　　　　　　　（　）
>
> 2.我的邻居越来越红火。　　　　　（　）
>
> 3.这个产品在世界各地都卖得特别红火。（　）
>
> 二、用"红火"完成句子：
>
> 1、这家小店_____。
>
> 2、随着人们生活水平的提高,_____。

PPT10

完成了对目标词语的重要知识点和使用规则的学习后,使用本张PPT展示出为检验学生学习效果和掌握情况而设计的练习题,以帮助学生及时巩固所学知识,强化对目标词的使用范围和使用方法的正确理解。

（2）用于巩固练习和检查学习效果的习题单（见PPT10）。

3. 教学步骤：

（1）使用PPT展示从语料库中选取的使用目标词语的例句。

（2）引导学生从例句所提供的语境中归纳出目标词的词义。

（3）提醒学生注意目标词语典型的使用语境,请学生在白板上划出各例句中目标词语的修饰对象。

（4）进一步引导学生归纳出目标词语的特定使用范围。

(5) 使用PPT展示出正式的使用规则。
　　(6) 下发习题单,学生完成其习题。
　　(7) 学生互相评价、讨论习题答案,巩固、强化对目标词语使用特点的理解。
　　(8) 重复步骤一至步骤七,介绍下一个目标词语。
4. 反思:

　　对高年级学习者而言,影响他们语言准确度的一个重要方面就是能否熟练掌握近义词或同义词的细微差别,对它们进行正确的使用。因而,强化学生对这类词语的确切使用范围的正确理解,成为高年级字词教学的主要教学目标之一。"深究细品"这个教学方法正是为了实现这一目标而特别设计的。其中所使用的语料库法,已经被研究证明了是帮助学生正确认识目标词语使用特点的有效方法。

　　在介绍这类词语时,教师不仅应该懂得如何从语料库中选择可以体现目标词语典型使用语境的例句,还应该知道怎样来引导学生抽丝剥茧,抓住学习的重点、难点。教师引导学生分析例句,归纳出重要的知识点,应该是层层递进,层层深入,具有清晰的条理性。每一遍阅读例句的具体目的是什么,学生需要特别注意的点在哪里,教师都应该做出清楚明了的交代,让学生感受到鲜明的层次。第一遍读例句往往是要学生理解词义;第二遍的阅读是要提醒学生注意目标词语特定的使用环境和对象;到了第三遍时,可以要学生找出目标词语在使用时的一些常用搭配;第四遍,则要学生体会包含目标词语的句子在意义或结构上的特点……另外,教师应该在学生完成体会、分析、归纳之后,进入巩固、练习之前,给出对所涉及知识点的简要总结,确保学生获得了正确的认识。这样做是为了避免学生将错误的观念带入练习,得到强化,形成影响长久的错误习惯。

方法四:辨析比词

1. 内容:
　　介绍"依据"等生词,并比较"依据"与"根据"等。
2. 设计:
　　这也是一个以语料库为基础的半语境化教学方法。为了减少学生在学习和使用目标词语时,因近义词之间的竞争而造成的混淆和错用情况,本方法特别突出了比较的内容。在比较中辨析、区别,完成对目标词语的深度加工,形成对其意义和用法的鲜明而深刻的正确印象。使用到的材料和教具有:

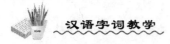

(1) 展示例句、介绍使用规则和进行练习的PPTs：

> 依据/根据
>
> 1. 市场经济要求企业严格依据合同协议办事。
> 2. 依据国家的人口政策，一个家庭只能有一个孩子。
> 3. 依据法律的规定，这种行为已经对他人构成了伤害。
> 4. 根据新闻的报道，我们可以想象出当时的情况。
> 5. 根据经理所说，公司会在春节前将工资发给职工。
> 6. 只有根据她现在的情况，医生才能决定怎样对她进行治疗。

PPT11

本课生词中有"依据"一词，而学生之前已经学过了"根据"一词。两词词义相似，但使用范围和方法上却不尽相同。为了提高学生在语言使用上的准确度，本教学法特别把两词成对提出，使用大量例句，在典型语境中进行比较，以确保学生对它们的不同用法有鲜明的认识。因此，上面的第一张PPT就展示出为这组近义词在语料库中各选取的三个典型例句，共六句。学生可以通过"根据"来了解"依据"的意思，但是教师特别提醒学生注意两词所搭配的对象的不同。

> 依据/根据
>
> 依据 ＋ 法律、规定、协议、政策、
> 　　　　合同等正式文件；
> 　　　（不可以与情况或某人说的话搭配）
>
> 根据 ＋ 协议、规定；情况、报道；
> 　　　　某人的话。

PPT12

学生通过分析语料，归纳出"依据"和"根据"这对近义词的不同典型搭配后，教师用上面这张PPT展示出两词不同使用范围、特点的正式规则。

> 练习:
>
> 用"根据"或"依据"改写句中的划线词:
>
> 1、<u>据</u>有关消息报道,这个市场的经济地位日趋重要。
>
> 2、<u>据</u>他分析,汽油价格还会继续上涨。
>
> 3、<u>据</u>相关协议规定,他去中国留学的全部费用都由中国政府承担。

PPT13

  上面这张PPT的用意是介绍完重要知识点和规则后,仍然用针对性鲜明的练习来检查学生的学习效果和掌握情况,巩固、加深学生的正确理解。

  (2)用于巩固练习和检查学习效果的习题单(见PPT13)。

3. 教学步骤:

  (1)使用PPT展示目标词语和其近义词以及为每个词所选的例句。

  (2)引导学生阅读两组例句,对这组近义词在用法上的细微差别进行辨析。

  (3)将学生分为两组,分别讨论其中一个词的具体用法。

  (4)学生报告讨论结果。提醒学生注意例句中影响到词语使用的关键词,引导他们归纳出这组近义词在用法、语境上的差别。

  (5)使用PPT展示出每个词正式的使用规则,强调它们之间的不同点。

  (6)分发习题单,学生完成上面的练习。

  (7)学生互相讨论、评价习题答案,巩固、加强对本组近义词不同的使用特点的正确认识。

  (8)重复步骤一至步骤七,介绍下一组进行辨析的词语。

4. 反思:

  这个立足于语料库,突出对近义词之间细微差别的辨析、比较的教学方法,也是为了达到强化学生对目标词语的使用语境的清晰认识和理解这一教学目标。研究证明,近义词之间界限模糊,相互影响和干扰,会给学习者在学习生词和正确使用上带来不小的困扰。所以,当生词中存在这类词语时,必须要引起学生的特别注意。使用典型例句,进行细致的比较,在第一时间帮助学生划分出近义词之

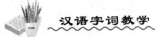

间鲜明的界限,清晰地知道它们的差别,非常有利于提升高年级学生的学习效果和语用能力。

在这里,对于练习题的设计,我也有一些建议。这种紧跟在学习之后,用于巩固训练的练习题应该是有着很强的针对性的。重点突出,直接考查学生对于目标词语的目标语言知识的掌握程度。这样的练习才能让教师及时发现学生认识上的薄弱环节,深化正确理解,形成清晰的印象。

方法五:以旧换新

1. 内容:

复习"随处可见、客流量、仍旧、照常、购销两旺、了不起、例外、车水马龙、自产、大多、决策、指令性、白手起家、日趋、绝对"等生词。

2. 设计:

作为复习、巩固生词环节中使用的第一个教学方法,在这里我设计的是一个以词为单位的,为新旧知识搭桥的半语境化方法,主要是对本课部分生词进行词义层面的复习:在一段例文提供的语境中,让学生进行新词与已知词汇、语句的配对活动,将旧的表达方式换成新的表达方式,从而达到复习新词,巩固所学知识及加深理解的目的。同时,本方法中使用的语料亦有一定的阅读量,可以训练学生的阅读技能。可以说,这是一个融合了直接的生词复习和间接的阅读练习的教学方法。以下是本方法中使用到的材料和教具:

(1) 展示例文的PPT:

> 汉正街小商品市场被称为"天下第一街"。这个市场非常著名,每天都有很多人慕(mù)名(míng)到这里来买东西,专门从外地过来的顾客也是(到处都看得到)。就算在很少市场营业的星期一,这个市场里的商店(还是)(和平常一样)营业,而且(买卖非常兴旺)。
>
> 汉正街市场里的经营者(大部分)是做批发生意的,只有少数几家(和别人不一样)。这里商店卖的商品一部分是由他们(自己生产)的,也有从南方购买回来的。
>
> 这个市场里的经营者们依据市场的情况来做出生意上的(决定),赔钱的买卖他们(肯定)不会做。随着市场经济的发展,汉正街小商品市场的经济地位(一天比一天)重要。

PPT14

本张PPT展示一篇与课文内容相似的短文,是由教师根据活动需要自己写作的。短文里用到的都是学生已经学过的旧词,其中括号中的词语和短语可以用本课所学的近义或同义新词来替换。因为短文共有三段,所以接下来的换词活动,学生也是分为三组来进行,每组负责一段。(见任务单)

(2)提供三组待选生词的展示板。不同的组别以不同的纸张颜色来区别。

随处可见	了不起	决策
客流量	例外	指令性
仍旧	车水马龙	日趋
照常	自产	白手起家
购销两旺	大多	绝对

上面生词板上展示的三组备选生词为每组学生提供了一个选择新词的范围,旨在帮助学生更准确地找到与旧知识相匹配的新词,以旧带新,实现复习、巩固的效果。

(3)三张分别包含有例文中不同段落的任务单:

任务单一:

请将下面一段话中括号里的词语换成本课的新词:

汉正街小商品市场被称为"天下第一街"。这个市场非常著名(mù míng),每天都有很多人慕名到这里来买东西,专门从外地过来的顾客也是(到处都看得到)。就算在很少市场营业的星期一,这个市场里的商店(还是)(和平常一样)营业,而且(买卖非常兴旺)。

任务单二：

请将下面一段话中括号里的词语换成本课的新词：

汉正街市场里的经营者(大部分)是做批发生意的,只有少数几家(和别人不一样)。这里的商店卖的商品一部分是由他们(自己生产)的,也有从南方购买回来的。

任务单三：

请将下面一段话中括号里的词语换成本课的新词：

这个市场里的经营者们依据市场的情况来做出生意上的(决定),赔钱的买卖他们(肯定)不会做。随着市场经济的发展,汉正街小商品市场的经济地位(一天比一天)重要。

3. 教学步骤：

(1) 用PPT展示学生在活动中将要阅读、处理的包含学生已有知识的例文。

(2) 根据例文的三个段落,将学生分为三个小组进行活动,布置任务,分发任务单。

(3) 每组学生负责处理一个段落,将括号中的旧词、旧语句换成合适的本课学习的新词。

(4) 展示提供待选新词范围的生词板,让三组学生通过讨论、合作,分别在不同组别的候选词中找出正确的可用之词。

(5) 每组派一个代表学生出来在生词板上勾出他们的答案。

(6) 请每组同学依次报告他们所选的每个新词所替换的旧内容,教师引导其他学生一起评价,共同复习。

4. 反思：

"以旧换新"这个复习生词的教学方法,从名字上就可以看出,它是通过联系新旧知识,将新字词纳入旧图式的手段,来完成帮助学生巩固新字词的相关知识,强化对目标词语的正确理解的教学目标。用学生的已有知识来促进他们对新知识的理解和吸收。

需要指出的是,在这一类教学方法中,所选取的语料是否合适成为决定整个方法成败的关键。大家可以看到,我在这里提供给学生的这篇短文语料与本课的课文内容十分相似。这样做的目的有二：一是将生词学习紧扣课文中的典型内容和语境,以获得更好的学习成果。前面已经谈到,高年级汉字词教学不应该孤立于课文学习之外,而应将两者紧密结合,激发它们相互促进,相辅相成的功效。二是补充材料与课文在语境上保持相当程度的一致性,有助于学生在复习过程中回想所学的新词、新知识,加速巩固和内化。而不至于因为引入了太多的新元素,给学生造成额外的、过重的认知负荷,对学习效果产生负面影响。

方法六:你说我接

1. 内容:

　　复习"可想而知"等新学的连词或关联词。

2. 设计:

　　由于连词、关联词,往往出现在复句或语段中,因此,为复习和巩固这类词语,我设计了这个由学生合作联句的半语境化教学方法,旨在深化学生对这类词语的使用环境和所连接的从句间的关系特征的认识。

　　本方法所需要的材料和教具非常简单,仅一张目标词语的生词卡:

可想而知

3. 教学步骤:

（1）教师向全班展示生词卡,检查学生对目标词语意义、用法及使用语境的理解情况。

（2）介绍活动设计,布置合作联句任务。

（3）学生根据任务进行准备。

（4）师生互动,演示联句活动。

（5）学生互动。一人说出开头的从句,而后随机指定合作伙伴,使用目标词语进行联句,补充完整复句或语段的后半部分。

（6）教师和其他学生进行评价、讨论和纠错。

4. 反思:

　　前面已经说过,本教学方法的目的就是为了通过学生间的互动活动,帮助他们复习目标词语的意义及用法。这种学生之间分工合作,共同来完成一个复杂句子的方法,能让学生很直观地体会到连词、关联词这类词语与一般词语不尽相同的使用语境;也能强化他们对使用目标词语时从句间的关系特征的认识,加深印象,实现对目标词语的意义、用法的正确理解,从而正确使用。这一点对连词和关联词的学习和真正掌握是非常重要的。

　　既然是学生间互动完成的活动,教师应特别注意帮助学生把握前后从句间在意义上和结构上的一致性和完整性,以确保合作创造出的句子在意义和结构上都通顺。这样才是对连词或关联词的有效练习。

方法七:视听搜词

1. 内容:

　　复习"日趋、红火、赔钱、自产、手头、行情、大多、决策、绝对、指令性、批量、可想而知、购销两旺、车水马龙、随处可见、日用小商品"等本课重点生词。

2. 设计:

　　在复习、巩固环节的最后,我设计了这个集生词复习和听力训练于一体的半语境化教学方法。运用多媒体视听材料和手段,让学生在听力活动中准确定位目标词语,从而帮助他们实现对所学生词的全方位认知、掌握和巩固,达到"四会"——会认、会说、会用、会听。本活动使用到的材料和教具如下:

(1) 展示听力活动的备选生词的PPT:

```
看录像,并选出你听到的生词:
• 第一段:
    随处可见    车水马龙    日趋
    日用小商品   大多       购销两旺
• 第二段:
    批量       自产       红火
    随处可见   决策       日趋
• 第三段:
    绝对       手头       指令性
    行情       可想而知   赔钱
```

PPT15

　　本张PPT展示的是为这个视听选词活动提供的备选答案。教师将录像分为三段播放,每段之间稍作停顿,给学生在活动单(见后)上作答的时间。学生在本活动中,看录像、听解说,并在备选生词中选出听到的词语。

(2) 展示听力活动的正确答案的PPT:

```
看录像，并选出你听到的生词：
• 第一段：
              车水马龙
    日用小商品    大多    购销两旺
• 第二段：
              红火
    随处可见            日趋
• 第三段：
              手头
    可想而知
```

PPT16

配合学生报告听力活动的答案，展示本张PPT。随着学生的报告，每段中多余的生词会隐去，只留下正确答案。

(3) 与本课主课文相配套的录像片段。(根据活动需要进行了再剪辑。)

(4) 提供备选生词的听力活动单：

```
听力活动单
    看录像，并选出你听到的生词：
    第一段：
    随处可见  车水马龙  日趋  日用小商品  大多
    购销两旺
    第二段：
    批量  自产  红火  随处可见  决策  日趋
    第三段：
    绝对  手头  指令性  行情  可想而知  赔钱
```

3. 教学步骤：

(1) 展示为本活动准备的提供备选生词的PPT。

(2) 布置在视听材料中搜索出所学生词的活动任务，下发活动单。

(3) 分三段播放录像，让学生边听边选出本课学过的生词。每段录像播放完后，稍作暂停，让学生有时间完成选词任务。

(4) 请三个学生分别说出他们在每一段录像中听到的生词，全班学生一起评价、讨论，得出正确答案。

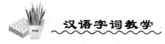

(5) 使用PPT依次展示出每段的正确答案。

4. 反思：

本教学活动旨在实现将新字词知识的学习、巩固与各种语言技能的训练相结合，使之相辅相成的教学目标，突出高年级汉语字词教学高度的综合性。同时，多种不拘一格的教学方法和活动的使用，也有助于增加课堂教学的多样性和丰富性，帮助学生保持注意力。

现代化语言教学的一大特点就是多媒体材料、教具和相关科技手段的广泛使用。以多媒体科技和材料为依托，现如今教师在语言教学中可以设计、运用的方法和活动较之以前都大大地丰富了。因此，当今的语言教师应该有意识地用多媒体技术来武装自己，以多媒体材料来装备课堂。与时俱进，因地制宜，根据具体的教学特点和目标，选择合适的科技手段来活跃课堂，促进学习，以收获更好的教学效果。

还需要指出的是，在设计一次汉语字词教学的复习环节中最后使用的教学方法时，应该注意其承上启下的作用。使之既承接之前的生词学习和复习阶段，并进行收尾；同时又成为向之后的生词应用环节和任务的铺垫与过渡。比如，设计两个使用同一材料的活动，分别作为复习环节的结束和应用环节的展开。这样能更加连贯、流畅地引导学生进入到应用生词的阶段，使整个教学过程更加行云流水。

方法八：解说录像

1. 内容：

应用"日趋、红火、手头、大多、可想而知、购销两旺、车水马龙、随处可见、日用小商品"等生词来解说录像片断。

2. 设计：

从这个方法开始，本次汉语字词教学进入到应用生词的环节。紧接着上一个"视听搜词"的活动，我设计了这个促使学生主动运用目标词语的语境化教学方法。在这里的活动中，学生需要扮演录像解说员的角色，使用在上个听力活动中找出的生词为录像配音。在这种模拟真实情况的语境中，促使学生应用目标词语来完成任务，并达到由词到句再到段落水平的语言创造。所使用的材料和教具有：

(1) 展示在每段录像中需要使用的目标词语的PPT：(也就是在上个教学方法中展示听力活动正确答案的PPT16)

由于教学法之间的连贯性，本活动直接保留、承接了上个听力活动所使用的材料和教具。在布置任务阶段依然展示的是这张听力活动正确答案的

PPT,用以提醒学生录像各片段的主要内容以及解说录像时必须使用到目标词语。

(2) 与本课主课文相配套的录像片段(在前一个方法中已经播放过,根据活动需要进行了再剪辑)。录像片段经过了消音处理,所以学生只看得到画面,但听不到解说。目的是让学生自己运用目标词来解说录像片断。

(3) 学生依然使用在上一个听力活动中完成的听力活动单。(已在上一活动中圈出了正确生词,可以为准备解说稿提供内容线索。)

3. 教学步骤:

(1) 教师展示囊括所有目标词语的PPT,并布置活动任务,让学生运用在上一活动中听出来的目标词语解说录像。之后,将学生分成三组,准备开始活动。

(2) 播放经过消音处理的同一录像(共三段),提醒学生注意画面中出现的场景和事物,为描述录像搜集线索。

(3) 给学生3到5分钟的时间,分组讨论,运用目标生词准备讲稿。每组学生解说一段录像。

(4) 再次播放无声录像,请三组学生依次为三段录像进行解说。教师和其他学生对目标词语的应用情况进行监督、评价,必要时进行纠错。

4. 反思:

本教学方法通过一个模拟真实情况的任务,创造出使用语言的需要和语境,从而促使学生主动、有意义地操练、运用目标词语,分组合作完成任务。这是为了达到帮助学生实现对目标词语的正确、熟练应用的教学目标而服务的,同时也是对任务型教学法理念的贯彻和执行。

为了获得预期的教学效果,使用本方法时需要注意以下几点:(1)选择合适的录像片段。录像内容应与使用目标词语的典型语境相符合,画面应对学生的语言创造和使用有正确的引导作用。(2)学生的语言创造应以正确运用目标词语为首要目标。在师生共同努力,确保这一目标完全实现的基础上,教师还应该鼓励和引导学生进行适当的语言拓展,使学生的语言创造达到高年级学生所要求具备的段落水平,兼顾到语言的正确度与复杂度。

方法九:采访准备

1. 内容:

运用"起家、机遇、挑战、行情、利润、依据、决策、先决条件"等生词。

2. 设计:

本教学方法同样贯彻了任务型教学法,使用的是一个开放式的语境化应用生词的活动。在这个任务中,学生需要扮演记者的角色,在接到采访私营企业或国营企业的员工的采访任务后,以小组为单位进行讨论。在给出的目标生词范围中选择生词,进行应用,设计出一份采访问题单,为后面的综合互动式采访活动做准备。这里用到的材料和教具有:

(1) 展示活动任务和目标生词范围的PPT:

> • 采访准备（第一组）
> 　请选用规定生词,设计一份采访<u>个体经营者</u>的采访问题:（至少使用4个生词）
> 　（起家 机遇 挑战 行情 利润 依据 决策 先决条件）
>
> • 采访准备（第二组）
> 　请使用规定生词,设计一份采访<u>国营企业员工</u>的采访问题:（至少使用4个生词）
> 　（起家 机遇 挑战 行情 利润 依据 决策 先决条件）

PPT17

在本教学法的开始,展示此张PPT,用以布置活动任务。将学生分为两组,分别根据此PPT和活动单(见下)的具体要求准备采访问题。

(2) 两份写有不同采访对象并提供目标生词范围的活动单:

> 活动单一:
> 　　　　　采访准备
> 1. 请选用规定生词,设计一份采访<u>个体经营者</u>的采访问题:（至少使用4个生词）
> 　（起家 机遇 挑战 行情 利润 依据 决策 先决条件）
> 2. 列出你的采访问题:

> 活动单二:
> 　　　　　采访准备
> 1. 请使用规定生词,设计一份采访<u>国营企业员工</u>的问题:（至少使用4个生词）
> 　（起家 机遇 挑战 行情 利润 依据 决策 先决条件）
> 2. 列出你的采访问题:

3. 教学步骤：

(1) 将学生分为两组，布置活动任务。要求学生以记者的身份，每组分别根据不同的采访对象，合作准备采访问题单。

(2) 小组讨论，完成任务。

(3) 每组学生分别报告所设计的问题，教师和其他学生对其使用目标生词的情况进行监督、评价，必要时进行纠错。

4. 反思：

　　本教学方法旨在为学生创造一个主动使用目标词语的语境，在完成任务的过程中强化他们对目标词语的正确应用。整个过程看似简单，但实际上较之于前面的任务，在难度上有了更大的提升，建构起了一定的学习坡度。在本次汉语字词教学的应用生词环节中，从"解说录像"到"采访准备"，在形式上是从相对控制型的语言活动向开放式的活动的过渡。后者使用的辅助材料更少，对学生使用语言、创造语言的限制也就更少。因而，学生在完成任务时需要进行更多的开放的主动性思维，自主决定所要运用的生词及应用生词创造语言的方向。这种更加自由宽松的使用环境，有助于培养学生根据实际需要正确选择和使用所学生词的能力，使其自主运用目标词语的能力得到进一步加强。因此，建立合理的学习坡度，促进学生学习成果的深化，也是教师在设计教学方法、组织教学时需要考虑的一个重要方面，应力求在任务要求和难度层面上减少不必要的重复。

　　另外，任务间的连贯性也是在设计教学方法和活动时所必须注意的。在任务型教学法的课堂中，一个教学目标的实现，往往是通过使用多种方法，设计多个任务，层层推进来完成的。在这种情况下，如果任务之间各个独立，每个语境和角色身份都互无联系，很容易就会流于杂乱，造成学生过重的认知负荷，影响其操练效果，也无法很好地实现每个任务的设计目的。因此，在为每次教学设计活动任务时，教师应有全局意识。不仅要使所用的任务与教学内容的特点相符合，还应该考虑到任务之间的联系，形成连贯性，使它们之间在语境、角色身份或材料上相互承接、发展。从而使整个教学组织逻辑清晰、脉络顺畅，让学生能够更好地理解任务、参与任务，实现教学效果的最大化。本次教学展示中的方法七和方法八，方法九和方法十都体现了这种任务连贯性的理念。

方法十：现场采访

1. 内容：

　　承接上一方法，继续训练学生应用"起家、机遇、挑战、行情、利润、依据、决策、先决条件"等生词。

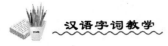

2. 设计:

在本次汉语字词教学的最后,我设计了一个综合型互动式的语境化教学方法。基于前一个活动的准备,在本任务中,学生分别成为采访者和被采访者,使用目标生词,进行模拟真实场景的采访问答活动。这里使用到的材料就是学生在方法九中完成的采访问题单。

3. 教学步骤:

(1) 学生仍然延续在上个活动中的分组(两个),互换在上一活动中完成的采访问题单。

(2) 各组学生根据得到的问题,共同讨论,运用目标词语准备答案。

(3) 两组学生轮流上前,接受对方同学采访,运用目标词语回答问题。教师引导学生注意对目标生词的理解和使用情况,全班进行监督、评价,必要时进行纠错。

4. 反思:

在教学的最后阶段使用这个学生互动问答形式的语境化活动的目的也是为了强化学生在更加复杂的情况下准确运用目标生词的能力。之所以说这里的语境更加复杂,是因为这个任务具有更大的综合性。模拟真实地采访和受访的互动过程,将目标生词的操练以及听力、口语等语言技能的训练有机地融为一体,互相促进,共同进步。这样不仅能帮助学生尽快实现运用新词的自动化,更有利于全面提升他们的综合语言水平。

在这种比较复杂的综合性活动中,为了真正达到教学目标,教师对学生语言的监控就显得更加重要。对于学生在语流中出现的错误用词情况,教师应给予及时、明确的提醒、反馈和纠正,加深正确的理解,避免错误习惯的形成,以提高学生准确地使用目标词语的能力。

其他方法举例

前面已经谈到过,高年级学习者本身已经具有相当的语言知识和语言技能水平,这为高年级字词教学的方法和任务设计提供了很大的操作空间和自由,使得一些综合性语境化的教学方法的使用成为可能。而这些相对综合和复杂的活动,也正是高年级课堂教学特点的重要体现。在实际的高年级汉语字词教学中,根据不同的课文内容和生词类别,可供使用的综合性语境化教学方法不胜枚举。关键一点还是要对每种方法的适用范围有清楚、正确的认识,务必使设计的方法和任务与课文内容和生词特点相适应,这样才能发挥出其应有的教学效果,对学生的学习产生积极的促进作用。

例如,针对本课特点,在应用生词阶段还可以使用的语境化教学方法有:

1. 唇枪舌剑:
   甲方:私营经济更能适应市场经济的发展
   乙方:国营经济更能适应市场经济的发展

   这个方法是采用辩论这种互动形式,让学生在支持和反驳不同观点的过程中主动操练目标生词,同时训练综合语言技能。教师可以在课堂中组织这个活动,以训练听说技能为主。也可以在课后,利用网络平台,组织学生进行网上合作、讨论以及辩论,这样还可以训练学生的中文读写技巧。

2. 就职演说:
   第一组:如果我是私营企业的经理……
   第二组:如果我是国营企业的经理……

   这是一个角色扮演进行演讲的语境化方法。学生将自己想象成私营企业或国营企业经理的身份,使用目标词语发表就职演说,对企业发展提出自己的想法和计划。相对于其他活动,这一任务的特点是:(1)语境更加正式,所以需要学生不仅能够正确运用新学生词,还要使用合适的文体和用语。(2)题目的范围更宽,更强调段落、篇章水平的语言创造。因此,具体的活动方法可以是学生准备腹稿,然后口头报告;也可以将写作与演讲相结合,先布置课外写作练习,然后在课堂上进行模拟真实情境的就职演说活动。

Appendix A
附录 A

Modern Chinese Character Stroke Chart

现代汉字笔画表

基本笔画(7) 笔画、名称、例字	十 一:横	中 丨:竖	人 丿:撇	主 丶:点	大 ㇏:捺	江 ㇀:提	日 ㇕:横折	
派生笔画(24) 笔画、名称、例字	又 ㇇:横撇	写 ㇆:横钩	月 ㇆:横折钩	记 ㇊:横折提	朵 ㇌:横折弯	凹 ㇎:横折折	风 ㇟:横折斜钩	公 ㇜:撇折
	九 乙:横折弯钩	队 ㇈:横撇弯钩	及 ㇋:横折折撇	乃 ㇉:横折折折钩	凸 ㇎:横折折折	民 ㇂:竖提	山 ㇄:竖折	戈 ㇁:斜钩
	小 亅:竖钩	酉 ㇗:竖弯	已 乚:竖弯钩	专 ㇞:竖弯撇	鼎 ㇞:竖折折	马 ㇉:竖折折钩	女 ㇇:撇点	家 ㇈:弯钩

根据《现代汉字教程》(31—32页，作者：张静贤，现代出版社，1990)内容复制。原文中是"基本笔画(6)"而不是"基本笔画(7)"，可能是笔误因为原文基本笔画的图示有七种。

Appendix B

附录 B

Rules for the Character Stroke Order

笔顺规则	例字	笔顺
1. 先横后竖	十	一 十
2. 先撇后捺	人	丿 人
3. 从上到下	三	一 二 三
4. 从左到右	做	亻 佐 做
5. 从外到里	月	丿 几 月
6. 先外后里再封口	日	丨 冂 日 日
7. 先横后撇	厂	一 厂
8. 先中间后两边	小	亅 小 小
9. 点在上方或左上角,先写点后写主体。	文	丶 亠 文
10. 点在右下角或下方或在里边,先写主体后写点。	术	木 术
11. 上左下包围结构,先写上、里,后写左下。	区	一 又 区
12. 上右包围结构,先写上右,后写里边。	司	𠃌 ㇆ 司
13. 左下右包围结构,先写上边,再写左下、右。	凶	乂 㓪 凶
14. 左下包围结构,当左下是 辶 和 廴 时,先写右上,后写左下,当左下是其他部件时,先写左下,后写右上。	进	井 进

根据《现代汉字教程》(38－39页,作者:张静贤,现代出版社,1990)内容复制。

Appendix C 附录 C
Types of Physical Structure of Compound Characters

部件书写顺序：1、浅黑 2、中黑 3、深黑

1. Left-Right Structure 左右结构

2. Top-Bottom Structure 上下结构

3. Half Encircled Structure 半包围结构

4. Encircled Structure 包围结构

Appendix D 附录D

100 Radicals According to Their Frequency
按频率排列的100部首

编号	拼音	部首	编号	拼音	部首	编号	拼音	部首	编号	拼音	部首
1	shuǐ	水(氵氺)	26	yī	衣(衤)	51	pū	支(攵)	76	jiàn	见(見)
2	cǎo	艹(艸)	27	quǎn	犬(犭)	52	gē	戈	77	sī	厶
3	kǒu	口	28	mù	目	53	shī	尸	78	máo	毛
4	mù	木(朩)	29	dāo	刀(刂⺈)	54	xué	穴	79	bǔ	卜
5	shǒu	手(龵扌)	30	yì	邑(阝在右)	55	lì	力	80	chǐ	齿(齒)
6	rén	人(亻入)	31	mián	宀	56	zhōu	舟	81	fāng	方
7	jīn	金(钅)	32	hé	禾	57	wéi	囗	82	hēi	黑
8	xīn	心(忄㣺)	33	mǎ	马(馬)	58	yǔ	雨	83	shū	殳
9	tǔ	土(士)	34	bèi	贝(貝)	59	hǎn (chǎng)	厂	84	rén (ér)	儿
10	yuè	月(肉)	35	chē	车(車)	60	yòu	又	85	shān	彡
11	mì	纟(糹)	36	fù	阜(阝在左)	61	niú	牛(牜牛)	86	qì	气
12	huǐ (chóng)	虫	37	shì	示(礻)	62	mǐn	皿	87	bāo	勹
13	yán	言(讠)	38	shí	食(饣)	63	bīng	冫	88	zhǎo	爪(爫)
14	nǚ	女	39	yǒu	酉	64	yǔ	羽	89	wǎ	瓦
15	zhú	竹(⺮)	40	bā	八(丷)	65	yáng	羊	90	zǒu	走
16	huǒ	火(灬)	41	yè(xié)	页(頁)	66	gōng	弓	91	fāng	匚
17	wáng(yù)	王(玉)	42	jīn	巾	67	è(dǎi)	歹(歺)	92	hù	户
18	rì	日(曰)	43	mén	门(門)	68	xiǎo	小(⺌)	93	gōng	工
19	shí	石	44	Yǎn (guǎng)	广	69	qiàn	欠	94	zhǐ	止
20	yú	鱼(魚)	45	dà	大	70	zǐ	子	95	cùn	寸
21	shān	山	46	mǐ	米	71	zhuī	隹	96	zhǐ	夂
22	zú	足(⻊)	47	tián	田	72	ěr	耳	97	shǐ	矢
23	niǎo	鸟(鳥)	48	shí	十	73	bái	白	98	jīn	斤
24	nè	疒	49	chì	彳	74	gǔ	骨	99	shé	舌
25	chuò	辶(辵)	50	gé	革	75	lì	立	100	shēn	身

From the textbook *Learning 100 Chinese Radicals*, p. 16. Authors: Helen H. Shen, Ping Wang, Chen-Hui Tsai, Beijing University Press, 2009.